102

Muslim Nationalism and the New Turks

PRINCETON STUDIES IN MUSLIM POLITICS
Dale F. Eickelman and Augustus Richard Norton, series editors

A list of titles in this series can be found at the back of the book

Muslim Nationalism and the New Turks

Jenny White

PRINCETON UNIVERSITY PRESS

PRINCETON AND OXFORD

Copyright © 2013 by Princeton University Press
Published by Princeton University Press, 41 William Street, Princeton, New Jersey 08540
In the United Kingdom: Princeton University Press, 6 Oxford Street, Woodstock,
Oxfordshire OX20 1TW

press.princeton.edu

First printing, 2013

New edition, with a new afterword by the author, 2014
Paperback ISBN 978-0-691-16192-1

Library of Congress Control Number 2013957457

British Library Cataloging-in-Publication Data is available

This book has been composed in Garamond Premier Pro

Printed on acid-free paper. ∞

Printed in the United States of America

10 9 8 7 6 5 4 3 2 1

In Memory of Elizabeth Warnock Fernea

1927–2008

Man is the child of customs, not the child of his ancestors.

—*Ibn Khaldun*, Muqaddimah, *1377*

Contents

Illustrations   xi

Abbreviations   xiii

Acknowledgments   xv

CHAPTER 1
Introduction   1

CHAPTER 2
Islam and the Nation   24

CHAPTER 3
The Republic of Fear   54

CHAPTER 4
The Missionary and the Headscarf   80

CHAPTER 5
No Mixing   102

CHAPTER 6
Sex and the Nation: Veiled Identity   136

CHAPTER 7
Choice and Community: *The Girl with Blue Hair*   163

CHAPTER 8
Conclusion   181

AFTERWORD TO THE NEW PAPERBACK EDITION   197

Notes   215

References   237

Index   249

Illustrations

FIGURE 1.1. Taksim subway station tile mural depicting the Turkish conquest of Byzantine Constantinople in 1453.   10

FIGURE 2.1. Director of an Islamist charity foundation in his office under a portrait of an Ottoman sultan, Ümraniye, 1994.   45

FIGURE 3.1. Cover of a weekly political news magazine with the caption "How did the Turks become Muslim?"   70

FIGURE 3.2. Children wearing Ataturk masks during National Sovereignty and Children's Day celebrations in Bursa in 2008.   76

FIGURE 4.1. Janissary band performing in the Istanbul district of Eyüp before an appearance by the AKP mayor, 2004.   98

FIGURE 5.1. Crowd at a 2008 demonstration marking the anniversary of Hrant Dink's assassination. The sign reads, "We are all half-breeds."   115

FIGURE 5.2. New housing squeezes out the last squatter homes in Ümraniye.   119

FIGURE 5.3. Iconic fish restaurant with patrons drinking rakı under portraits of Ataturk.   121

FIGURE 5.4. Department store display for New Year's celebrations, with fir tree, tinsel, reindeer antlers, and Santa.   125

FIGURE 5.5. Woman sitting in the window of an Istanbul restaurant rolling out dough.   130

FIGURE 6.1. Postcard showing a man and his mother, typical of photomontage souvenirs created for men going off to military service.   155

FIGURE 7.1. Young woman in fashionable *tesettür* with jeans coat and unconventional semitransparent headscarf.   168

FIGURE 7.2. Shoes belonging to different generations before the door of a conservative, working-class home in Ümraniye.   172

Abbreviations

AKP	*Adalet ve Kalkınma Partisi* (Justice and Development Party)
CHP	*Cumhuriyet Halk Partisi* (Republican People's Party)
CUP	Committee of Union and Progress
DTP	*Demokratik Toplum Partisi* (Democratic Society Party)
FP	Felicity Party (*Saadet Partisi*)
MHP	*Milliyetçi Hareket Partisi* (Nationalist Action Party)
NSP	National Salvation Party (*Millî Selâmet Partisi*)
PKK	*Partiya Karkerên Kurdistan* (Kurdistan Workers' Party)
VP	Virtue Party (*Fazilet Partisi*)
WP	Welfare Party (*Refah Partisi*)

Acknowledgments

THIS BOOK is literally the product of decades, as I have incorporated insights from various periods of my research in Turkey since 1975. Some of the kind people who shared their time and thoughts with me during this project are people I have known for years; others are new acquaintances. Some I sought out specifically to discuss the subject of this book; others I met accidentally. I would like to thank them all for their hospitality, and their willingness to engage me and to answer my questions. A number of colleagues in the United States and Turkey helped me think these matters through, although it is important to mention that they are not responsible for my conclusions. I am particularly indebted to Şahin Alpay, Betty Anderson, Kimberly Arkin, Laura Graham, Haldun Gülalp, Roberta Micallef, Roger Owen, Ayşe Önal, and Merry White, as well as my students in Boston University's 2011 AN462 theory class. My thanks as well to an anonymous reviewer for helpful suggestions. Michael Freeman, who has perfect pitch when it comes to writing, edited the entire manuscript with a deft hand and his usual attention to detail. I would like to thank the Fulbright-Hays Program and the American Research Institute in Turkey for funding this research. The conclusions are entirely my own.

Muslim Nationalism and the New Turks

Introduction

SOON AFTER my arrival in Turkey in January 2008 for a year's research stay, the country was abuzz about a group of twenty high school students from the city of Kırşehir in central Anatolia that had painted a Turkish flag with their own blood—a broad red field about eighteen inches wide, with a white sickle moon and star at center. The students had presented it to Turkey's top military chief, General Yaşar Büyükanıt, as a gift to commemorate the deaths of twelve soldiers killed in clashes with Kurdish separatist PKK[1] guerrillas two months earlier. The general displayed the flag to journalists and praised the students, pointing out that not only had they made a flag of their blood but had also given him a petition to "please take us immediately as soldiers." "This is the kind of nation we are," he said, visibly moved. "We are a great nation. Truly our martyrs have died for a holy purpose. That holy purpose is to protect the country we live in as one and undivided."[2] The young people, boys and girls, posed with the framed flag for an adoring media, and the right-wing newspaper *Tercüman* distributed promotional copies of the blood-flag to its readers.

Some voices in the media expressed qualms about the potential health risks—the children, after all, had injured themselves, drawing blood from their fingers with pins. A few protested on moral grounds. Psychologist Serdar Değirmencioğlu pointed out that "in countries where militarism is intense, blood is not seen as something to be treated carefully, but something to be spilt."[3] Political scientist Baskın Oran argued that it was dangerous to condition children in primary school to believe that the Turkish nation is based on bloodlines. "We saw the recent attacks by young people directed at Christian priests," he added, drawing a parallel between Turkish blood and Muslim identity.[4] In her column in the centrist newspaper *Radikal*, journalist and writer Perihan Mağden condemned the general's approval of the blood-flag and the "militarist, war-mongering and violent atmosphere" that had inspired the children's act. Another journalist, Ece Temelkuran, wrote in *Milliyet*, "If only this noise, which makes flags out of children and dead children out of flags, would end."[5]

Public reaction was swift against those critical of the blood-flag.[6] Both Mağden and Temelkuran were attacked in the media, with *Tercüman* calling Mağden a "flag-enemy" whose "ugly words" are remote from a Turkish identity, and accusing Temelkuran of committing a crime. The journalists took *Tercüman* to court for insulting them, and the paper's editor was fined. But by April 2009 Mağden faced at least ten other cases against her in court, mostly insult cases, including one brought by two Turks who made a YouTube video Mağden had criticized that praised the murderer of Armenian-Turkish journalist Hrant Dink.[7]

Dink was assassinated in front of his office in 2007 by a young nationalist who had accused the journalist of insulting Turkish blood in a news article he had written. Dink had been tried in court for that crime in 2005 under Article 301 of the Turkish Penal Code, which makes it illegal to insult "Turkishness" (*Türklük*), a concept so vaguely defined in legal terms that it has encouraged hundreds of prosecutions against journalists, authors, publishers, and others. Despite an expert report that Dink had not insulted or denigrated anyone in his article, four months later the court found Dink guilty and sentenced him to six months in jail, suspended. Arguing that his words had been taken out of context, Dink was preparing to appeal his case before the European Court of Human Rights when he was assassinated.[8] Ironically, in the original text, he had been urging the Armenian diaspora to rid themselves of their enmity ("poisoned blood") against the Turks.

For the young killer, Ogün Samast,[9] it was enough that Dink was Armenian and Christian, making him an enemy of Turkishness and the Turkish nation. As Samast was running away he reportedly shouted, "I killed the non-Muslim." His crime was met with some sympathy in nationalist circles. In a photo that police officers had taken with Samast while he was in custody, the suspect is holding a Turkish flag, and on the wall behind them are the words "Our country is sacred—its future cannot be left to chance." In 2008, under pressure from the European Union (EU), the Turkish parliament (Grand National Assembly) reformed Article 301 of the Penal Code, replacing "denigrating Turkishness" with a more specific term, "denigrating the Turkish nation." This does not appreciably change the nature of the crime, however, since the concept of nation, as we shall discuss later, itself is premised upon a racial understanding of Turkishness and Muslim identity. In his introduction to a collection of essays comparing race and ethnic systems around the world, Paul Spickard writes that race in the context of nationalism is always about power. It is "written on the body" as a product of culture, not as a self-evident biological fact.[10]

I relate the incidents of the blood-flag and Hrant Dink's murder in some detail because they exemplify a number of the issues I discuss in this book—the physicality of Turkish national identity with its emphasis on blood, purity, boundaries, and honor—and the cultural work that underlies them; the gendered nature of nationalism; its sharply contested profile; the link between being Turkish and being Muslim; a substratum of militarism, hostility, suspicion, and authoritarianism; and a heightened discourse of fear and the polarization of society. This polarization, I suggest, is in part a consequence of the vacuum created by the weakening of the state Kemalist project over recent years and the increasing inability of the state—despite prosecutions under Article 301, and the banning of websites like YouTube—to control the definition of Turkishness and thereby shape the identity of Turkish youth. Kemalist national identity has been challenged by new heterodox forms of nationalism emerging from increasingly powerful and self-confident Muslim networks rooted in economic and political life that privilege Muslim identity and culture over race.[11]   *Kemalism*

Kemalism refers to the vision of Turkey's founding figure and first president, Mustafa Kemal (later given the honorific Ataturk, meaning Father/Ancestor of the Turks), of a culturally unitary, Westernized, secular society in which state institutions and the military play a special tutelary role as guarantors of Kemalist democracy. The orthodox Kemalist vision of the nation imagines solidarity as unity of blood and race in which being Muslim is considered to be an essential component of having Turkish blood.[12] This vision is accompanied by intense fear of dissolution of racial unity and thereby of national unity. Community is thus a product of a sense of continual threat, and a strong state and military are presented as crucial guarantors of the health and safety of the national family. When asked what being Turkish means, many men across the nation will respond, "*Hepimiz askeriz.*" ("We are all soldiers.") These words also appear on banners during national holidays and other occasions. The militarism and emphasis on the masculine nature of national identity that is indicated by this slogan make it difficult for women to define their place as national subjects, an issue to which I will return.

Just over half of Turkey's population is under age thirty.[13] Young people are increasingly expressing themselves through new media, civic activism, and consumerism, searching for arenas of belonging, of which the nation is but one. While subjective freedom of choice may have expanded with globalization, individualism tends to be framed within a collective logic. Belonging to a group, whether family, community or nation, continues to be essential for social survival, as well as social identity.[14] Muslim networks, especially those surrounding the Islam-rooted Justice and Development Party (AKP, *Adalet ve Kalkınma Partisi*), which has been in power since 2002, and the ubiquitous Fethullah Gülen Islamic movement, are beneficiaries of this search for alternative collectivities. Against Kemalism's message of continual embattlement, Islam appeals to youth with its rootedness in networks that promise to help them gain education, skills, and connections needed to succeed economically, and that give meaning to individual lives within a distinctly Muslim brand of national community.

As new forms of nationalism emerge and identities and loyalties become contested, people struggle to maintain the physical and metaphorical boundaries that mark their territories of belonging. But the process of change is far advanced. Turkey is now a vastly different place than it was when I first visited in 1975, a time when Kemalism was embattled by leftist ideas but retained a powerful appeal across classes and generations. That challenge was met by the military with a coup in 1980 that was meant to reset the republic on the Kemalist path but, as I explain in chapter 2, ultimately sowed the seeds of its own diminishment. Today, it is not so much Islam that has challenged the status quo, I suggest, but rather what Islam has become in the postcoup urban, modern, globalized environment where, for many, religious and national identities, like commodities, have become objects of choice and forms of personal expression.

TURKEY'S THIRD REPUBLIC

Turkey has entered an era of social and political revolution. Indeed, scholars and pundits refer to the period after the 1980 coup as the Third Republic, a time during which something entirely new was being created in Turkish society and politics. (The period after the 1960 coup so transformed Turkey that it is called the Second Republic.) Yet, in a puzzling counterpoint, it seems that Third Republican Turks also are firmly patrolling the boundaries that define their membership in familiar social and political categories, and attributing to others membership in demonized groups. Society appears to be divided into militantly opposed secular and Muslim forces, and this division tends to be valorized by observers who bring to bear preconceived ideas about what secularism and Islam mean.

I define secularism and religion in historically and culturally specific terms. José Casanova has pointed out that while modern secularism posits that religion in the abstract is a transcultural phenomenon against which secularism can set itself, in reality, non-European practices of both religion and secularity are highly culturally specific.[15] Furthermore, secularism is not necessarily modern, nor is religion marginal or superfluous to a modern life. Instead, religion itself can become secularized (individualized, privatized) while the secular sphere becomes sacralized as profane images and practices are imbued with attributes of the sacred, and religious meanings and legitimacy are extended to new practices. Turkey's tense confrontations, then, might not be examples of secularism versus religion, as these terms are generally understood, but might better be described as struggles over blasphemy of the sacred, with secularists and the pious fighting over the designation of what is sacred, what is intrinsic to tradition and inviolable, and what lies outside the boundaries of identity sacralized by tradition. Adam Seligman observed that what scholars gloss as religion and secularism, and even identity, are really "traditions of practices" that as nation-states emerged in Europe, were subsumed within national identities. People, he pointed out, do not "do" religion, secularism, or identity, but rather, they follow a tradition of specific practices.[16] This means that traditions (and, thus, what is glossed as religion, secularism, and identity) are open to transformation in practice, as when religion in the modern context becomes a form of self-expression or a touchstone of national identity. Religion may be forced to redefine itself in competition with other faiths and ideologies.[17]

As a result of their encounters with global cosmopolitan secular modernity,[18] Casanova writes, religious traditions are reinterpreted not as accommodations to the West or as fundamentalist reactions, much less in a triumph of modernity over tradition, but as what he calls *aggiornamentos*, practical adjustments of tradition that blur the line between sacred and secular. As an example, Casanova cites the sacralization of the discourse of human rights by the Second Vatican Council, a reinterpretation of tradition that in effect allowed Catholic resources around the world to be mobilized for democratization. He suggests that in countries like Turkey and Indonesia, democratization is unlikely to thrive until political actors are able to "frame" their discourse in a publicly recognizable Islamic idiom, rather than insisting on the privatization of Islam as a precondition to modernity as the Kemalists did, a stance that Casanova argues elicits only antidemocratic responses. In other words, in responding to the challenges of global modernism, Islamic publics may elaborate their normative traditions to generate new forms of public civil Islam that are conducive to democratization. In a sense, the Arab Spring revolutions of 2011 set up a living laboratory to examine the process of Islamic *aggiornamento* as a path to democratization in a variety of political and cultural settings. The experience of Turkey described in this book suggests that reinterpretations of modernity as much as of tradition have led to public interpellations of piety and democratization previously unimagined.

Religion in Turkey has become secularized and the secular sphere sacralized, resulting in a struggle over the definition of what is sacred, accompanied by accusations of blasphemy (phrased as disloyalty to the nation and even treason[19]). Indi-

vidual choice—the choice to be *şuurlu*, a "consciously" believing Muslim, as opposed
to blindly following tradition—has become highly valued as a sign of Muslim modernity. Islamic practice increasingly has come to be expressed as participation in
economic networks and through a commodified lifestyle of self-consciously Muslim
fashion and leisure. Meanwhile, Kemalist secularism has taken on aspects of the sacred. Turkish blood represents the nation and is surrounded by taboos. In Mustafa
Kemal Ataturk's speeches, the earth of Anatolia is sacred "because it is drenched in
the blood of those who gave their lives for the country."[20] Busts and statues of Ataturk
mark sacred ground and may not be moved or destroyed. It is against the law even to
criticize Ataturk. A shadow that resembles his silhouette thrown by one hillside onto
another in the remote village of Ardahan every summer draws thousands of viewers
and representatives of the army and media.[21]

Turkey is riven by disputes over what is sacred to the nation and where the boundaries of national identity are drawn. While the categories of secular and Islamic have
a long history in Turkey, their specific meanings and how they are experienced have
developed in response to particular events and societal changes. What they represent
today in practice arguably is new. The secularists and pious Muslims of the Third
Republic are not the secularists and Muslims of the Second or First Republics, nor
do their words and costumes signify what they did in the past.

I will suggest in this book that much of the tension and anxiety that has come to
dominate daily life and discourse in the Third Republic arises from a radical revision
of the most basic category of all—what does it mean to be Turkish, to be a member
of this nation? Popular answers have been naturalized through decades of Kemalist
Republican education: We are a Turkish race, of Turkish blood, of Muslim faith; we
are all soldiers; our historical roots lie in Turkic Central Asia; we believe in Ataturk's
project of modernization; we are laicist (laicism in Turkey means a secular lifestyle
within a system of state-sponsored Sunni Islam). Many of these elements are felt to
be under siege as a result of changes occurring in Turkish society. This view occasions
fear and, in consequence, intensifies the perceived need for tests of belonging and
loyalty.

Community membership these days is often accompanied by an increased search
for enemies and monitoring of members' conceptual purity. As an anthropologist, I
generally have tried to examine issues from many sides, rather than take a stand
about right and wrong. In years past I had the opportunity to think through conten-
tious issues with Turkish friends and colleagues who were willing to examine the
causes and consequences of a variety of social and cultural practices and political
events. But by the late 2000s, the number of people willing to entertain that middle

ground had shrunk. Even many of my liberal friends expected me to take a stand—with them or against them. As a result, I lost a friend of thirty years because I had written an article about the headscarf for the Islamic news daily *Zaman*, a theoretical piece that, to my mind, took no sides. But my friend, a fervent Kemalist, claimed that simply by writing for an Islamic newspaper, I had demonstrated that I supported "the Islamists." She has not spoken to me since. One secular colleague at a major Turkish university forbade the discussion of politics at his dinner table because he too had lost a friend to the face-offs that ensued. The most incendiary issue is the headscarf, which acts as a key marker of identity for those who wear it and for those who despise it. A brother and sister, both liberal academics, reportedly argued about whether the headscarf should be allowed on campus (it was banned at the time). Thereafter the siblings shunned each other, the brother not even telling his sister when he contracted a fatal illness.

On the "other" side, several studies have documented intensified "community pressure" around the country to veil, to follow Islamic rules of comportment, and to participate in Islamic networks.[22] Polls show that intolerance has grown toward non-Muslims and generally toward anyone different, and attitudes toward other countries have become more negative, not only toward the United States, but across the board.[23] In such an atmosphere, where people are reaffirming membership in value-laden communities and patrolling for correct principles and behavior within well-worn social and political categories like Islam and secularism, what does it mean to speak of revolutionary change?

The three most dramatic changes that put their mark on the Third Republic—and contributed to its revolutionary transformation—were

1. the 1980 coup that radically reshaped the political landscape;
2. the opening of Turkey's insular, state-led economy to competition in the world market by the first party elected after the coup—the Motherland Party (*Anavatan Partisi*), led by the economist Turgut Özal; and
3. the rise of Islamist political parties that showed ever stronger election results through the 1990s.

None of these changes could have been predicted by the military. The Motherland Party had not been the military's favored candidate in the postcoup election. In the early 1980s, the army encouraged Özal's government to allow more freedom for a modest, state-defined form of Turkish Islam to counter the appeal of socialist and communist ideas to Turkey's youth. The government duly incorporated Islam in school texts and built more preacher training schools. This "Turkish-Islamic Synthesis" was not without risk, however, as the freedom to discuss Islamic ideas coincided with the deregulation of the media—which allowed an explosion of magazines, newspapers, and radio and television channels devoted to things Islamic—and with the rise of a Muslim political and economic elite.

Small- and medium-sized businesses in the provinces, many owned by pious Muslims, benefited from the economic opening and became so successful that the press named them the Anatolian Tigers. Their wealth created a market for Islam-friendly bourgeois products and lifestyles (an Islamic economic sector) and initiated a Muslim cultural renaissance in fashion, lifestyle, leisure activities, novels, media, and music. To be Muslim within this consumer framework, for the first time in Republican history, could be interpreted as urban and upwardly mobile.

The pious elite's wealth also supported overtly Islamic politicians and their programs throughout the 1980s and 1990s. One beneficiary was the Justice and Development Party (AKP), a moderate offspring of a series of more radically Islamist parties of the 1990s. The AKP won the 2002 elections and has remained in power through three election cycles, increasing its share of the vote to 49.9 percent in 2011. Although led by openly pious Muslim politicians, AKP claims not to be Islamic but, rather, a center-right conservative party that serves a broad and varied constituency across Turkey.

The economic opening vastly expanded the variety of available commodities and lifestyles, the extent and manner in which personal choices could be expressed, and the categories to which one could affiliate. The pious Muslims and politically engaged Islamists of the 1980s were augmented by new Muslim publics—pious political pragmatists;[24] an Islamic bourgeoisie;[25] the self-contained yet global socioeconomic networks of the preacher Fethullah Gülen;[26] a nationalist-racist Islamist fringe; and what the journalist Mustafa Akyol referred to as "free-lance Muslims," young pious Muslims like himself experimenting with religion and lifestyle, and shopping among Islamic forms and communities.[27] To be a "conscious" Muslim means that one is a modern, thinking individual. In our conversations, pious men and women often would point out that although they were born Turkish, they had chosen to be Muslim, making that identity more valuable.

One of the most revolutionary consequences of these changes, I would argue, has been a contestation of the nature of Turkishness and the Turkish nation not seen since the founding of the Republic. What does it mean to be a Turk in the face of this proliferation of identities and onslaught of unorthodox ways of being Turkish? The rise of a pious elite has seriously undermined the social and political leadership that had been enjoyed until then by the secular urban part of the population. Kemalist control of the educational system and urban economic and social life had provided and promoted an orthodox national identity. The emblematic citizen was a Turkish Muslim with a secular lifestyle, dedicated to a state-led program of modernization believed to be Ataturk's design. (A common secular nationalist banner at demonstrations reads, "*Ata'nin izindeyiz*" (We step in the footprints of our father/ancestor, that is, Ataturk).

The AKP and its pious supporters, in contrast, have developed and implemented an unorthodox alternative definition of Turkishness and the nation that imagines Turkey not as a nation embattled within its present political borders but as a flexibly bounded Turkey that is the self-confident successor to the Ottomans in a rediscovered (and reinvented) past. The new Turkish identity, which I call Muslim nationalism, is that of a pious Muslim Turk whose subjectivity and vision for the future is shaped by an imperial Ottoman past overlaid onto a republican state framework, but divorced from the Kemalist state project. In other words, everything from lifestyle to public and foreign policy are up for reinterpretation, not necessarily according to Islamic principles (although Islamic ethics and imagery may play a role), much less Islamic law (in which few Turks have any expertise[28]), but according to a distinctively Turkish postimperial sensibility. In this vision, Ataturk's footprints are an anachronism.

Instead of commemorating the 1923 founding of the Turkish nation, the new Turks pay public tribute to historical events like the 1453 Ottoman Muslim conquest of Christian Byzantium. This event is reenacted by municipalities and visually depicted in public places; the date is celebrated with festivities. Istanbul's new central Metro station in Taksim, at the epicenter of Turkish secular culture and nightlife, is decorated with enormous tile murals depicting various aspects of the conquest. In 2009 the Istanbul Metropolitan Municipality opened the Panorama 1453 History Museum at a cost of 1.2 million dollars, where visitors can "relive" the fall of Constantinople to the Turks in 3-D. "You can be a soldier in Sultan Mehmed II's army," the brochure promises.[29] Several years ago, the AKP government introduced a new public holiday, Holy Birth Week (April 14–20), to celebrate the Prophet Muhammad's birthday. Many see this as a countercelebration to the Kemalist-themed National Sovereignty and Children's Day (April 23).[30] In May 2012, the government overhauled national rituals, eliminating official stadium events of costumed and choreographed youth, ten-story banners of Ataturk, and military displays. The secularist newspaper *Milliyet* reported that heavily veiled, lower-class Islamists were flocking to the World War I Gallipoli memorial as an alternative to paying tribute at Ataturk's tomb in Ankara. There, the outraged reporter wrote, they prayed for the Turkish martyrs and picnicked on the graves of foreigners. A "know-nothing" tour guide related that "a cloud descended from the sky and the enemy was lost into that

Figure 1.1. Taksim subway station tile mural depicting the Turkish conquest of Byzantine Constantinople in 1453.

cloud." Saints smashed the enemy's bullets. Gallipoli was presented as a jihad against the heathen; Ataturk, the heroic frontline commander at Gallipoli, wasn't even mentioned.[31]

At one level, Turkish society appears to be divided into secular and Muslim positions whose proponents are circling the wagons and demanding ideological and behavioral purity from their members. But neither term—secular or Muslim—does justice to the variety of possible positions and their sometimes surprising combinations. For instance, to an outside observer who assumes Islam is anti-West, it would appear counterintuitive that it is the Islam-rooted AKP, the Muslim bourgeoisie, and other Muslim publics, such as the Gülenists, that are enthusiastic developers of a globalized economy and that support political liberalization, international political alliances, and in many cases EU membership. Hard-line secularists, however, including some in the military, oppose these same things in favor of an isolationist, globally unplugged "Turkey for the Turks." These secularists feel deeply their loss of influence and fear the spread of Islamic conservatism and ethnic separatism that might result from more liberal laws and uncontrolled freedom of speech and religion. Globalization and EU membership would erode the final vestiges of state control over what they believe to be divisive religious and ethnic identities, spelling an end to Turkey as a coherent and unitary nation—"one and undivided," as General Büyükanıt put it.

These attitudes don't map neatly onto AKP membership or Kemalism. A 2007 survey examined some new categories of political identity that had recently gained currency.[32] Forty-four percent of Turks defined themselves as "new right" or "modern rightist," meaning prodemocracy and pro-West. The majority (66 percent) of AKP supporters chose this category. The rest said they were "traditional rightists," skeptical of democracy and the West, a category shared by a quarter of the survey population. Another quarter of the population identified with "traditional left," also skeptical of democracy and the West, but for different reasons. In other words, while half the population is skeptical of democracy and the West, a majority of AKP supporters are pro-West.

Rather than understanding secular and Muslim nationalisms as yet another set of binary categories, I see them as shorthand for relatively distinct patterns of self-identification as national subjects based on certain forms of knowledge about what it means to be a Turk.[33] This knowledge can be acquired in many ways, from school or the media, by way of authority figures or neighborhood chat. In some ways, which I discuss in chapter 7, secular and Muslim understandings of national subjectivity converge. The unique qualities of Muslim nationalism, however—particularly its unorthodox definition of the nation and its boundaries—are important for understanding a number of issues in Turkey, including the increase in social and political tension and the AKP government's unprecedented political and economic adventurism inside and outside the country. Some pundits have mistakenly glossed this as Turkey's turning to the East and away from the West because of the Islamic sympathies of its government. They fail to understand that the new Turks are motivated not by Islam but by postimperial political and economic ambitions that extend far beyond the Muslim Middle East.

OTTOMANISM AND ITS DISCONTENTS

Under the AKP, Turkey became an active, independent international player, engaging in diplomacy with countries as far afield as Brazil and Venezuela, as well as countries outside the comfort zone of previous Kemalist governments. These governments tended to be suspicious of Muslim states as potentially threatening secularism, and of European states, especially Greece, as potential enemies wishing to undermine Turkey's integrity, possibly with the help of Turkey's Christian and Kurdish minorities. The mutilation of Ottoman territory before and after World War I by European powers has been neither forgotten nor forgiven. By contrast, since coming to power in 2002 the AKP government has lifted visa requirements to dozens of countries—many in the Middle East and North Africa—and forged strong ties with regional states like Russia and Iran, including those with whom it has had problematic relations in the past, like Greece and Armenia. Turkey has been opening new embassies in sub-Saharan Africa and building schools, signing trade deals, and leading relief efforts there. The AKP's willingness to consider a Cyprus settlement, treating it as a subject of international negotiation, flies in the face of decades of Kemalist insistence that any solution that "gives up" Cypriot territory would be dishonorable and would expose the island's ethnic Turks to danger.

The architect of Turkey's foreign policy, Ahmet Davutoğlu, denies that Turkey wishes to re-create the Ottoman Empire, an idea that would not sit well with other regional nations, but he is clearly inspired by this history. "Reintegration is the most important issue for us," he said, referring to Turkey's policies in the Middle East. "The foundation for it is in our history and geography." He wishes "to bring back the golden era, which produced many important civilizations."[34] The desire to change society in order to recapture a golden era thought to have existed in the past resonates at many levels, from AKP's postimperial ambitions to the longing of ordinary people for a "golden age" of communal solidarity and cosmopolitan civility in which moral values coexist with affluence. Turkey's Ottoman past, long ignored under the Kemalist regime, now romanticized and consumed uncritically, has become a touchstone for these desires.

The Ottoman model, for instance, has provided Muslim nationalists with a rationale for integrating Jews and Christians within the nation. Under the Ottoman *millet* system, non-Muslim religious communities were assigned places within the Ottoman system that allowed them semi-independence in daily affairs, but not equality with Muslim subjects of the empire. AKP politicians often refer to the millet model when discussing outreach to Christian communities. They do so largely ahistorically, without acknowledging the supremacy inherent in the historic system.

Furthermore, the Ottoman model does not provide a framework for encompassing Turkey's other minorities, like Kurds and Alevis.[35] The Ottoman state tried a number of different strategies to co-opt or control Kurds and Alevis, whom they saw as potentially rebellious subjects, with only intermittent success.[36] It is not surprising, then, that today's Muslim nationalists lack an ideological framework for incorporating these groups into the nation.[37] This lack of direction has led to inconsistent policies and false starts.

For instance, the AKP initially attempted to appeal to the Kurds as fellow Muslims and, as did previous governments, focused on developing the largely Kurdish southeast region economically. Kurds make up about 20 percent of the population, with a majority living in the impoverished east and southeast regions bordering Iran, Iraq, and Syria. The mountainous area also provides a haven for the PKK, which has been engaged in an armed struggle with the Turkish state since 1984 over Kurdish autonomy and greater political and cultural rights for the country's Kurds. The PKK continues to draw fighters from the local population, which has been brutalized by poverty, years of warfare, extrajudicial killings of Kurdish notables by rogue elements of the Turkish military, and curtailment of their rights by an unsympathetic state. The PKK goes through periods of quiescence, then steps up attacks against security forces and civilians that draw a violent response in a seemingly endless cycle of reprisals that have taken more than forty thousand lives. Kurdish political parties participate in elections, but they are widely seen as the political arm of the PKK and are routinely closed down by the courts.[38]

In 2009 the AKP government began to take steps toward what it called a "democratic opening," restoring Kurdish language rights, permitting a Kurdish television station, allowing politicians to campaign in Kurdish, offering a more generous amnesty for PKK rebels, and returning village names that had been Turkified to their original Kurdish. Although many voters in the southeast supported the AKP initially, it soon became clear that the human rights situation did not improve as a result of the AKP's brotherly embrace, and voters returned their support to Kurdish parties. Kurdish politicians, journalists, and protesters, including children, continued to be arrested and given extensive jail terms for supporting the PKK, not infrequently for holding a poster, throwing a rock, or writing a news article. That December, the Democratic Society Party (DTP, *Demokratik Toplum Partisi*), whose Kurdish deputies were seated in parliament, was closed down by the Constitutional Court for threatening the state's unity. As reflected in both the Islamic and secular media, there was little public support from the start for the government's "democratic opening." Somer and Liaras attribute these cynical and defensive reactions, particularly of the elites, to a belief that ethnic pluralism is backed by external powers and that its political expression causes disunity and weakness. The public is unable to differentiate between demands for regional and cultural autonomy and separatism.[39]

At the same time, the PKK stepped up its deadly attacks on Turkish soldiers, police, and civilians, causing an outpouring of anti-PKK nationalist fervor that swung easily into anti-Kurdish feeling. After the PKK killed twenty-four soldiers early in October 2011, the military opened a massive offensive against PKK members in Turkey and their bases over the border in Iraq. While the streets and media convulsed with nationalist outrage, calling the concessions of the "democratic opening" "treason," it is notable that inside the parliament building in Ankara a committee quietly began its work to design a new liberal constitution that is expected, among other things, to guarantee ethnic rights.

The Alevi are a heterodox religious community that combines elements of Shi'i Islam and pre-Islamic religious practices. The Turkish census does not record religious affiliation, so estimates of the Alevi population range widely from between 15 percent to 25 percent of the population, with considerable overlap with the Kurdish population. Alevis tend to have a more secular, liberal lifestyle than their Sunni neighbors.[40] Women play a central role in religious ritual, which involves music and dance and takes place in an assembly house (*cemevi*) rather than a mosque. Alevis suffered centuries of oppression under the Ottomans, who accused them of not being truly Muslim and suspected them of colluding with the Shi'i Persians against the empire. Alevi Kurds were victims of the early republic's Turkification policies and were massacred by the thousands in Dersim in 1937–39. In the 1970s, Alevis became associated with socialist and other leftist movements, while the political right was dominated by Sunni Muslims. An explosive mix of sectarian cleavages, class polarization, and political violence led to communal massacres of Alevis in five major cities in 1977 and 1978, setting the stage for the 1980 coup.[41]

Today, some Alevi communities have reinvented themselves around cultural foundations; others have revived Alevi rituals and spirituality. Alevis have petitioned to have their *cemevleri* officially recognized by the state as houses of worship (at present they have the status of cultural centers), which would bring them tax benefits and government assistance. Although the AKP has reached out to the Alevis, attending ritual events and listening to their demands, official recognition has not been extended. Alevis themselves remain conflicted about state recognition, and the issue is mired in questions about the status of other non-Muslim houses of worship.[42] However, another Alevi demand, that the state school curriculum incorporate the study of Alevism as well as the Sunni faith, was implemented in October 2010 in the context of teaching pluralism of religion.

The AKP also has pushed the EU accession process forward. Responding to the requirements for membership, Turkey has revamped many of its laws and institutions. A parliamentary commission has been established to draw up a more liberal constitution based on individual human rights (that would, in effect, no longer allow the state to limit religious and ethnic expression, for instance, by banning headscarves at universities or use of the Kurdish language).[43] The AKP also has passed laws improving women's rights that have long been sought by women's groups.

It is important to point out, however, that liberal impulses regarding minorities and women have been almost continually contradicted in practice. While the state has returned confiscated properties to Christian owners, others are dispossessed through the courts or by slight-of-hand. AKP officials, the military, and the media have stoked a fear of missionaries, creating a hostile climate in which a number of Christians have been murdered; there have been violent community riots, sometimes supported by local officials, against Kurdish and Roma citizens; women's legal rights have been diluted by judges and officials acting out normative, rather than legal, standards; and AKP officials have expressed open hostility toward gay, lesbian, and transgendered citizens and their organizations. How can this discrepancy between liberal impulse and illiberal practice be explained? Secularists would say that the AKP is showing its true face, that it was forced to carry out liberal reforms to appease the Europeans and gain the support of liberal Turks who wish to join the European Union. Now that the party has a wide power base in the electorate and is essentially unopposed, they argue, it no longer needs to curry favor with outsiders and can reveal its true motive, which is to undermine democracy and replace it with shari'a law.

I would suggest a different explanation, for it is not only pious AKP supporters that are full of contradictions. In a society characterized by powerful group identities and norms, belief in the desirability of individual liberty almost inevitably collides with collective norms. This does not mean that people give up all individuality and personal goals but, rather, that daily life operates at several levels at once. A typical response in my conversations about identity with pious Turks was the following. They chose to be Muslim, and because it is a consciously chosen identity, being Muslim is superior to being Turkish, an identity into which a person is born. Yet, the same speaker might well deny choice to his or her daughter who wishes to unveil in order to train for a profession. Similarly, a secular young woman might profess a belief in human rights and desire that Turkey join the European Union yet be intolerant of women wearing headscarves, of Jews, or of the open expression of Kurdish ethnicity. While choice and liberal individualism may be valued, shared beliefs and practices that are markers of group membership are lines that cannot be crossed except at risk of losing group membership, being exiled from your family, no longer being invited to dine with friends, and being marked as a person without honor.[44]

INDIVIDUAL LIBERTIES AND COLLECTIVE LOGIC

Whether secular or pious, Turks must continually negotiate between individual liberties that allow innovation, and a collective logic that demands that they demonstrate group loyalty and adherence to community values. It is a logic that cannot be denied without threat of losing the support of constituents and community. In other words, individual strategies must fit a cultural logic. Such alignment, I suggest, is considered honorable, Turkish, and patriotic. Individual strategic action without a normative frame is seen to be dishonorable, impure, non-Turkish, and a threat to the morals and unity of society. In the coming chapters, I will discuss how these issues affect the constitution of the national subject. Here I would like to make the point that contradictory practices and discourses in Turkish politics and daily life result in part from the dissonance between practical, cognitive decisions made in the best interests of the nation or oneself (or one's party) and the pull of conservative collective norms that require that every individual put his or her group first. Judges and police officers may have a grasp of the law on the books but also a duty to uphold the ethics of their communities, even if these contradict one another. Thus, judges and prosecutors admit to placing the welfare of the state above the law,[45] and police regularly return battered wives to their husbands because that is the culturally appropriate thing to do, although the law requires police to protect women, even from their families.

Turks have always pursued their personal choices and motivations within powerful collective frameworks provided by family, community, and nation. In my first book, set in Istanbul's squatter areas in the mid-1980s, I discussed how categories of people—mothers and fathers, mothers-in-law, sons and daughters-in-law—used different strategies to obtain access to or control of the resources and labor of others, and how family relations acted as a template for everyday business dealings.[46] In the 1990s, I examined the way in which Turkey's Islamist movement mobilized people to support a political party by setting political relations within the framework of neighborliness, which contained elements of the mutual obligation that characterized family ties. Personal motivations created contradictions within the Islamist movement but also served strategically to paper them over. Female activists, for instance, seemed to have quite different motivations for participating than male activists. When I pointed out to some of the women that their male colleagues had told me they were interested in changing the law so they could take more than one wife, the female activists, who were much more interested in gaining an education and careers, dismissed this by saying, "That's just their personal opinion. It has nothing to do with the party."[47] In other words, individual goals were represented strategically as being either aligned with or deviant from movement norms.

The coexistence of subjective freedom and the demands of the collectivity lead to sometimes surprising and contradictory discourses and practices that cross social divisions. For example, it is not uncommon for people to claim to be simultaneously liberal (*liberal*) and conservative (*muhafazakâr*). In other words, they believe in a general framework of individual civil liberties and yet live (and demand that others live) according to a collectivist logic that denies certain rights. This is as true for well-meaning secularists who believe that veiling oppresses women, and therefore support the ban that keeps covered women from attending universities, as for pious Muslims who try to ban alcohol consumption "for the good of society." Others point out proudly that all Turkish citizens, regardless of ethnic origin, can succeed in Turkish society—as long as they participate as Turks, rather than Kurds. These same people, whether secular or pious, are likely to support education for girls and at the same time believe that mothers should stay at home with their children. There is room for individual self-development, but within the limits of a communally defined moral world.

People, in other words, can simultaneously be global liberals and local chauvinists. They can be true to type, loyal group members, yet in the pragmatic negotiations of everyday life exhibit unlikely similarities with the "other" type, whether defined socially or politically. Such code-switching between individual rights and community demands is aptly demonstrated by the AKP in its contradictory discourses supporting universalist principles of human rights while at the same time curtailing freedom of speech and openly opposing lifestyles that do not conform to a conservative worldview. Secularists point to these contradictions as an example of AKP's duplicity and a sign of the AKP's hidden intention to turn Turkey into an Islamic state, but at base they express the dual nature of political and social life as open to innovation while being communally limited. Secularists exhibit similar contradictions between a freewheeling Westernized lifestyle and limited communal tolerance for difference, as when they demonize the expression of nonorthodox ideas and identity markers (for instance, wearing a headscarf, refusing to drink alcohol, or speaking Kurdish). The effect is heightened by a majoritarian understanding of democracy in which the electoral winners, having obtained a majority, get to determine what is allowed and what is banned in social life according to the norms of their communities, with no room for tolerance of nonconforming practices (whether alcohol consumption or veiling).[48]

In practice national subjectivity is highly situational. It is the product of individual motives, the position and perspective of the actor, the intended audience, and the multiple frameworks (civilized, modern, conservative, Kemalist, secular, Muslim, liberal, and so on, as these are defined locally) within which an individual is situated while projecting his or her identity at any given moment. As Fredrik Barth demonstrated in his work on Balinese identity, the definition of a culture must proceed from the individual's understanding and expression of cultural categories, which are always strategic.[49] Consequently, this book does not aim to develop a coherent definition of "Turks" or Turkishness but, rather, presents sketches of competing and overlapping cultures of Turkishness and other forms of national subjectivity.

Being Turkish, like being Balinese, is a form of knowledge acquired and filtered through socialization, education, and other life experiences. Such knowledge is rarely unitary but has layers of shared meanings and expected characteristics, sometimes of a contradictory nature. These can be implemented, consciously or unconsciously, by the individual to fit the social context.[50] Nationalism, like religion, has affective, as well as communal and cognitive dimensions. Certain sources of knowledge are considered more acceptable than others, and certain criteria of validity apply, what Barth calls touchstones for truth. These too will vary, appealing to emotion, reason, or the authority of a text, group, or leadership figure. Nationalism, like religion, draws on stylized performances and key metaphors to scale its message and values up from the individual to the larger public. All cultural descriptions, in other words, are positioned evaluations and, at the same time, political assertions. As such, they are ideally studied when expressed as discourse in particular settings.

It is important to point out, as Barth does, that although individuals project identities that are motivated and strategic, these are recognizable to others within the same national framework. In Bali, a Hindu farmer might have little in common with a Muslim urban professional, but both will claim to be Balinese. The debates about Turkishness, however fierce, take place between individuals—and sometimes family members or friends—who would all claim to be members of the Turkish nation. As much as Turks might reject nonconforming cultural assertions of Turkishness, they nevertheless recognize one another as acting within a national framework, even if that acknowledgment elicits shame or aversion. Turkish national culture, the sociologist Ferhat Kentel once told me, is like a balloon with lots of bulges. When you inflate it, the bulges disappear.

CONCLUSION

To all appearances, Turkey's Third Republic is caught in a fierce battle between secularist and Muslim sectors of the population. Although each side invokes traditional categories of political and social difference, the outcome has been revolutionary in its transformation of Turkish society. This transformation is not easily read from the categorical labels, since liberal and conservative impulses and actions do not map neatly onto what is expected of a "secular" or "Muslim" government or population. Furthermore, each "side" is rife with contradictions. What is clear is that since the 1980s a new self-consciously Muslim elite has not only mounted a powerful political and economic challenge to the traditional secular elite but has developed an alternative, nonorthodox definition of the nation and the national subject based on a post-Ottoman, rather than Republican, model.

Muslim nationalism, I suggest, is largely based on a cultural Turkism, rather than blood-based Turkish ethnicity, and imagines the nation as having more flexible Ottoman imperial boundaries, rather than historically embattled Republican borders. This view creates quite a different understanding of Turkish national interests and allows Muslim nationalists the freedom to open borders to Arab states, make alliances globally, and pursue economic interests without concern for the ethnic identity of its interlocutors or the role they played in Republican history (with former enemies Greece and Armenia, for instance). Not surprisingly, such actions have occasioned great tension and a backlash from Kemalist secularists, who have consolidated forces with the military. Hundreds of officers and members of civil society have been arrested over the past three years in what has come to be known as the Ergenekon trial, accused of fomenting national chaos through assassinations and other means in order to pave the way for a coup against the AKP government.

Both secularists and "conscious" Muslims share a belief that to be Turkish means to be Muslim, and that Turkish Islam is the better form of Islam. Both desire to be modern, and each faction in its own way wishes to connect to the West. Both emphasize cultural and ideological purity. I will suggest as well that the association of sexual purity with national boundaries makes it difficult for women to imagine a place for themselves within the nation, as mothers of martyrs or as citizens perhaps, but not as national subjects. Indeed, *nationalist*—whether secular or Muslim—is a masculine term with which few women are able or willing to affiliate.

An important aspect of the term *Muslim nationalism*, then, is that it describes primarily a male experience of the relation between religious subjectivity and the state. Women may share many of the characteristics and ideas described previously, but their experience of Islamic modernity does not weld their identity to the nation-state. If the interface between nation and women is powerfully shaped by cultural discourses about their sex, in other ways, the distance between women's experience and nationalist expectations means that their ideas can afford to be less predictable and leave room for an appreciation of pluralism and debate.

Turkey arguably is becoming more socially conservative, and its traditional emphasis on maintaining group solidarity remains intact, although the constitution of such "groups" and networks has in some cases changed dramatically. This is true especially among the young, who are creating new roles within what appear on the surface to be traditional social and political frameworks. Surprisingly, Turkish society also may be becoming more liberal, as bourgeois expectations and practices and global connections transform daily life for "conscious" Muslims and others. One cannot say, however, that Turkey is becoming more democratic, as long as electoral success does not bring with it tolerance of nonconforming practices and identities. It may well be modern Muslim women who hold the most promising key to greater pluralism and tolerance, although they have been kept far from any door to national leadership.

Road Map

This discussion is largely based on research carried out in Turkey in 2008 that included participant observation as well as formal interviews and countless informal encounters. I spoke with individuals of both sexes—young and old, pious and secular, educated and working class, villagers and city dwellers, and of different faiths. Many of the people I spoke with I have come to know over the years as a result of repeated visits in the service of various research projects. Some have aging family photos in which I appear, noticeably younger. It is this trust and familiarity that I rely on to allow me some modicum of depth and insight into people's explanations of who they are. I am immensely grateful for their thoughtful answers and discussions among themselves to which I have been privy. Unless the speakers are public persons and have permitted me to use their names, I have used pseudonyms to protect their privacy. I was disappointed not to have been able to speak with right-wing nationalist youth. Despite introductions, in this polarized climate I was unable to overcome their suspicions. Although the method was less satisfactory, of necessity I relied on survey data to flesh out their views.

I make no attempt in this present study to be representative, but I wish to discuss certain discursive patterns that emerged from my conversations. I define as "Muslim" those who responded to my questions about their identity (*kimlik*) by volunteering Muslim before Turk, and "secularists" as those who made a point of placing a Muslim identity second to Turkishness, however they defined it. Other scholars have examined this difference between Turk-first and Muslim-first self-attribution. Most recently, in 2010, concerned about social "othering" of people of different origins in Turkey, the Educators Labor Union (*Eğitim Bir-Sen*) commissioned a national study of Turkish identity. Among other things, respondents were asked how they presented themselves in terms of cultural identity. Fifty-three percent chose Turk, and 33 percent chose Muslim.[51] In another 2010 study, in which respondents were given more choices, they selected the following as their "most important identity": Turkish citizen, 36 percent; Turkish *millet/ulus* (nation, people, tribe), 29 percent; devout Muslim who obeys Islamic precepts, 18 percent; modern (*çağdaş*) Muslim with laic mindset and lifestyle, 9 percent; ethnic, 5 percent; regional, 1 percent.[52] When respondents in a different study were asked whether they were modern Muslims using the term *modern*, instead of *çağdaş*, which is associated with Kemalism, 63 percent chose that over "traditional Muslim".[53] In a 1998 national study of Turkish youth, respondents who chose to identify themselves as religious-traditional nearly always chose Turkish-national as the second point of reference, and vice versa.[54] What is clear from the many surveys on identity is that being Turkish and being Muslim are primary, overlapping expressions of belonging. What is not clear is what it means to be Muslim or a Muslim Turk or a Turkish national subject.

In surveys respondents are generally asked to select from a list of prepared choices. In contrast, I did not specify answers but simply asked people who they were and how they presented themselves to others, then asked them to elaborate upon their relation to the nation and national culture. It is interesting that, despite not being prompted, most men began with either Muslim or Turkish as their primary form of self-identification, and with Turkish or Muslim second. Women and some liberals were an exception to this, and this is part of the story I wish to tell here. Since the Muslim-first and Turkish-first identity division was so powerful and seemed also to predict how people related to the nation and national culture, I framed the larger discussion in this book in those terms. I took the liberty of substituting "secular" for "Turkish," as in "secular nationalism," since that more clearly reflected the complex of meanings associated with "Turkish" in this context. My conversational partners generally marked their choice of a "Turkish" identity by making a point of placing Muslim second, sometimes deliberately highlighting their secular lifestyle.

This is not an attempt to reduce the present social conflict to secular versus Muslim (although these are powerful constituent elements) but, rather, to try to understand *de novo*, with as few preexisting expectations as possible, how people with different characteristics and positions in society perceive of themselves as part of a nation. That is, what forms of knowledge make up their national subjectivity, under what circumstances, and why? And, finally, what can we understand about the present social tensions—which are expressed in discourses about Turkishness—by grasping what this means to people in practice? This method displaces a wide variety of indigenous differentiations of national and nationalist identity but has the benefit of encouraging people to describe what they know about who they are in relation to the world without reproducing preexisting nationalist categories. This approach was designed to allow people to loosely position themselves along a continuum of self-defined values. I hoped in this way to capture the strategic and potentially contradictory aspects of national subjectivity.

Chapter 2 takes a look at the relation between Islam and the nation in Turkish history. I focus particularly on social and political developments since the 1980s—the rise and decline of Islamism as a political movement, its replacement by a new generation of Muslim democrats and pious modernists, and the development of what I call Muslim nationalism. These are discussed in part as outcomes of macropolitical factors, such as the U.S. invasion of Iraq and the EU's lukewarm response to Turkey's membership bid, but also within the context of Turkish national culture.

Chapter 3 examines secular nationalism. Approaching nationalisms as forms of knowledge embedded in discourses, I begin the chapter with a deconstruction of my conversations with prominent and powerful nationalists. I also ask where and how nationalist forms are produced and reproduced in society. This topic entails discussion of schoolbooks, rituals, and military service, which act as criteria of validity, and structure reception of particular "truths." Media, advertisements, cinema, popular culture, and word of mouth also play a role, and are discussed here and in the following chapters.

Chapter 4 examines two key emblems of fear—the missionary and the headscarf—as axes of Turkey's social and political polarization.

Chapter 5 discusses the role of boundaries and purity in reproducing Turkish identity. I begin with conceptions of "the enemy" and the often violent attempts to "unmix" the population. Fears of boundary penetration and loss of the nation are kept at bay through purity rituals and taboos. I examine objects that are perceived to be "out of place" (like the headscarf), the purification of space through placement of images, rehearsal of in-group/out-group membership in festivals, food preferences, and notions of the purity of blood, custom, language, religion, and music. I also examine entanglement and hybrid (*melez*) forms within society and the expression of these forms within national identity(ies) and political ideology. Liberalism, for instance, can be considered an ideological form of hybridity that, by its very nature of accepting boundary crossing, engages the defenses of the militarist nation.

Chapter 6 takes up the gendered aspect of nationalism and the nation. Two tropes of national identity are soldier and mother of soldier. The link between masculinity and the nation is summed up by the phrases "We are all soldiers" or "Turks are born soldiers," two common male refrains heard throughout Turkish society. The discourse of nationalism uses the same language and imagery as that of sexual purity or honor, that is, the shame brought about by penetration of sexual boundaries. The effect of such discourses, I suggest, is that men and women position themselves differently in the national imaginary.

In Chapter 7, I discuss the dual and contradictory nature of Turkish social and political life as it accommodates individual choice and motivations while validating the primacy of family and community in determining ethics and norms. The collision of individual liberties with the collective logic of Turkish society is played out on a national scale in the contradictory policies and practices of Muslim nationalists and Kemalist secularists. The final chapter examines the concept of Muslim nationalism in relation to the interplay of religion and nationalism in other countries. For instance, Turkey has been widely touted as a model for Arab countries building democratic systems after the Arab Spring. What lessons can be drawn from this analysis of Muslim nationalism about the future course of the Arab Spring?

CHAPTER 2

Islam and the Nation

> Men make their own history, but they do not make it just as they please;
> they do not make it under circumstances chosen by themselves, but
> under circumstances directly found, given and transmitted from the
> past. The tradition of all the dead generations weighs like a nightmare
> on the brain of the living. And just when they seem engaged in
> revolutionising themselves and things, in creating something entirely
> new, precisely in such epochs of revolutionary crisis they anxiously
> conjure up the spirits of the past to their service and borrow from them
> names, battle slogans and costumes in order to present the new scene of
> world history in this time-honoured disguise and borrowed language.
> —Karl Marx, *The Eighteenth Brumaire of Louis Bonaparte*[1]

TURKEY'S THREE REPUBLICAN ERAS all were preceded by coups—political earthquakes that resulted in a substantial shifting of the political and eventually cultural ground. This upheaval included reinterpretations of national identity and what constitutes Turkishness as the state and various governments attempted to shape the subjectivities of their youth through education, rituals, military service, and other forms of socialization, and as new populations gained a voice in this process. These transformations often remained embedded within discourses and practices of the past, especially those related to group membership, whether family, lineage, tribe, or religion, thus providing familiar cultural knowledge that could be mapped onto political and social transformations.

THE FIRST REPUBLICAN ERA

In a series of coups beginning in 1908, the Ottoman sultan was stripped of power by a group of young bureaucrats, officers, and professionals, the *Ittihat ve Terakki Ce-*

An earlier version of a portion of this chapter was published in *Current History* (White 2007).

miyeti (Committee of Union and Progress, CUP); the sultanate was abolished in 1922. The CUP was dedicated to reinstating the Ottoman constitution and parliament that had been abrogated by the sultan. Many of its members had spent years in exile in France, where they called themselves *Jeunes Turcs,* Young Turks. After World War I, when the Ottoman Empire was occupied by the victorious European powers, an army led by Mustafa Kemal (Ataturk) and other army officers linked to the CUP liberated the heartland of the empire (the provinces of Anatolia and Thrace) and in 1923 established the Turkish Republic in those territories. Prior to this, the term Turkish had been used simply to describe people who spoke Turkish or in a pejorative way to refer to rural peasants.[2]

The new Republic of Turkey was vastly reduced from the empire that had once covered most of northern Africa, what we now call the Middle East, the Balkans, Hungary, and southeastern Europe. The government was faced with the task of providing a unifying national identity to these remnants of empire that had encompassed people of many backgrounds, and conflicting regional, sectarian, and tribal loyalties.[3] It did so by distancing itself from its imperial Ottoman past and constructing a new national identity. The basis for a unified nation was debated—should it be Islam, Turkic culture, or race? Meanwhile, prior identities, networks, and hierarchies, far from being displaced, were structurally absorbed into the nation.[4]

Although citizens of many faiths had once populated the Ottoman Empire, by 1923, most non-Muslims had migrated, been expelled, killed, or in the case of the *Rum,* "exchanged" in return for Greece's Muslim population. Eissenstat writes that "At this point, at least, there was a consensus regarding the non-Muslims. They were not part of the nation, even if they could not all be forced out of the national boundaries. The range of possibilities for Muslims was in greater dispute. Now that the Turks had won their independence, it remained to be decided who the Turks were."[5]

Ataturk initially experimented with Islamic language and imagery as a means to unify the mostly Muslim nation, but after several religiously inspired revolts against the new state, he banned Islamic brotherhoods and closed Islamic educational institutions. The state absorbed the wealthy and powerful Islamic foundations that under the Ottomans had offered social services, like education, health care, and social security. Although these services were expected of the modern state, they long remained outside the impoverished nation's ability to provide. In the meantime, people continued to rely for their basic needs on family, clan, community, and religious orders that henceforth operated clandestinely.

Under the influence of ideas about nationalism popular in Europe and Russia at the time, the Turkish state set itself to producing—or, rather, "proving" the prior existence of—a nation homogenous in language, culture, and religion. Interestingly, most of the important participants in these debates about Turkish national identity were from peripheral or mixed areas, some from Turkic areas of the Russian Empire; "the most ardent Turkish nationalist Tekin Alp was a Jew from Seres, the Westernizer Abdullah Cevdet a Kurd from Arapkir, Ziya Gökalp half Kurdish from Diyarbakır, and Sait Nursî a Kurd from Bitlis."[6]

In the first two decades of the Republic, Ataturk mobilized the intelligentsia of the nation to "discover" its long and glorious national history, collect the nation's folklore,[7] and develop a common Turkish language to replace the cosmopolitan Ottoman used by the bureaucratic elite.[8] Archaeology was harnessed to reinvestigate and rewrite history to give Turks a rich past and to counter the identity of "Mongolian-type" barbarians they believed Western scholars had assigned them, referring to the eleventh- and twelfth-century Turkic migrations into Anatolia that had initiated the Ottoman dynasty.[9] As the Republican intellectual Selahattin Kandemir explained in the introduction to his 1933 book about the Hittites, "the root of national power is national identity. What creates national identity is national history."[10]

The Turkish Historical Society (*Türk Tarih Kurumu*) was founded in 1930. Ataturk gave the society the mission to develop a scientific thesis about the roots of Turkish history. Scholars were assigned different segments of world history to study for their relevance to Turkish history. The result was a manuscript completed in 1930, *Outline of Turkish History* (*Türk Tarihinin Ana Hatları*), which included discussions of China, India, Mesopotamia (Hittites, Phrygians, Lydians, and Seljuks), the Aegean Basin (Greeks), Italy (Etruscans), Iran (Achamenids, Parthians, Sassanians), Central Asian Turkic states, and the Ottoman Empire. This book, of which only 100 copies were printed, formed the basis for the Turkish History Thesis (*Türk Tarih Tezi*) that was incorporated into school textbooks.[11] It posited that Turks were an ancient people that radiated out of Central Asia in successive waves of migration long before the eleventh century, crossing many areas of the world, populating and bringing civilization to native peoples of China, India, the Middle East, northern Africa, the Balkans, and parts of Europe. According to the Turkish History Thesis, the Turks were direct ancestors of the Sumerians (2900 BC) and the Hittites (1600 BC), and contributed significantly to the development of Greek civilization. A similar linguistic theory, the Sun Language Theory, was developed that proposed that these emigrants spoke an ancient form of Turkish that contributed loanwords to every primitive language in these regions, providing concepts necessary for abstract thought. While the flurry of archaeological activity that resulted from the Turkish History Thesis gained international approval for its professional quality, the Sun

Language Theory was a fiasco. When presented at an international conference of linguists, it was severely criticized.

It is noteworthy that these early attempts at creating a national identity did not focus on blood or a single Turkish lineage, or on Islam. Even the reference to Central Asian origins was couched in a larger civilizational project. "Rather than isolate a single culture or historical lineage as the ancestor of the Turks," the contemporary scholar Tanyeri-Erdemir suggests, the aim of this all-embracing nationalism was to create "a common ground for all the citizens of the newly established nation-state" and to help intellectuals "to imagine 'Turkishness' as a general, inclusive concept." [12]

Archaeological investigations were undertaken to provide supporting evidence for the Turkish History Thesis and to validate the nation by tying its citizens to the land it encompassed. The Turks of the First Republic created unity out of their inherited diversity by positing that the Turks were the legitimate heirs (and in some cases, progenitors) of numerous other civilizations. Until the 1980s, the capital city, Ankara, was officially represented by a Hittite sun disk.

Ankara was built largely from scratch on the windswept Anatolian plateau, far from the minarets and palaces of the corrupt Ottoman capital, Istanbul. The city's master plan was laid out by Hermann Jansen, a German urban planner. The government adopted the international style of modernist architecture as "Turkish" national style [13] and hired European architects to help build it. "International" was taken to mean that the style was not representative of any particular country and thus was available as a building block for Turkish identity. Similarly, Western practices and lifestyles were incorporated into Turkish modernity as civilization (*medeniyet*), "a rational, international system of knowledge, science and technology." [14] By participating in this globally shared civilization, the sociologist Ziya Gökalp wrote at the time, Turkish society could rescue its unique culture from the medieval, partly Arabian Islamic, and partly Byzantine Christian civilization in which it had become mired during the Ottoman period. [15]

Gökalp's writings influenced Ataturk and his circle, and his ideas were incorporated into the founding ideals of the Republic, although Gökalp died soon after it was established. He imagined national culture to be composed of certain essential values and habits and a form of Islamic worship that was unique to Turks. Rather than considering Islam as faith, he viewed it as a set of beliefs and mores that would socialize Muslims into the collective values of a culture that included a common education, morality, and aesthetics. [16] In this way, a Turkish national essence, consisting of an ethical and egalitarian Muslim culture cleansed of Arab and Byzantine pollution, could coexist with modern, Western lifestyles and technology (part of an international language of civilization). This distillation also had the effect of reimagining aspects of Turkey's Ottoman and imperial past—the influence of non-Muslims and non-Turkish Islam—as polluting national identity.

According to the official historical narrative still taught in Turkish schools, under Ataturk's enlightened leadership and guiding hand, every aspect of the new Turkish nation constituted a definitive break from its Ottoman imperial past, from women's roles in society to clothing, the alphabet, and the calendar.[17] These were radically Westernized and cut off from Islamic references. The language was purged of Arabic and Persian terms to create a more "authentic" Turkish vocabulary that required invention of new terms by a Turkish Language Association (*Türk Dil Kurumu*) created for this purpose. For a while, even the call to prayer was in Turkish. Since communication between the capital and the mostly rural population was limited, for a long time these changes mostly affected the already Westernized urban population.[18]

The Young Turks, who had been in exile in France before the war, had been strongly influenced by the French Revolution and its Jacobin tradition of anticlericalism and state-enforced secularism, or *laïcité*. *Laiklik*—state Islam—became a central pillar of Republican national identity. The Turkish term *laiklik* means state control over religion and a strong state role in keeping religion out of the public sphere. For the Kemalists, religion was a dangerous, divisive force in society that could not be eliminated and so had to be kept under the thumb of the state. Instead of formally separating religion and the state, as France did in 1905, the Kemalists established the Directorate of Religious Affairs (*Diyanet İşleri Başkanlığı*), which trains and oversees all religious specialists; supervises mosques, religious schools, and Islamic education; vets sermons; and translates religious texts and interprets them.[19] The Diyanet also issues advice about how to be a good Muslim that the state feels is compatible with a rational, scientific, secular society. The display of religious symbols in public places, such as schools, state buildings and hospitals, was banned. Priests were forbidden to wear their collars in the street, and imams their turbans. Western clothing became compulsory for men, and women were prohibited from covering their heads in public institutions, like the Grand National Assembly and the civil service. Turkishness, in other words—the ideological clothing for the naked citizen—was conceived as a common state-produced national, culturally ethnic, territorial, linguistic, and Muslim identity. The role of each of these elements in national identity, however, has fluctuated over time.

Ataturk's definition of the nation did not exclude non-Muslim citizens, so long as they met three minimum conditions: they spoke Turkish as their mother tongue; adopted Turkish culture, including Turkish names; and accepted the ideals of Turkism. Turkification was based on "language, sentiments, and ideas," but part of this process meant disbanding their own community structures, like religious schools, and dissolving their ethnic/religious identities into the new national Turkish identity, becoming Turks of Jewish or Christian faith, indistinguishable from Muslim Turks. Many minority groups accepted the Kemalist project as a way to participate on equal terms in building the new nation. Prominent Jews started a "Speak Turkish" campaign among their fellows and wrote books explaining how to be a Turk. Feroz Ahmad's analysis of the cooperative relationship between Jewish political elites and the CUP between 1908 and 1918 supports the view that there was little anti-Semitism during this period.[20]

But by the end of the 1920s, nationalist discourse had shifted from language and culture to race, and this change had an immediate effect on non-Muslims. In his study of the Ottoman *Dönme*, or Muslims descended from seventeenth-century Jewish converts, Baer describes the community as completely assimilated and very active in the CUP and in the founding of the Turkish Republic. Indeed, as Muslims, the Dönme were forced to move from Salonica to Istanbul as part of the 1923 population exchange between Greece and Turkey. But soon after their arrival, Republican leaders and elites began to question their Turkish credentials and to ask who their ancestors were. If their ancestors were Jews, then clearly they were not really Muslims and not "real" Turks. Consequently, the Dönme community, despite its ties to the Republican leadership, was harassed, Baer writes, to the extent that the community ceased to be a corporate entity, and the remaining members have ever since hidden their Dönme identity.[21]

Cagaptay describes 1924 debates in the Grand National Assembly about what constituted a citizen. Non-Muslims speaking other languages were differentiated as *Kanun Türkü* (Turks-by-law), thus opening an institutionalized gap between Turks-by-citizenship and Turks-by-nationality.[22] During this period, members of the Turkish national movement alternatively defined Turkishness by race (Turks were white[23]), blood, territory ("residing within our borders"), ethnicity, culture and language, and religion. The government was faced with resolving concrete dilemmas about whether to award citizenship to Arabs, Circassians, Albanians, Kurds, Chechens, Laz, Uzbeks, and other Muslim peoples, some of whom had fought for the Ottomans but now lived outside Turkish borders. Should they be considered Turks?

The switch from Ottoman cosmopolitanism (in which religion was perceived to be one form of cultural group identity among others) to religio-racial exclusion was a drawn-out process, a response to the increasing Muslim homogeneity of the population and a (largely failed) attempt to use Islam to unify the Ottoman state and then the Turkish nation. Enacar compared schoolbooks, storybooks, periodicals, and poetry from the Abdulhamid period to those published after 1908, when the Young Turks took de facto control of the Ottoman government. The earlier texts emphasized the equality of all Ottoman citizens regardless of origin or religion. In one text, an Ottoman Jew explains that he speaks Turkish and extols the Ottoman discipline he has received. However, by 1913, at which point the empire had lost most of its European provinces in the Balkan wars, the texts had a decidedly racial and Muslim cast, urging Turkish children to become "protectors of the Turkish race and all Muslims in the lost Ottoman lands."[24]

Spickard writes that race becomes significant only when communities "begin to see themselves as fundamentally and irrevocably different," a turning point that he calls "the racial moment."[25] The losses of the Balkan Wars, compounded by the humiliation of World War I, and the political and cultural ascendance of nationalist elements within the CUP provoked such a "racial moment" at the end of the Ottoman period. What "race" meant in the Turkish context, however, would continue to be culturally elaborated and structurally consolidated throughout the rest of the twentieth century.

Eissenstat suggests that Ataturk's assimilationist ethnic definition of Turkish national identity did not resonate with the vast majority of men and women engaged in the national struggle, who believed they "were defending the 'nation' of Islam, not an ethnic identity that had little political value to them."[26] Kemalists used "Muslim" to address the public during the World War I period, when they relied on an alliance with Muslim Kurds against Armenians, Greeks, and the Allied Forces, but after 1924 the term largely disappeared from Republican texts.[27] Challenged by the possibility that Islam might form the basis for a rival political identity, the new state increasingly secularized and incorporated public Islam into its own institutions.[28] To better address ethnic diversity among Turkey's Muslims, Republican nationalists elaborated a definition of Turkish identity that imagined a nation of Muslim "brothers" and "sisters" belonging to the same lineage (soy). "The success of Turkish nationalism," Eissenstat writes, "has rested in large part on its ability to overlap a preexisting and deeply felt Islamic identity."[29]

All Muslims were considered potential members of the early Republican national community. This meant that non-Turkish Muslims, such as Kurds and Balkan Muslims, theoretically could assimilate by learning the Turkish language and culture. But Kurds, although Muslim, were considered poor candidates for assimilation because of their strong tribal loyalties and so were among the groups that Cagaptay found were denied naturalization papers, along with Arabs, Albanians (who also were considered difficult to assimilate), and Jews and Christians who had left the Ottoman Empire during the war years and wished to return. The principles of national membership were not always consistently applied, as other interests and economic and security issues intervened. For instance, Muslims from the Balkans were given preferential treatment, even if they were not Turkish, because the Republican elite drew heavily from there, and the region represented a gateway to Europe.[30] Cagaptay concludes that the national community in the 1930s was defined primarily through "ethnicity" (which he defines as race or soy, plus language) and, secondarily, as nationality-through-religion.

The promised equality as assimilated citizens was undercut by two things—Turkification of the economy and racism. The early Republican elite wished to make Turkey's economy independent of Europe. During Ottoman times, European powers had contractual concessions, called Capitulations, that gave them economic rights and privileges within the empire that were humiliating to the Ottomans. The new Republic focused on making Muslim Turks dominant in sectors, like banking, trade and manufacturing, that until then had been dominated by non-Muslims. The latter were to be replaced by Muslim Turks, who had shed blood in the war and thus had earned the right to be masters of their nation. Non-Muslim Turks were fired and banned from many jobs and professions, and quotas were imposed. Laws were passed that clearly aimed to rid the nation of what it perceived as foreign elements. For example, men and women were stripped of their citizenship if they had not served in the national struggle and had failed to return to Turkey before 1927.[31] In these and other measures against minorities, the term "Turk" was interpreted not as a nationality based on language and assimilation but as an amalgam of race and faith, that is, a person of the Turkish race (soy, or bloodline) and of Muslim faith.

Ankara, in other words, viewed Muslims as Turks, and non-Muslims as outsiders, regardless of their willingness to assimilate. As Muslims, Kurds were by definition Turks, whether they agreed with that designation or not. Their status as Turks was conveniently explained by the Turkish History Thesis, which claims that the Turkish race founded the ancient civilizations of Anatolia. The Kurds, therefore, were simply Turks who had forgotten Turkish.[32]

The elaboration of a religio-racial national identity naturally affects the status of non-Muslims, although the racial component tends to be obscured by historical arguments used to explain their exclusion. Cagaptay surmises that "the contemporary antagonism vis-à-vis Christianity in the country seems to be rooted more in nationalist feelings than in religious intolerance."[33] Rıfat Bali agrees, suggesting that Turks were never able to overcome the fact that the minorities had not fought in the War of Independence and that some had cheered the Allied Forces as they occupied Istanbul and Izmir during World War I.[34] I would add the caveat that the religio-racial definition of the Turkish nation as a Muslim tribe bonded by blood and ancestral roots has made assimilation all but impossible. The historical prejudices to which Bali refers are kept alive in schoolbooks and public discourse. The narrative about the disloyalty of Turkey's non-Muslim citizens, despite the century that has passed since World War I, legitimates the continued exclusion of non-Muslim citizens from the nation by placing the blame on them (as the enemy within) while obscuring the religio-racial nature of the antagonism.

Although race came to play a dominant role in Turkey's national identity, the religious component retained Gökalp's notion of Islam as a quintessentially Turkish cultural identity, rather than a faith. Cagaptay writes, "There is a tension in Turkey between Islam as a religion and Islam as an identity.... While nominal Islam is a marker of Turkishness, Islam as a faith is outside the public sphere."[35] Over the intervening decades, Islam as faith has reentered the public sphere, challenging the notions of Islam as culture and Turkishness as race.

THE SECOND REPUBLIC

After more than two decades of single-party rule, Turkey held its first multiparty elections in 1950, which opened a Pandora's box of unanticipated effects. The elections empowered the rural population to bring their concerns, conservative traditions, regional and clan-based affinities, and local expressions of Muslim faith[36] into the political arena, challenging the narrow parameters of state-defined laicist Islam. Religious brotherhoods and dervish orders had continued to operate clandestinely after being banned early in the Republic, but after the introduction of multiparty political contests in 1946, they began to play a more open role in the Turkish national arena. Politicians appealed to Islamic sentiment and courted religious leaders who could deliver the votes of their followers. Even the starkly laicist government, led by the Republican People's Party (*Cumhuriyet Halk Partisi*, CHP) founded by Ataturk and unopposed until then, was prompted by competition for votes in the lead-up to the election to add voluntary religious instruction to the elementary school curriculum in 1948, and to build more mosques, preacher-training schools, and a school of theology.

The center-right Democrat Party, which pushed out the CHP in the 1950 election, continued these policies. It also built roads to connect the countryside to the cities for the first time, leading peasants to migrate in search of work in the many state-subsidized factories that aimed to meet the nation's every need, from tires, shoes, and glassware to tobacco, tea, and alcohol. Migration created vast squatter areas around the cities and changed the nature of urban life.[37] The opposition CHP and the Kemalist intelligentsia accused the Democrat Party of undermining secularism and the laic nature of the state, leading to a prolonged battle for control over the government.

In 1960, officers in the army carried out a long-planned coup, sending the Democrat Party prime minister, Adnan Menderes, to the gallows.[38] For the first time, the role of the military as Kemalist watchdog was formally acknowledged. Given what it saw as the treacherously populist nature of elected governments, the military assumed the role of guardian of the Turkish state, with the right to intervene if it deemed laicism under threat. At the army's behest, what became known as the Second Republic was fitted with a more liberal constitution and an independent Constitutional Court. A National Security Council was created, a bureaucratic perch from which the military would guide the government.

This long-standing split between the state and the popularly elected government runs like a geological fault beneath Turkey. The state (and its institutions, like the military, judiciary, and education administration) presents itself as the guardian of the laicist system and secular national identity and of the cultural and territorial integrity of the Turkish nation-state. Governments, by contrast, see themselves as representing the interests of their party and of the electorate, a substantial percentage of which is devout in belief or conservative in lifestyle.[39] State and government have clashed almost continually. Since 1950, there have been three coups against elected governments, and several operations just short of a coup. The Constitutional Court has shut down twenty-four political parties—many after they won popular elections—primarily for being too Islamic, although ideological divisions between left and right played a prominent role between 1960 and 1980.

The innovations following the 1960 coup aimed to prevent a power monopoly of the kind the military believed had developed under the Democrat Party. What ensued instead were twenty years of political instability (another coup in 1971) and bloodletting between ideological factions of the left and right, fueled by economic crises, unemployment, social inequality, political fragmentation, and—to quote Marx, in "time-honoured disguise and borrowed language"—an overlap between ideological and traditional cultural motives that mapped political onto communal boundaries.

What made the political extremism in Turkey so exceptionally violent was the fact that it overlay a traditional culture in which honour and shame, an extreme contrast between one's own family or clan and outsiders, and vendetta played a prominent role. Traditional conflicts were given political connotations.[40]

Cultural notions of honor and shame and powerful group identities, the boundaries of which are assumed to be contested and hostile, I suggest, continue to shape national politics today and provide a form of cultural knowledge that defines membership in the national community, as much as in family and clan.

Political rifts in the 1960s and 1970s tore Turkish society apart at every level, from school to workplace. Everyone, even school children, was forced to choose a side, or risk being attacked by those on the "other" side. This was no easy choice, since "left versus right" did not do justice to the many splinter groups that formed. The left was split into socialists, Che Guevaraists, Maoists, and other ideological persuasions. These groups would attack each other for their lack of ideological purity; extremists of all stripes battled with guns, bombs, knives, and whatever else came to hand.[41] At one point, the left-wing mayor of the small Black Sea town of Fatsa officially repudiated the authority of the government and, with his supporters, declared the town an independent Soviet Republic.[42]

On the "right," fundamentalist and secular nationalist youth groups fought for control of the streets, campuses, and neighborhoods. The ultranationalist Gray Wolves acted as the shock troop of the far-right Nationalist Action Party (*Milliyetçi Hareket Partisi*, MHP), a party that was represented in parliament while shielding its radical members. The Gray Wolves carried out drive-by shootings of leftists and Alevis, who were associated with the left, sometimes choosing their victims simply by the style of their mustache. (Leftists liked to sport a Fu Manchu mustache that drooped at the sides of the mouth.)[43] The violence and ideological extremism were inescapable, whether one lived in a village, shantytown, or middle-class housing. In rural areas particularly, ideological differences overlay clan and family feuds, sometimes resulting in high body counts. An attack on an Alevi neighborhood in Maraş organized by the Gray Wolves in 1978 started a raging battle that went on for days and in which more than a hundred people—mostly leftists—were killed. Superimposed on these opposing ideologies was a feud between regional clans, who had taken this opportunity to settle scores.[44] That same year, a student at Ankara University, Abdullah Öcalan, founded the Marxist Kurdish Worker's Party (the PKK), which aimed to establish a socialist Kurdish state in southeastern Turkey, thus mapping ethnicity onto a political identity.[45]

Around the country, as police and local authorities became increasingly helpless to stop the violence, martial law was imposed, which eventually led to a military takeover.[46] Having lived through three years of street violence in Ankara, where I was studying at Hacettepe University, I pocketed my master's degree and left the country in 1978.

THE THIRD REPUBLIC

The coup in 1980 inaugurated the Third Republic with brutal efficiency. The stated aim of the coup was to stop the street violence that was costing dozens of civilian lives a day, and to wrest control from an ineffectual parliament that had become so fractured it was unable to make important decisions. The military banned existing parties and their politicians and set in place a new political system. It appointed a committee that designed a more restrictive constitution. Hundreds of thousands of people were hunted down and arrested, especially on the left, although members of the Gray Wolves were also brought in. Many of those arrested or fired from their jobs were ordinary people—professionals, teachers—who had expressed even vaguely leftist or Islamist views. Dozens were executed, many were tortured, hundreds died in custody, and many more disappeared or were exiled. The military also strengthened its role in the National Security Council to oversee future governments. Elections were held again in 1983.[47] The Motherland Party, led by Turgut Özal, won the election by a substantial margin. The election of Özal set in motion a series of fundamental transformations of Turkish society.

The Motherland Party, while secular,[48] oversaw the expansion of Islamic institutions and liberalization of Islamic discourse under a joint government-military policy called the "Turkish-Islamic Synthesis." This policy was designed to heal the left–right rifts of previous decades and to give Turkish youth an alternative moral universe that, it was hoped, would make them resistant to communism and other ideas of the left. An unanticipated consequence of the liberalization of Islamic expression was the beginning of an Islamist movement that heralded an extraordinary explosion of self-consciously Islamic politics and public discourse.

The expanding Islamic presence in public life was the outcome of a number of factors that came together in the 1980s. The Turkish-Islamic Synthesis coincided with the de facto deregulation of the media in the early 1980s. State-controlled radio and television were challenged by multiple private stations, cable, and other technologies that the state was no longer able to control. A much-discussed television skit at the time acted out an attempted coup that failed as Turkish soldiers ran from one radio and television station to another, unable to take over all of them. It was the first time a military coup had been portrayed in the media as comedy (walking a fine line, since it is illegal to insult the Turkish military). Before long, Islamic radio shows and television stations became popular and discussed long-forbidden topics, including shari'a law and the ideas of Egyptian and Indian Islamist thinkers like Mawdudi, Hasan al Banna, and Sayyid Qutb, whose works had been translated into Turkish in the 1970s. Their ideas gained a following and began a radical trend that advocated a political project and control over the state to set up an Islamic government. This trend was expressed in a series of Islamist political parties that will be discussed later.

Meanwhile, the youth of the postcoup Third Republic threw themselves with gusto into the opportunities afforded by the newly opened economy.[49] Buildings went up, foreign brand names appeared in the shops, and young people sat in cafes, worked in banks, set their sights on success. The mayor of Istanbul at the time, Bedrettin Dalan, talked proudly about Istanbul as a city of yuppies and his plans for making it the conference capital of the world. While this rhetoric ignored the reality of widespread poverty and unemployment, it did capture the sense of possibility that Özal's new policies unleashed even among the poor. Squatter areas became factories without walls, producing for export.[50] Entrepreneurial activity soared, especially in regional cities in Anatolia that had effectively been left out of the state-led economy of earlier years, which had focused primarily on big industry. In the 1980s, by contrast, government policies supported even the smallest export initiatives. Indeed, so generous were the subsidies that some businessmen initially made a killing by exporting loosely knit loops of yarn, claiming they were manufactured goods for export and receiving a subsidy per item exported, then unraveling them, shipping them back, and starting all over.

Neoliberal capitalism and a well-oiled door to the world market liberated the pent-up creativity and entrepreneurship of small and medium-sized businesses. Their owners tended to be more pious and conservative than big-city industrialists. Labeled the Anatolian Tigers by the press, they built their own business networks and professional organizations (for instance, MÜSİAD or *Müstakil Sanayici ve İşadamları Derneği*, Independent Industrialists and Businessmen's Association) that bore the stamp of their conservatism and piety. In a documentary about the Anatolian Tigers, one businessman pointed to his Mercedes and said, "Allah allowed it, so I bought one."[51] Their work ethic and belief that their success is the will of Allah led the press and academics to call these pious businessmen Islamic Calvinists.[52] They and their families provided a market for stylish Islamic fashions, commodities, leisure activities, and gated communities suitable for a middle-class or elite Muslim lifestyle, a lifestyle that was shaped as much by the market as by Islam. The only precedent for a pious Muslim Turkish elite class was in Ottoman times, so businesses invented a Muslim elite lifestyle, replete with cultural references to a romanticized imperial Ottoman past, but also self-consciously modern and even trendy.[53] One company marketed its pious clothing as being reminiscent of Ottoman court dress, but made of European-quality materials.[54]

Less visible associations also sprang up, founded equally on religious affiliation and business ties, like the many independent foundations set up by a global network of modernist Muslims who follow the teachings of a charismatic Turkish preacher, Fethullah Gülen.[55] The foundations have non-Islamic names that make them hard to identify as Gülenist (in Istanbul, the Journalists and Writers Foundation; in Chicago, the Niagara Foundation). Their main function is to coordinate the global charity and investment activities of Gülenist businessmen and other participants, many of them teachers and students. The Gülenist foundations support schools that act as springboards for training what Gülen has called a "golden generation" of youth with know-how and knowledge to excel in the modern world, but with the civic and moral values of good Muslims. In many ways, the Gülenist foundations carry out the functions once associated with Freemasonry—organizing in semi-independent chapters around certain nonreligious, although religion-referenced, rituals (Gülenists meet in reading circles to discuss Gülen's writings); requiring moral uprightness of members; carrying out charitable work; and developing both local and international fraternal networks of mutual assistance that play themselves out in politics and business, often in secret. The main differences may lie in the custom that expects Masons to believe in an unspecified Supreme Being, while Gülenists are clearly Muslims, and in the latter's emphasis on building schools. In any case, like Freemasonry, the Gülenist movement has created widespread networks that support the political and economic ambitions of its members, who are bound less by religious ritual than by lifestyle and success.

Gülenist networks overlap with the Anatolian Tigers and the rising Islamic bourgeoisie, flush with money and power, although it is impossible to tell to what extent. Some pious businessmen may choose to vote for secular parties, especially if they are made uncomfortable by competition from Gülenists. A recent study indicated that some pious businessmen feel pressured to join these networks or face ostracism and loss of customers.[56] Some AKP members are Gülenists; others are not. Gülenists insist that one cannot be a "member" of their movement, only a sympathizer, since foundations (unlike associations) do not have members. This makes it impossible to calculate the extent of Gülenist influence. AKP politicians with whom I've spoken tend to be friendly to the movement, recognizing the contribution Gülenists make to Turkey's education through their high-quality schools. Among working-class Sunni Muslims of my acquaintance, however, Gülenists are relatively unknown and often considered an undesirable cult. This may be due to the middle-class quality of the movement that to my knowledge is not well represented among the working poor and unemployed, who thus remain ignorant of its goals and organization. It may also be due to competition between traditional Muslim brotherhoods like the *Nakşibendi*, who are active in working-class neighborhoods, and the upstart and nontraditional Gülenists who are not organized in any recognizably Islamic manner. The Gülenists, however, were but one strain of Islamic practice and discourse that came to characterize Turkey in the 1980s and 1990s.

In contrast to the Gülenist associations, which were not openly political, several political parties arose during this period that introduced Islamism as a national discourse, directly confronting the laicist Kemalist state and secular society. This period of about fifteen years ended with the election of the AKP, a descendant of these Islamist parties, but one with a different understanding of Islam in politics. The Islamist movement, however, left a legacy of identity discourses, from a resurrection of Ottomanism to a focus on business, that continue to color Muslim nationalism today.

Rise and Fall of an Islamist Movement: *Milli Görüş*

Turkey's population today is almost entirely Muslim, with small minorities of Jews and Christians. About four-fifths of the Muslim population are Sunni Muslims; the rest are Alevi, a non-Sunni syncretistic Muslim minority. A survey in 1999 showed a high level of religious practice in Turkey, with nine of ten adults fasting during the holy month of Ramazan and almost half praying five times a day.[57] Between 40 percent and 60 percent of all respondents rated themselves as religious, and 40 percent defined themselves as Muslim or Muslim Turk before Turkish citizen.[58] Muslim identity, however, is not a homogenous category in Turkey and also offers a code for expressing political ideas, social class position, or general life philosophy, in addition to specific religious beliefs or affiliation.[59] Its elements are incorporated into an individual's national subjectivity, partnered with a distinctly Turkish ethical culture and political history.

Let me begin with definitions of the well-worn categories Islamist and Kemalist. Islamists are Muslims who, rather than accepting an inherited Muslim tradition, have developed their own self-conscious vision of Islam and the ideal Islamic life, which they then bring to bear on social and political events. In many parts of the world, Islamists who wish to inject their religious values into the political sphere push for shari'a law. Even if their aims fall short of introducing Islamic law, Islamists usually desire some form of systemic social and political change, even if the group operates within a secular party system, as in Turkey.

Supporters of Mustafa Kemal Ataturk's laicist reforms are referred to as Kemalists. The Kemalist position combines a kind of authoritarian democracy with a Westernized secular lifestyle. Kemalists have tried to ensure a laic state and secular Turkish society through the government, judiciary, educational system, and military. The army, for instance, closely vets its officer corps, purging anyone who refuses to drink alcohol, whose wife wears a headscarf, or who demonstrates other Islamic tendencies. Both Islamism and Kemalism are self-ascriptive terms representing group boundaries based on shared beliefs about the proper role of religion in society and politics.

As self-referential expressions of group loyalty (or aversion), these discursive categories assume internal coherence and extreme difference. They also assume a lack of change over time. However, the meanings of Islamist and Kemalist have changed over the past decades, and, whatever their differences, as national subjects they share certain characteristics.

Turkey has had only one Islamist movement, *Milli Görüş*, or National Vision. The term refers to the party platform the politician Necmettin Erbakan wrote in 1975 that laid out his vision of a form of modernization that was authentically Turkish and based on Muslim ethics. He proposed a Just Economic Order (*Adil Düzen*) to eliminate socioeconomic inequality and corruption. He called for state withdrawal from economic activities in the heavily state-led Turkish economy and instead espoused the promotion of individual small enterprise. In other words, Milli Görüş wasn't against capitalism, except in its monopolistic form. Rather, its supporters wanted a share. This probusiness approach continues to characterize mainstream pious Muslim discourse today in both business and politics.

Milli Görüş linked Islam to nationalism and had a strong chauvinist and racialist component based on Turkishness and Turkish blood and history. The Ottoman Empire was posited as the originating locus of the civilization of Islam. In this way, Islam provided an authentic Turkish justification of modernization that did not rely on the West. In other words, Milli Görüş used Turkey's Ottoman-Muslim heritage to construct a modern religio-ethnic Turkish national identity.

Milli Görüş was not an underground revolutionary movement but a legitimate strain of political thought within a democratic party system. Erbakan founded a se-

l parties explicitly rooted in these principles. Before Milli Görüş, Islam
.. the form of functional appeals to Islamic forms and practices to curry
.. or with voters but was not a basic building block of party policy. It was the laicist
state that oversaw the functioning of Islam in society. The Diyanet built and ran
mosques and religious foundations; imams or prayer leaders were civil servants. Erbakan's Welfare Party (WP, *Refah Partisi*), was the first Islamist party, that is, a party
rooted in Islamic principles, to do well in elections.[60] Throughout the 1980s Welfare
added to its supporters, including members of an expanding Islamist business and
professional community that did business explicitly within a framework of Islamic
principles. They provided a stable economic underpinning for various aspects of
an emerging Islamist movement in the form of contributions to political parties,
support for charitable organizations, scholarships, and the building of schools and
gender-segregated dormitories, putting into practice both the economic and moral
principles of the Milli Görüş movement. In nationwide municipal elections held in
1994, Welfare won half of the mayoral seats in provincial capitals, including six of
Turkey's largest fifteen cities. Istanbul and Ankara both elected Islamist mayors.
These events shocked and galvanized Kemalists, who organized to counter what they
perceived to be a fundamentalist threat that would culminate in a restrictive shari'a-
based state, which they feared was Welfare's ultimate aim.

Erbakan fueled these fears by speaking against laicism and Westernization and
criticizing Turkey's military cooperation agreement with Israel. He pledged to with-
draw Turkey from NATO and the European Union Customs Union signed in 1996,
in favor of political and economic alliances with other Muslim countries. He said he
planned to pursue a brotherhood of Muslims around the world, replacing Turkey's
ties with and reliance on the West. After the 1994 elections, several attacks were reported on women in Western dress in Istanbul, and attempts were made to separate
women from men on public transport. Some Welfare mayors had statues of nudes
removed from parks and tried to close or restrict restaurants and nightclubs that
served alcohol. In a direct affront to the institutional legacy of Kemalist secularism,
party zealots proposed building an enormous mosque in Istanbul's Taksim Square
beside the modernist Ataturk Cultural Center, which hosted Western-style opera,
ballet, and symphonies. While this plan did not succeed, other emblems of Kemalism were transformed. When Welfare won the 1994 municipal elections in Ankara,
the new mayor changed the official city symbol from the Hittite sun to a design that
included the cupola and minarets of a mosque, a move that was challenged in the
courts. (In 2007 the court demanded the resurrection of the Hittite logo.) Istanbul's
tulip symbol was replaced by a quartet of minarets. These markers were incorporated
in public works, fences, and signs all over the city.[61]

The Welfare Party's antisystem stance heightened public anxiety about the ultimate aim of the party. The party tried to move hundreds of secular-minded judges to posts in rural districts and replace them with judges who might stretch the interpretation of Turkey's secular legal code, especially in the area of family law. This prompted a public outcry, and the move was blocked by a government supervisory council. The press kept a watchful eye on Welfare's actions, and public and civic organizations were quick to mobilize and demonstrate their displeasure. After winning municipal elections, Welfare closed some community libraries and educational centers for women, sometimes replacing them with Quran courses.

The reasons for Welfare's success in elections are multifold. In part, support for the party was a protest against the corruption and incompetence of the other parties. Welfare appealed to widespread religio-cultural values. Despite the concessions made under the Turkish-Islamic Synthesis, the laicist state's continued repression of religious expression led to public demonstrations and political activism, particularly by the conservative sector of the population aspiring to education and economic upward mobility. The ban on wearing headscarves at universities rankled and was seen as an attempt to keep conservative young women from getting an education and entering the professions. Issues of poverty and social class fueled what appeared on the surface to be a purely religious issue. The ban was inconsistently applied, so some covered female students appeared for their final exam or graduation ceremony, only to find that the rules had changed and they were unable to finish their education.

The Welfare Party also appealed to some nonreligious voters. Two-fifths of those voting for Welfare in 1995 identified themselves as secularist.[62] WP's election advertisements avoided religious language and presented it as a forward-looking party with a vision that encompassed all strata of society, regardless of their views about political Islam.[63] Political advertisements referred to issues like pensions, affordable housing, health care, and the environment. Religious themes and images were, for the most part, avoided. The Welfare Party mayor of Istanbul at the time, Recep Tayyip Erdoğan, brought some order to municipal services, and his administration seemed, on the surface at least, to be less corrupt than previous ones.

The party had a face-to-face, personalized political style that mobilized voters through a system of associations, foundations, and informal organizations. The metaphor of family and its associated responsibility and obligation was carried over to the neighborhood and work place, where it meshed with cultural and religious norms that gave neighbors, employees, and so on, rights to communal assistance and just treatment. In other words, human rights and citizens' rights were presented as personal obligations. People were asked, as their religious duty, to take personal responsibility for their neighbors, and businessmen for their employees. This policy carried over into a lack of support for labor unions—they shouldn't be necessary. Unlike the other top-down, highly centralized parties that brought their projects to the voters for support, Welfare built on local solidarities, and wedded local projects and sensibilities to the party's project. The involvement of grassroots organizations lent flexibility and endurance to the Islamist political project, even in the face of the banning of the Welfare Party and jailing of its politicians.[64]

The party also had the advantage of the strong Milli Görüş message, which appealed across class, ethnic, and gender divides. Islamists took over the role of champions of economic justice from the left that had been decimated in the 1980 coup, although the Islamist conception differed quite substantially from the class-based ideas of the left. Milli Görüş with its Just Economic Order appealed to the working class and to marginal people in the squatter areas, as well as to small businessmen and entrepreneurs. In the 1980s, Turkey opened its economy to the world market, creating new opportunities for small and medium-sized businesses. At the same time, the government began to privatize industry, thereby increasing unemployment, and to dismantle the already thin social safety net. The segment of the population left behind by the economic transformation found a voice in the Welfare Party, which emphasized issues like social justice, unemployment, poverty, and social security while respecting the more conservative lifestyle of the masses.

In sum, Welfare's political success reflected the increasing role of Islam in Turkish public life, as evidenced by the growth of Islamic schools and banks, Islamic businesses, and a politicized Islamist movement with its own organizations, distinctive dress, and publications. The state ban on headscarves at universities galvanized Islamist activism. Welfare's success also expressed voter dissatisfaction with government corruption and the performance of the centrist parties. Support for the Welfare Party came not only from the smaller towns in its traditional strongholds of central and eastern Anatolia but also from major cities.[65] Welfare expanded its voter base from conservative rural people and small businessmen to include big business owners, young urban professionals, women, intellectuals, and crossovers from the left. In a pragmatic move, the party began to present itself not as a religious party but as a modern party with a vision that encompassed issues of concern to all strata of society. Campaign advertisements depicted people like pensioners, civil servants, and unveiled women. The party's approach to organizing took advantage of local grassroots organizations that brought it closer to the people.

Despite these moves, some of Welfare's activities and Erbakan's speeches continued to reflect Milli Görüş radicalism. The activities of the Welfare Party came under intense scrutiny by the military, and the party's radicalism eventually led to Erbakan's ouster as prime minister and the party's demise. In June 1997 the military engineered what has become known as a "soft coup," using the National Security Council to edge Erbakan out of power without actually taking over the government itself. In January 1998 the party was closed down by the Constitutional Court for violating the laicist nature of the state, and Erbakan was banned from politics for five years.

The demise of the Welfare Party was by court order, but the death of Islamism as a viable movement can be attributed to a number of factors. First, by this time, Turkey had a long history of fair multiparty elections and had developed a political system that allowed for competition and change. Polls showed very little support in the population for Islamic law or even for Islam in politics.[66] This lack of support is partly due to the continuing diversity of Islamic thought and practice across the country that does not lend itself to a consensus about what Islam is, how it should be practiced, and how it relates to the state.[67] Turkey has no powerful religious class or *ulema* outside of the state-run Diyanet, nor have Saudi-funded *madrasa* schools found a foothold. For the most part, religious education takes place in state-supervised classroom settings, so ordinary Turks have little orthodox religious training, and even theologians have quite varied understandings of what constitutes Islamic law.[68] Some, including Erdoğan, refer to shari'a law as "a metaphor for a just society."[69]

Nationalism is a check on Islamic ideas and practices perceived to be Arab in origin, further limiting the influence of transnational Islamic movements. There is more familiarity with democracy than Islam as a political system, and because of Turkey's history as an empire, rather than colonized, Western ideas and systems of governance and law are not tainted as impositions by outsiders. And until now, the judiciary and the military have controlled the parameters of political opportunism, so no group, whether leftist or Islamist, has been able to hijack the system for very long before the state has stepped in. Importantly, banned political actors are able to reform and get back in the political game rather than being forced underground. In other words, the political context allows, indeed demands, moderation. In 2011, however, Kemalists felt that many of these safeguards that keep the nation safe from Islamist tampering were weakening. This topic is the subject of the next chapter.

Muslim Secularists: The Justice and Development Party (AKP)

The Welfare Party was succeeded by the Virtue Party (VP, *Fazilet Partisi*), which Erbakan helped lead from behind the scenes. Welfare's experience of persecution pushed the Virtue Party's platform and rhetoric in the direction of democracy and human rights, political freedom and pluralism. While Welfare was a political party defined by its relation to Islam, its successor, Virtue, represented itself as a Muslim party defined by its relation to politics. It claimed to be a moderate, modern meritoc-racy—populist, environmentalist, and open to women and minorities in its organi-zation. Kemalists were cynical about the party's sudden discovery of democratic principles and saw it as self-serving, given the party's precarious legal state. It was also perceived to be yet another example of *takiyye*, of hiding one's true purpose in the interest of achieving one's ultimate goal, presumably to remake the Turkish state into an Islamic one.

Younger leaders like Istanbul mayor Recep Tayyip Erdoğan began to dominate the party. Unlike the older, more elitist Erbakan, Erdoğan was a charismatic populist who appealed to the new self-consciously Islamic constituencies—young, middle-class professionals, students, and intellectuals. The younger Islamic generation was invested in current political issues, not loyalty to regional patrons and religious brotherhoods. Many were urban youth in their twenties and thirties, educated in secular institutions or theological schools, desiring upward mobility and economic security, but with few opportunities to participate in the global economy and boom-ing service sector. They were open to new ideas and models of society that would incorporate these aspirations while retaining a Muslim lifestyle and moral values. Fully 63 percent of respondents to a 2007 survey described themselves as "modern religious" rather than "traditional religious" (37 percent). They tended to be young, upwardly mobile, nationalist (*milliyetçi*), pro-European Union, and liberal in their views of Muslim practice.[70]

Erdoğan's rise to leadership of the Islamist movement, Turkey's globalizing econ-omy, and new Islamic publics made the Milli Görüş movement increasingly irrele-vant. Leadership and networking functions in the Muslim economic sector moved from Milli Görüş to the Gülen movement. Like Milli Görüş, the Gülen movement posits a moderate form of distinctively Turkish Islam and promotes self-improve-ment, religious outreach, education, and business development, but without Er-bakan's antisystemic and anti-Western discourse. In the Virtue Party and the Gül-enists, the Islamist movement moved toward the mainstream, distancing itself from Erbakan's Middle East–focused Islamist agenda in favor of a distinctively Turkish form of Islam. In recent years, Erdoğan and the AKP (the successor to Virtue) have rediscovered the Middle East as a special arena for Turkish politics and trade, but in the framework of former Ottoman dominions rather than the *umma*, the global community of Muslims.

Although the young upstart in the Virtue Party, Recep Tayyip Erdoğan, enter-tained Islamist ideas, he and Abdullah Gül, at the time a forty-nine-year-old former

Figure 2.1. Director of an Islamist charity foundation in his office under a portrait of an Ottoman sultan, Ümraniye, 1994.

economics professor from Kayseri, edged Virtue ever further away from an "Islam-referenced" party to what they called a "new politics" based on democracy and freedom of belief. Nevertheless, in April 1999 the Constitutional Court opened a case against the party on charges of antilaicist activities. The Virtue Party was banned in June 2001, with the conservative faction under Erbakan and the reformists under Erdoğan going their separate ways, each founding a new party. Erbakan's Felicity Party (FP, *Saadet Partisi*)[71] continued to represent Milli Görüş views but did not do well in subsequent elections. It was unable to pass the 10 percent vote threshold to take a seat in parliament. Erdoğan founded the Justice and Development Party

(AKP), claiming to have abandoned Milli Görüş altogether, including both its ethno-nationalist and Islamist views, and to have become a conservative democratic party.[72] This proved to be a winning formula, propelling AKP into government leadership with an ever-increasing segment of the vote (47 percent in the 2007 elections), with Erdoğan as prime minister and Gül as president.

The 2007 parliamentary election marked a historic turning point, giving the ruling AKP a stunning mandate to intensify its fundamental makeover of everything from Turkey's constitution to its legal and economic systems and culture. This change came about despite saber rattling by the Turkish military, suspicious of AKP's Islamic credentials and the pious lifestyle of the party's candidate for president, Abdullah Gül. The AKP had been shedding its Islamic identity and now styled itself as a conservative democratic party having no quarrel with secularism, but secularism to the AKP meant something quite different from the laicism that had been the leitmotif of Turkish politics since the founding of the Republic. AKP defines secularism as a hands-off principle in which government keeps an equal distance from all beliefs. AKP politicians sometimes clarify their conception of secularism by referring to it as "the American system" to avoid confusion with *laiklik*, which is generally translated as "secularism." Current laicist law forbids wearing a headscarf in state institutions, including parliament and some universities, and at official government events, causing wrenching scenes as mothers wearing headscarves are turned away from their children's graduations, and creating bizarre protocol problems for AKP politicians, including the president and prime minister, who must leave their covered spouses at home. In 2009 Hayrünnisa Gül, the wife of Turkey's president, was denied entry to a military hospital, where she had gone to visit a sick friend, because she was wearing a headscarf. AKP would like to change this situation, moving from state control of religious expression to a "secularism" that removes the state's interest in religion.[73] It is, however, a line that cannot yet be crossed because, as we shall see in chapter 4, the presence or absence of a headscarf has become emblematic of much broader issues in a power struggle between segments of the population.

THE BLACK TURKS

In the 2007 elections AKP did well in every region of the country, demonstrating that it had become a party that represented national interests, not just those of a subset of rural conservatives or rural migrants in the booming cities. The party's early association with these populations, however, has stuck, in large part because the wives of many AKP politicians wear the headscarf. Since the founding of the Republic, secular urbanites have associated headscarves with backwardness, rural origin, and an uncivilized lifestyle. Despite the AKP's centrist discourse, it is still seen by many as the party of the Black Turks. The term "Black Turk" is used by Kemalists to disparage Turks of lower-class or peasant heritage, who are considered to be uncivilized, patriarchal, not modern, and mired in Islam, even if they have moved into the middle class.[74] Black Turks are suspected of harboring a secret agenda to impose Islamic law, and thus pose a threat to the westernized lifestyle championed by Ataturk and guaranteed by the military.

Both Prime Minister Erdoğan and President Gül were born on the wrong side of the Kemalist tracks. Erdoğan grew up in a gritty Istanbul neighborhood and was a semiprofessional soccer player before earning a Marmara University degree in accounting and management. Gül comes from a working-class family in Kayseri, a provincial city in central Turkey. He studied in Turkey and England and earned a PhD in economics. While the charismatic Erdoğan speaks no English and retains a rough touch of "the people" that is part of his appeal to some, Gül is a dapper, multilingual cosmopolitan. Their religiosity and the fact that their wives cover, however, erase any differences between them, as these are unforgivable sins in the White Turk canon. To secularists, this makes them Black Turks, no matter their other qualities. Prime Minister Erdoğan has turned this to his electoral advantage, proudly proclaiming that he is a Black Turk like many of his constituents, although his wealth and opulent lifestyle as prime minister belie those origins.

Senior military officers and traditional Republican elites entrenched in state institutions and monopolistic holding companies that have flourished under state subsidies have been calling the shots for decades. The upstart AKP not only has a corner on political power, but the socially conservative majority that forms its core support has begun to do well enough to challenge the Republicans in globalization and economic development and in defining national culture. They have become confident enough to fuel a highly visible Muslim cultural renaissance. These days women in fashionable Islamic dress drive SUVs from their gated communities to upscale shops—and the presidential palace—that had previously been the province of secular elites. However, a stylishly dressed professional woman driving an SUV will be marked as a Black Turk if she wears a headscarf, which has become the key symbol of perceived threat, a subject to which I return in chapter 4. Now that pious men have discarded the rounded beards and distinctive clothing that used to distinguish them as Islamists, they are no longer marked and have become socially invisible, leading to a greater sense of danger, a fear that invisible hands are taking control of the levers of society.

It is interesting to note that the language of Black Turk/White Turk (as Kemalists call themselves) references people by social class, membership in which is defined not by income or even political and social power but by whether the person inhabits a Kemalist definition of contemporary civilization (*çağdaş medeniyet*). The term *çağdaş* (of the age, contemporary) also means modern and has become associated with Kemalist modernism; Muslim nationalists tend to use the more global term *modern*, which delinks civilization (*medeniyet*) from the Republican period and allows reference to both Islamic civilization and modern Western/European civilization.

Both "sides" consider themselves to be Muslims as well as Turks, but in a different order. (Such categories do not map onto actual practices and beliefs, of course, but crystallize certain attitudes and expectations about what people consider nonnegotiable aspects of national identity.) Much as Gökalp desired for the new Republic, for White Turks of the Third Republic, Muslim culture should be expressed in everyday values that mark one as Turkish (for instance, in the importance of extended family), while a person's lifestyle should be marked by secular standards of international civilization (which include drinking alcohol and not covering one's head). Muslim nationalists have kept the first part of that equation intact but substituted an invented Ottoman tradition for international civilization as the framework for both lifestyle and public action.

MUSLIM CULTURE, OTTOMAN CIVILIZATION

Since 2002, when the AKP won its first major election, an Islamist vision of political life has given way to a Muslim nationalist vision that is focused less on a shared global umma and more on a structured relationship with the Muslim world in which Turkey takes a leading role, as it had in Ottoman times. This reference to an Ottoman past is not based on ancestry, as in the Turkish History Thesis, but rather on two ideas reminiscent of Ziya Gökalp: (1) that Turkish culture (consisting of ethics and values) and Turkish Islam are central to national identity, as long as they are purified of Arab cultural influences; and (2) that the Turks have a superior (in this case, post-Ottoman) civilization that allows them to take a leadership role in the world. Islam as a specifically Turkish religious sensibility has moved to the center of national identity, where it intersects with Turkish moral and ethical practices.

AKP politicians, activists, and supportive Muslim theologians have developed a unique national view that posits pious Muslims running a secular government and state system.[75] Islam enters the picture as a quality of personhood that the politician brings to his or, more rarely, her work in the form of ethics, rather than as an ideological position or a desire to change the system to impose Islamic law. The emphasis on Muslim interiority does away with the assumption of a unitary body of Islamic thought, goals, or practices (thereby reinforcing the decline of an Islamist movement in Turkey). Instead, the rise of a model of personal Muslimhood implies a pluralist vision of an Islamic public sphere that allows people to position themselves in a variety of ways within an Islamic idiom.

The Muslimhood model constitutes a major transformation in the way in which an Islamic identity is experienced on a personal level and as a national identity. The personalization of Islam as a public identity, which I discuss in a later chapter, has encouraged experimentation in public expressions of faith and faith-based lifestyles. In the oppositional atmosphere of today's Turkey, however, the term "Islamist," like "Black Turk," is still used by many secularists to refer to all pious public Muslims, regardless of differences in belief and lifestyle.

The assumption of Muslim interiority requires that a distinction be made between religion and culture. When I visited the prominent reformist theologian Ömer Özsoy in his office at Ankara University's School of Theology in 2002, he explained why this was necessary. "Since Islam has been an imperial religion from the beginning, it has the capacity to take on different cultural forms. This allows nations to preserve their characteristics after becoming Muslim. This is, in fact, the result of Islam being a humanistic and realistic religion. Of course, we should not make the mistake of equating ethnic and national character with Islam. In the final analysis, Islam is nothing but the average of what contemporary Muslims are. However, I have always weighed the significance of this. I mean, while reading the Quran, to what extent am I facing an Arab reality and to what extent the demands of Allah? We have to distinguish between these."[76] The separation of religion from culture and the personalization of Islamic identity, I suggest, has shaped a new understanding of the nation based not on bloodlines and Muslim heritage but on Turkish culture/civilization and Muslim faith. Although the traditional nationalist emphasis on Turkishness remains intact, the meaning of being Turkish and being Muslim arguably has changed. This new nationalism has had consequences for policies at home and abroad.

Since coming to power, the AKP government has broken a host of twentieth-century taboos: Both non-Muslim and Alevi minorities have been allowed to open institutions and maintain their properties. The government agreed to negotiate on divided Cyprus. An international scholarly conference to discuss the 1915 Armenian massacres received government support. Kurds have been permitted to teach and broadcast in their own language. Although one can still be prosecuted in Turkey for using the term "Kurdistan" (the assumption is that the speaker is advocating Kurdish secession from Turkey), the Turkish government has regular contact with officials in northern Iraqi Kurdistan, and private businesses have invested heavily in the region; a Gülen-sponsored university was recently opened there, along with ten other Gülen schools.[77]

I have suggested that AKP's willingness to make these (in the Turkish context, historic) concessions is due to their unorthodox view of the nation and its borders and populations, modeled on a more flexible and inclusive Ottoman past rather than the Kemalist understanding of a nation whose borders and integrity are continually under siege by outside powers and by Turkish minorities suspected of helping them. Foreign Minister Ahmet Davutoğlu is a political scientist whose book *Strategic Depth*[78] lays out the basis for Turkey's post-Ottoman activism. In it, he advocates a more self-confident role for Turkey as a former imperial power, emphasizing the country's strategic importance. "We used to have hard power, muscles, but an empty stomach . . . and a head with a small brain that just thought Turkey was surrounded by enemies because of history. What we need instead is strategic thinking. We had a heart that just feared being attacked. Instead, we need self-confidence." Davutoğlu aims to replace such Cold War thinking with "a revival of these historical facts" that the Turkish nation within its borders includes people from all the surrounding regions.[79]

Consequently, he desires a "zero-problem" approach to relations with both Muslim countries and the West, followed by "maximum cooperation." This policy involves reaching out politically and economically, but especially to those states that were once part of the Ottoman Empire and with whom Turkey has a special relationship and for which it believes it has a certain responsibility. Turkey is trying to reintegrate the region, he said at a speech in Egypt in August 2010. The countries of this region should "combine our assets in order to bring back the golden era, which produced many important world civilizations."[80]

Davutoğlu objects vehemently to the use of the term "neo-Ottomanism" to describe his policies, as some Western scholars have done, pointing to Turkey's equal status with countries of the region and its activities in other parts of the world. Turkey should not be defined by the term "China to the Adriatic," he insisted. "Ottomans are part of our history. Islam is one of our cultural elements. Westernization was part of our historic experience, as was the Turkishness movement (*Türklük hareketi*)." Pax Ottomania is an acceptable term to describe Turkey's policy, he conceded, if the emphasis is on Peace.[81] Davutoğlu is right to be wary of appearing to endorse a new hegemony, as Arab memories of Ottoman rule are as much alive as their memories of European colonialism. Local Turkish politicians may not be as sensitive to the repercussions. At the invitation of the Turkish government, a delegation of high-level officials from Dubai with their families toured the Black Sea coast in 2008, accompanied by journalists. The mayor of one small town greeted them by enthusing about the new Ottoman Empire, and assuring the disconcerted visitors that Turkey would be their elder brother, just as in the past.[82]

Nonetheless, many of the participants in the Arab Spring revolutions of 2011, from the Egyptian army and Muslim Brotherhood to Tunisia's Ennahda party, have mentioned Turkey as a model for the new governments they envision. Each group has its own expectations of what a Turkish model involves—a strong army, an Islamic democracy, a secular democracy run by Muslims. It is important to ask, however, what are the factors that have shaped Turkey and made its recent enviable successes possible, and what are the forces that might undermine them. Despite Turkey's leadership, how likely is it that other countries can follow? I return to this last question in the conclusion.

The AKP government's expansive actions at home and abroad have triggered a Kemalist nationalist backlash that has been given oxygen and credibility by an impressive array of actual and perceived threats and insults to the nation. These include continuing EU refusal to recognize northern Cyprus despite Turkey's concessions; the perennial Armenian Genocide Resolution in Congress; PKK attacks from northern Iraq and the fact that for an extended period the United States did not allow Turkey to pursue PKK fighters across the border despite Turkish casualties; and perceived U.S. support for an independent, oil-rich Kurdistan on Turkey's border that might lure Turkey's own impoverished Kurds to secede, although such fears have receded as Turkish businesses have invested heavily in Iraqi Kurdistan and become shareholders in its stability and development. The U.S. invasion of Iraq, and its tense relations with Iran and Syria, made Turks wonder whether they were the next domino in U.S. imperialist expansion.

To make matters worse, after its 2007 election victory, a confident AKP appeared to focus on Islamic concerns—for instance, rescinding the headscarf ban and, at the local municipal level, restricting the sale of alcohol. Reforms dealing with minority rights, freedom of speech, and so on, languished, providing fodder for those arguing that the AKP was just using democracy to undermine Turkey's secularism and make it into an Islamic state. In February 2008 the AKP-dominated parliament moved to approve a constitutional amendment to allow university students to wear headscarves. Although the targeted law was stalled in the courts and was not implemented, the amendment formed the centerpiece of a case against the AKP in the Constitutional Court.

The Court accused the party of undermining the laicist nature of the state and sought to close it and ban 71 members and former members of the party from politics, including Prime Minister Erdoğan and President Gül. Other "crimes" against secularism mentioned in the indictment were statements by Erdoğan in which he called Turkey a Muslim society, a statement by former U.S. Secretary of State Colin Powell calling Turkey a "moderate Islamic republic," and Erdoğan's participation in the U.S. "Greater Middle East Initiative," which the indictment defined as an American project aimed at installing moderate Islamic regimes in the region. The indictment claimed that in its almost six years in power, the AKP had hidden its true intentions of imposing shari'a law, by violence if necessary, behind a façade of interest in human rights, democracy, and freedoms of religion and conscience. The headscarf was a banned symbol of religious fanaticism, the indictment continued, that the AKP had tried to pass off as a right reflecting freedom of religious belief.

The AKP presented its defense, which argued that the indictment was politically motivated and not based on legal grounds. If seven justices on the eleven-member Constitutional Court had voted to convict, this would in effect have toppled the popularly elected government. Some considered the court case to be a slow-motion coup attempt. With the nation holding its collective breath, the Constitutional Court announced its decision on July 30, 2008. The court backed away from what journalist Andrew Finkel called "the nuclear option"[83] by one vote, deciding that the AKP should not be closed down. Instead it cut some of the party's state funding, a relative slap on the wrist.

By the end of 2008, the AKP's reform process had effectively ground to a halt, and Prime Minister Erdoğan had begun to use militantly nationalistic language in his speeches. He stopped calling for "cultural rights" for minorities and reminded a Kurdish audience that Turkey is "one nation, one flag, one country" and "whoever doesn't like it can leave."[84] This change in language was likely an attempt to harness increasing nationalist fervor for upcoming local elections in March 2009. AKP did well in those elections and immediately embarked upon a much touted "Democratic Opening" (referred to as a "Kurdish Opening" in the press), putting the first Kurdish-language television station on the air and allowing villages to reclaim their original Kurdish place names. These and other reforms did not go smoothly, though, as national policy was often contradicted by local community values or the interests of local bureaucrats tasked with putting the reforms into practice. I discuss these contraditions further in chapter 7. As Karl Marx observed, at the very point of transformation, old categories and ways of doing things can appear to block change.

The government's vacillation between support for individual, cultural, and minority rights and hard-nosed "Turkey for the Turks" nationalism continues. Placed within a post-Ottoman framework, this appears to be less of a contradiction, since Muslim nationalism, despite its greater sensitivity to minority and individual rights (especially as these affect religion), shares with Kemalist nationalism a belief in the superiority of Turkishness. Muslim nationalists, however, define Turkishness primarily as a Sunni Muslim cultural identity, which is potentially inclusive of Kurds as fellow Muslims within the Turkish realm, making a "Kurdish Opening" plausible. In contrast, Kemalist nationalism excludes Kurds from the nation unless they reject their roots (their tribal lineage or soy, their language and culture) and become fictive Turks. In the next chapter I deconstruct the language of Kemalist ultranationalists—supporters of a strong state and military and a national scenario based on a pan-Turkish identity and bloodline.

CHAPTER 3

The Republic of Fear

Turks have no other friends besides Turks.
—Turkish saying

IN THE SPRING OF 2008 I was invited to an anthropology conference at Yeditepe University, a private university set up by former Istanbul mayor Bedrettin Dalan. In his mid-sixties with the demeanor of an aging boxer, Dalan is known for his strong opinions and has a reputation as an ultranationalist (*ulusalcı*)—Kemalist, Ataturkist, secularist, supporter of a strong state and military and a pan-Turkish national identity with a hefty dose of racialism. When Yeditepe University was built under Dalan's direction, its otherwise modern architecture incorporated emblems of ancient Turkic Seljuk design. Special-event dinners are hosted in a large tentlike yurt on the lawn, another Central Asian Turkic feature. In his opening speech to an audience of Turkish anthropology scholars and graduate students (and one visiting American anthropologist), Dalan linked the field of anthropology to the cultural knowledge passed down to present-day Turks by their Central Asian ancestors, the Alperenler, a reference to Turkic military commanders of ancient times, whose name means "heroic saintly soldiers," as in *ghazi*. "The first anthropologists were Turks, Alperenler," Dalan said. "We learned about them in schoolbooks. They went to live in villages and got to know and understand Central Asian ethics and culture."

Before long in his speech, Dalan began suggesting that anthropologists were working with unspecified outside powers to undermine Turkey's integrity. "The Kurdish problem emerged in the southeast after the Peace Corps came," he said. "Guns aren't enough to fight the PKK. I told the military, 'There are a hundred thousand anthropologists behind the PKK.' . . . Someone comes to take an X-ray of us, finds the small cracks and learns how to break us apart." The solution, Dalan implied, was to train Turks in the methods of the West so that they could protect Turkey:

Our job is to find out where they took the X-ray. The state is blind and dumb. We need anthropology even in high schools. The French in Africa—anthropologists told them how to get one tribe to fight another. In the USSR, anthropologists created separate states, even though their language was similar. In foreign countries in the last five years, how many studies were done on Turkey? More than two thousand. I bet we don't know ourselves as well as they know us.

Dalan lashed out at students who carried out research in Turkey to earn degrees at foreign educational institutions, implying that their knowledge would be used against the country:

Foreign departments take Turkish children, give them good grants on condition that they study Turkey and show them the results. They even use our children against us. . . . Anthropology is the science of identity. Anthropology is a knife that cuts both ways. They bring Kurds against us. Why? We're brothers. They play games that they need anthropology to play. So we need anthropology too.

Turkey's first International Anthropology Conference was held later that year at a different university in Istanbul, this time in the presence of a scattering of senior anthropologists from Europe and the United States, who listened to simultaneous translations of the proceedings. In her conference presentation, the head of the Turkish Anthropology Association revisited the themes broached by Dalan, waving in the air a copy of a recent ethnography of the Black Sea region written by two European anthropologists.[1] This was evidence, she declaimed, that foreign anthropologists were out to undermine Turkey's national integrity. In the book, the authors had used the Ottoman administrative name Lazistan to refer to the region encompassing speakers of the minority Laz language, an area that is now part of the Turkish provinces of Rize and Artvin. Nationalists understand the use of this term to be an incitement for Laz speakers to secede and create their own state of Lazistan, although no suggestion of the sort appeared in the book in question. "Lazistan?" the Turkish anthropologist shouted angrily from the stage. "Is there such a place as Lazistan? No!"

Dalan's introductory speech at the Yeditepe conference had warned about a loss of identity and cultural integrity, already diluted by contact with Arab society, corrupted by the Ottomans, and then undermined by Western foreign intrigue. He began his narrative of loss with the gold standard of Turkish identity, the Turkic Oghuz peoples of Central Asia, ruled by tribal khans who, beginning in the ninth century, crossed the steppes into the Balkans and what is now present-day Turkey, establishing a reputation as warriors. In later centuries they established empires and states that led inevitably to the "Turkic warrior nation," the Turkish Republic.

"The founding father, Oghuz Khan," Dalan explained, "set out traditional social custom (*töre*): Be master of your hand, your loins, your language (*Eline, beline, diline sahip ol*). Loins means your lineage, your clan, your nation." (For these, Dalan used the terms *soy sop* and *millet;* soy, or lineage, also refers to race and being of pure blood.) "Hand means soil, fatherland. Language means Turkish," he continued. "We are on the brink of the decay of custom. I see the games being played on our Turkishness."

Dalan lamented that Turkish foundational concepts like Ergenekon and gray wolf had been "emptied out." "Here if you make a wolf sign, people call you *kafatascı* [one who measures skulls, i.e., racist], a bad term for nationalists. We need more anthropologists," he called out to the audience of anthropology faculty and graduate students from around the country. "Anthropologists—you are the new Alperenler." This appeal was met by sustained applause.

Ergenekon refers to the origin myth of the Turks, in which a gray wolf showed them the way out of their legendary Central Asian homeland Ergenekon. The gray wolf has long been a symbol of ultranationalists, who at their rallies hold up the forefinger and little finger of both hands in the sign of the wolf while chanting allegiance to the fatherland. As a result of a prominent court case that began in 2008, the term *Ergenekon* now refers to a diverse group of shadowy figures, including active and former military officers, secret police, journalists, civic activists, and others, accused of plotting to overthrow the Turkish government, preparing to assassinate the Turkish novelist and Nobel Laureate Orhan Pamuk for his comments about the Armenian genocide, and being involved in the murder of other prominent Turkish figures, including Hrant Dink. The investigation also uncovered decades of rogue military assassinations of Kurdish leaders and citizens in the southeast.

The issue around which the Ergenekon gang is alleged to have organized its activities was the protection of Turkish blood and identity against foreign powers whom they believed to be acting against Turkey through its Armenian, Christian, and other minorities (like the Kurds) and through missionaries, a subject I revisit in the next chapter. As radical secular Kemalists, they were also against the Islam-identified AKP government, and evidence for several coup plots in the mid-2000s has been presented to the court. (The plots have colorful code names like Blond Girl, Moonlight, Sea-Sparkle, and Glove.) The group (or network of groups) is thought to have ties high up in the state apparatus. Turks call this shadowy network the "deep state."

Almost three hundred people were arrested in the hydraheaded Ergenekon case, many receiving heavy sentences.[2]

The Yeditepe anthropology conference continued with the awarding of an honorary doctorate to Kazim Mirsan, an engineer born in South Turkistan, whose hobby is the study of ancient Turks. Mirsan, an elderly man with a wizened face, set forth his argument that based on the similarity of words in both languages, the ancient Sumerian language was really Turkish. For good measure, he added that there had been no other people besides Turks in Anatolia, Turkey's heartland, and that in the Byzantine cathedral of Hagia Sophia there was no Greek (*Rumca*) writing, only Turkish. This elision of native populations and thousands of years of history was enthusiastically applauded by the audience of anthropologists.

I felt for a moment as though I had stepped back in time to the period after the founding of the Republic when anthropology, archaeology, history, and linguistics were politically manipulated to create a national identity. That identity today clearly still has the force of truth, validated—as it was then—by its professional, academic setting.[3] The Turkish History Thesis, the Sun Language Theory, and Ziya Gökalp's ideas about Turkish culture and the international language of civilization resonate in today's conference halls. (At the International Anthropology Conference, Bozkurt Güvenç, one of Turkey's first and most prominent social anthropologists, gave a slide show demonstrating that in terms of material civilization, Turkey was already "European" and "modern" even before the founding of the Republic in 1923.) I mentioned my reaction to a highly educated and well-traveled colleague after the Yeditepe conference, expecting her to join me in scoffing at Mirsan's idea that Sumerian was really Turkish. She looked surprised. "Why not?" she responded. "It could be true."

The themes that Turkishness and the Turkish nation were under threat and that outsiders gaining knowledge about Turkey was dangerous found their way into many of the talks at both conferences. Knowledge needed to be in one's own hands only. Ideally, Turkish culture should not be visible to outsiders, but at the very least Turks should know as much about themselves as outsiders do.

In some sense, this was a plea to Turks to take up anthropology in self-defense so that it would be they who defined themselves, not others. Modernity entails a claim to self-definition: We are the definers, not the defined. Güvenç, who is in his eighties, related the following story about Ismet Inönü, who followed Ataturk as Turkey's second president. In 1940, while Inönü was opening the Village Institutes the government had set up to train teachers for village schools, he reportedly said, "I don't know anything about villages. Tell me about villages." Someone from the official

Language Institute (*Dil Kurumu*) responded, "We have a translation of an encyclopedia entry in English that we can give you."

I end my account of the Yeditepe conference with a conversation I had with Bedrettin Dalan in his office. He had made some anti-American comments in the course of his speech, and afterward I confided in a Turkish colleague that I had been somewhat offended. This remark appears to have been relayed to Dalan, who invited me and the conference organizer to his office. A Turkish flag stretched almost the entire length of one wall. The remaining space was taken up by a framed larger-than-life, full-length portrait of Ataturk in military garb. Dalan was seated behind a massive wooden desk. My colleague and I settled ourselves in facing chairs before the desk, dwarfed by its expanse. Two young women waited demurely on a nearby couch. Dalan introduced them as students at an Istanbul conservatory who also attended Yeditepe University, and asked them to regale us with Central Asian folk songs. After about fifteen minutes, he signaled the singing to end.

We chatted for a while about the music as I wondered where this was leading. Finally, leaning toward us across his desk, Dalan said, "America has done many good things in its two hundred and fifty years." There was a pause, during which I was relieved that we were coming to the point of the meeting, which I assumed would be an attempt to make amends for his earlier anti-American statements. I was concerned that my colleague, the conference organizer, was being kept away so long from the event. Taking a breath, Dalan continued, "but they have too many blacks, and they treat them badly." Not knowing how to respond to this rather contradictory statement, I suggested that we might have a black president soon. Dalan responded, "Obama isn't black. He's Jewish." Nonplussed, I asked why he thought so. He pointed to the name Barack, which he said was Jewish, and asserted that Obama's mother was Jewish. I found it interesting that, as in Mirsan's talk, language itself became a criterion for validity, overriding other forms of knowledge.[4] In 2003 Dalan caused a furor when he claimed that the Kurdish language contained only 600 words, leading to angry counterclaims by Kurdish intellectuals that the language consists of between 70,000 and 100,000 words.[5]

This was a classic example of the "We are complex; they are not" claim and counterclaim to modern self-definition in which the civilized or civilizing culture defines itself as complex, meaning modern, while defining "folk" or minority cultures as simple ("only 600 words"). In the early 1990s, I interviewed a German official of Turkish descent in Berlin, whose origins could not be guessed from her clothing, speech, or demeanor (which was standard bureaucratic frostiness). When I mentioned in passing that I thought Turkish culture was complex, the official became incensed. "*We* are complex," she insisted, referring to Germans and including herself. "*They* are not." Cultural complexity is part of a hierarchy of values, made equivalent to civilization, to which other cultural identities are deemed subordinate.

Some months after the Yeditepe conference, an arrest warrant was issued for Bedrettin Dalan after a cache of weapons was unearthed on land belonging to his foundation. He stands accused of being party to Ergenekon-linked plots against the AKP government. As of this writing, he is still at large, after traveling to the United States for medical treatment, then to Russia and Germany.

TURKEY FOR THE TURKS

A similar discourse, one that defines Turkey as a singular, unitary nation that is under continual threat from within and without, can be found in the Turkish military. The journalist Fikret Bila interviewed a number of high-level generals and found that they shared a deep mistrust of the United States, of which they expected the worst, including an outright occupation of Turkey. According to Bila, the generals spoke of the United States in the same terms as they did of the USSR during the Cold War.[6] Ersel Aydinli writes that the majority of officers view the military's role as guarding "the achievements of the early Republican revolution" and coping with the security concerns occasioned by Turkey's "social fragmentation." The military is a closed institution with a culture and lifestyle that strips officers of their ethnic, regional, and religious identities and isolates them from society within their own compounds. Alienation from ordinary citizenry, combined with a focus on security risks, leads officers to distrust civilians and politics, and to be ever on guard against internal ethnic and ideological movements and "foreign enemies." A number of civilian associations and individuals loosely connected with the security establishment or sharing its ideological position have helped "securitize" public opinion, so that the military's role is widely seen as not only defending the country's borders but also the identity and embattled integrity of Turkey itself.[7] These views are also represented in the educational curriculum, an issue that will be taken up later.

Soon after the Yeditepe conference, I had an opportunity to speak informally with several high-level Turkish military officials.[8] When I explained that I was studying nationalism, the officers responded almost immediately with the threat paradigm. Turkey had enemies within and without, they told me. I asked them who these "enemies within" were and mentioned that I had read that schoolbooks cited Greeks and Armenians in that role. The officers denied that there was any specific mention of these in schoolbooks or that "enemy within" meant any specific group. Instead they individualized—and generalized—the threat: "It could be you or it could be me. Anyone can be an enemy." But "if you wipe out Turkishness," one officer insisted, "a small sprig will emerge and flower again."

When the group dispersed, one of the officers lingered; he said he wanted to explain nationalism to me. In his view, the term *ülkücü* (a term meaning right-wing ultranationalist that I had not brought up in the conversation) had been given a bad name by the MHP (the ultranationalist Nationalist Action Party) because it had injected racism (*ırkcılık*) into nationalism. "A real nationalist," the officer said, "believes that Turkey should be completely independent [*bağımsız*, a Republican neologism meaning "without connection"].... Turks are a special people. There has always been Turkishness, from the beginning of history. Turkey should be independent economically and politically. It should be independent of the United States and of the EU." I asked him whether that included NATO. His answer: "Once we've completed our duties in Afghanistan, why not?" When I asked him how Turkey could disconnect from the global economy, he responded that the key was education. You could educate Turkish youth to become independent, to focus on Turkishness instead. "Turkishness is enough," he insisted. When I asked him how one could control the influence of television and the Internet, he replied confidently, "These things can all be dealt with."

On another occasion, an American officer who has had extensive high-level interaction with the Turkish military told me that "The Turkish military is anti-U.S., worse as you go down the ranks." He didn't think that this was simply due to U.S. policies regarding Iraq and the PKK. "It's also anti-American, that is, anti-globalization, anti-American consumerism and culture, not just anti-policy." He explained that most officers are Anatolian lower middle class:

> They work their way up in the ranks. Within the ranks, there's a sense of solidarity, supported by an artificial, segregated lifestyle.... Every year officers in the officer training school, or War College, are taken on a trip around Turkey to all of the historic sites of the War of Independence. At the sites, lectures are given by a group of retired generals who invent history out of whole cloth.
>
> At Greek and Roman ruins, they said these were Turkish ruins because the Turkish people migrated from Central Asia [centuries] before the eleventh and twelfth century migration. [They said that] in fact, the Anatolian civilizations were Turkish.... Some of the younger officers were skeptical, but many swallowed it.

The American told me he knew of officers of Alevi descent and one of Armenian "extraction," but all presented themselves in public as "Sunni Muslims." What they were in private remained unknown to most of their fellows.

The spread of wireless Internet, the American officer guessed, might change what officers believe. "In the past, Internet connection at the officers' school was only in the library, two connections, and censored. You could look up very little on the Web. But now officers have wireless in their homes." I found it noteworthy that increased access to the Internet didn't seem to effect an embrace of globalization, but the reverse. Perhaps given the officers' hermetically sealed social, cultural, and political environment, the Internet appeared to open a portal onto dangerous chaos. The military prunes all personal practices and beliefs, whether ethnic or religious, that deviate from the Kemalist national narrative, even going so far as to purge officers whose wives wear headscarves. Turkish military officers—and their wives— literally embody the nation.[9]

I found the Turkish officers' emphasis on disconnecting Turkey from the world disturbing, but when I mentioned this conversation to a liberal, secular Turkish friend who works in the bazaar, he partly agreed. "You have to be part of some agreement like NATO, but to be independent, to have no debts, to stand up straight—I can't tell you what it feels like for a country that's been accused of every shit. It gives us back our honor." Honor and shame are forms of cultural knowledge widely characteristic of expressions of national subjectivity, regardless of the individual's political stance. In chapter 6 I argue that such layers of shared meanings and expected characteristics make up the framework for a shared national culture that unites secular and Muslim nationalists across all their categorical permutations, but at the expense of alienating women from the nation.

ATATURK'S MILITIAS

On April 12, 2008, an estimated twenty-five thousand to forty thousand people marched in Tandoğan Square in Ankara. Similar protests, called Republic Meetings (*Cumhuriyet Mitingleri*), were held in Istanbul and other major cities. There had been other well-attended Republic Meetings the previous year. Their purpose was to support Kemalism and secularism and to protest perceived threats to the state, particularly the Ergenekon trial and the AKP government's moves to allow headscarves to be worn on campus. Demonstrators suspected the government of having a secret agenda to impose Islamic law and believed that the Ergenekon trial was a trumped-up pretext to arrest the opposition. Among the Tandoğan speakers were members of the secularist opposition Republican People's Party, retired military officers and veterans, artists, and professors. Protestors held signs that read, "Turkey is laic and will remain laic"; "Ergenekon is a lie, it's a U.S. game"; "The code to Ergenekon is Fethullah [Gülen]." (Note the equivalence of U.S. interests with those of the Islamic Gülen Movement, which many Kemalists believe is funded by the CIA.)

One of the speakers, an officer of the Ataturk Thought Society, lamented that Turkey's independence had been destroyed by U.S. and EU politics after 1990. "For us to find Ataturk's luminous[10] road, we need national unity; we have filled this square in order to take back complete independence. We are the raving Turks who have emerged from the spirit of *Kuva-i Milliye*."[11] These were Turkish militias formed after the defeat of the Ottomans in World War I and the occupation of the empire by Allied armies. The term "raving Turks" (*çılgın Türkler*, as in, raving mad) has become a common cultural reference to romanticized ideal soldiers of Ataturk's war, taken from the title of Turgut Özakman's best-selling novel about the War of Independence.[12]

A middle-aged secretary, dressed in slacks and short-sleeved shirt, her blond hair cut in a bob, told me that she had attended the Republic Meeting in Istanbul to protest the AKP government. "Their lifeblood is Saudi money. [President] Gül worked there in Saudi Arabia.[13] Tayyip [she referred to the prime minister by his first name in a voice that made clear her desire to strip the reference of dignity] visits the Saudi king in his hotel room to give him the Medal of the Republic, instead of vice versa. He [the Saudi king] didn't even visit Ataturk's tomb." Tayyip was corrupt, she continued; he gave contracts to his own people. She accused him of having stolen the election and of harassing the media. In a later conversation, she made scathing reference to Prime Minister Erdoğan's manner of speaking, mustache, and style of suit, which she said weren't suitable for a Turkish prime minister, implying that they were lower class.

"Millions came [to the demonstrations] because we've reached our limit," the secretary said. "Enough is enough." She worried about Turkey's future:

> They want to erase Ataturk. They're eliminating music and art courses. [The concert pianist] Fazıl Say is afraid. We've become a minority. [To that] AKP says, "Whoever wants to go should get out." . . . Everyone used to be against YÖK [the state's Higher Education Council] because it stifled the university, but now we feel the need for a strong hand.

In Tandoğan Square, the protestors chanted militant slogans that called for Turkey to turn inward, away from both the East and the West: "Neither U.S. nor EU, totally independent Turkey" and "We are Mustafa Kemal's soldiers."

One could see displayed in these demonstrations fear of a Turkey transformed by an uncontrolled nonnormative Islam injected by outside enemies that ranged from the United States to Saudi Arabia, and fear for Turkey's future under the sway of CIA and Saudi money. The demonstrations also channeled anxiety about loss of control—over the elections, over the constitution of Turkish social life and values—and fear of decivilization, reversion to a rural, low-class *a la Turka* culture that the Kemalist national project had spent decades rehabilitating in the *a la Franga*[14] image of the West. The demonstrators also expressed a longing for a strong leader—like Ataturk—to whose authority the nation could submit, to whom national subjects could offer mind and body as soldiers ready to die for the leader's cause.

Indeed, the language of nationalism speaks as much about social class as about cultural divisions. The sociologist Ferhat Kentel observed that "Nationalism (*milliyetçilik*) is a metaphor we've learned for differentiating ourselves from those others." Over time the term became associated with MHP militants, many of whom came from central Anatolia:

We saw them as *kıro* [rubes], murderers, droopy-mustache types, as men who wore white socks and, in fact, didn't know at all how to dress. *Milliyetçi* was a sort of label for people. At the time, MHP members spoke about protecting Turkey: The Russians are coming, the communists are coming. Now it's: The Americans are coming, the Kurds, the Armenians, the Islamists. Because of these associations, the term *milliyetçilik* is unusable for the upper/middle classes who differentiate themselves using the new Turkish term *ulusalcılık*. After all, Ataturk encouraged people to use the new Turkish (*Öztürkçe*). It's like in the 1960s and '70s. Every word you used was judged according to whether it was leftist or rightist. In the same way *ulusalcılık* has come to mean the modern (*çağdaş*) lifestyle.[15]

A Discourse of Divisiveness

One could point to many other internal and external reasons for a perception of continual threat: a continuing hot war with the separatist PKK; EU reluctance regarding Turkey's membership bid; the U.S. invasion of neighboring Iraq and belligerence toward Turkey's other neighbor, Iran; U.S. reluctance to allow Turks to pursue PKK terrorists into Iraq; and fears that the United States is supporting an independent Kurdish state in northern Iraq. Add to this the tensions created by the power struggle between secular, urban, state-linked elites and newly emergent pious social and economic elites, a feud that has engaged parliament, the Constitutional Court, and the army. The divisiveness is amplified by a divided media and has spilled onto the streets in the form of public performances, demonstrations, and confrontations.

But the 2000s were also a time of relative economic and social stability, hope for the future, a raised profile abroad, and better infrastructure at home in the form of roads, buses, subways, trams, tunnels, trains, and communication. Even with the dark cloud of a 10 percent unemployment rate, business in the provinces was doing well, and there was pride in Turkey's economic accomplishments and a sense of forward momentum in society, with EU membership a potential goal supported by nearly half of the population, despite setbacks.[16] Some pious and secular businesses and nongovernmental organizations (NGOs) joined forces to pursue common political and economic goals.

Yet, public discourse over these years—both in the media and personal conversations—became almost exclusively black and white, infused with ever more vitriol and rage and directed increasingly not only against other Turks but also against the West. It was as if the entire nation had choked itself with a noose of terms that strangled any real discourse and narrowed vision to an ideological pinprick. Just as the Inuit have many terms for snow, Turks have multiple words to represent being a Turkish national subject, each with minutely differentiated ideological characteristics, ancestral voices, genealogies, narratives of threat and redemption, and discursive scripts: *Kemalist* (broadly, follower of the principles of the nation's founder Mustafa Kemal Ataturk, secularist, laicist) and the related and equally potent *Atatürkçü* (Ataturk admirer, secularist); *Islamcı* (adherent of politicized Islam); *milliyetçi* (rightist nationalist); *ülkücü* (right-wing ultranationalist with Islamist or pan-Turkist tendencies); *ulusalcı* (left-wing or neonationalist, secularist, supporter of a strong state and military, anti-West); *liberal* (supporter of cosmopolitanism and freedom of speech); *devletçi* (supporter of a strong state); and *Türkiyeli,*[17] a recent rather unpopular neologism that aims to circumvent the ethnic assumptions inherent in the term Turk without bleaching it of communal identity altogether.[18] *Vatandaş,* citizen, is often used to refer to non-Muslim citizens who, according to the religio-racial national narrative, cannot be Turks. The term *vatandaş,* as we shall see in chapter 6, also is used by women to describe their problematic relation to a heavily masculinized national culture. When I asked the woman who attended the Republic Meetings whether she considered herself to be a nationalist, she responded tentatively, "I suppose I'm a milliyetçi or a devletçi," but she seemed unsure. "We're more concerned about issues; don't distance us from Ataturk."

It is left to the citizen to attempt to assume the "correct" category, like donning a coat of a single color that allows one to stand in solidarity with others in one's community, family, or group. Liberals, in accepting a variety of positions and values, put on a coat of many colors and so stand with no one. Such creolization has negative implications for the credibility of liberal ideas in a society in which personal as well as national honor is signaled by purity and the maintenance of essential boundaries. This topic is discussed further in the next chapter. Women, because of the masculinist nature of much nationalist discourse, also have more difficulty in spontaneously representing themselves in terms of such categories.[19]

One of the aims of this book is to look beyond these categories of debate that shape discourse in Turkey and, reflecting the embeddedness of these terms in academic discourse, much of the discussion of Turkey abroad. Each of the descriptive terms listed is a category of knowledge that makes up one element among others of a person's national subjectivity. Each term has its own set of shared meanings, expected characteristics, and touchstones of truth—criteria of validity that may consist of personal experience, education, family or community consensus ("everyone says"), or particular voices considered to be authoritative, for instance, in media or education.

Beneath these categories of identity and knowledge, however, the sands of cultural identity are continually shifting so that what was "known" to be characteristic of an ülkücü or Islamcı in the 1970s may be quite different in 2010. As Fredrik Barth noted, an individual's understanding and expression of cultural categories are always situated and strategic. For instance, a recent study of the political identity of Turkish youth indicates that while the categories described remain important markers of identity, young people make political choices that confound category-based expectations and may identify with more than one category. A quarter of those who identified themselves as leftist secular nationalists (ulusalcı), for example, said they would support the Muslim-oriented AKP, and four of every ten youths supporting AKP defined him-/herself as Ataturkist/Kemalist. Conversely, a substantial percentage of youths that put their Muslim identity first (over a Turkish identity) said they would vote for the secularist (ulusalcı) Republican People's Party.[20] Even within organizations based on specific political or ideological definitions of identity, the elements of Turkishness (blood, culture, language, Muslimness, secularity, Westernness) that constitute them are often in dispute or differently realized, or their significance within the organization waxes and wanes over time.

GREEN WOLVES

Nationalist political parties and movements base their discourse on some combination of Islam, blood, and history, although their members might disagree about the precise definitions of these terms and their importance for Turkish national identity. Despite appearances of longevity, with the same party leaders surviving decade after decade in one party after another, the political scene is characterized by continually shifting political identities and platforms. These changes can be demonstrated by examining Turkey's most established ultranationalist (ülkücü) party, the Nationalist Action Party (MHP). In fall of 2008 over lunch at a sleek, orange-themed kebap restaurant inside one of Istanbul's high-rises, I met with Ali Doğan, who in the 1970s was MHP leader Alparslan Türkeş's right-hand man. Türkeş, a former army officer who acted as spokesman for the 1960 coup, was chairman of the MHP from 1965 almost until his death in 1997. Doğan is fifty-nine, a broad-shouldered man with a mustache, friendly brown eyes, and a courtly manner. When we met he was assistant chairman of the right-of-center Motherland Party (Anavatan Partisi). Doğan told me that he had left MHP because of the racism that had crept into the party. He considers himself to be a milliyetçi nationalist—a conservative, religious rightist with a cultural understanding of Turkishness:

> Before the 1980s, Turkishness wasn't racist, but cultural. It was enough to feel like a Turk; it wasn't blood. There were shamanists [in the party] and there were blood Turkists (*Türkçüler*). These fought amongst themselves. The *Bozkürtler* were soft Turkist.

Doğan was referring to the Gray Wolves, MHP's feared, violent youth group, known for assassinating members of the left, Alevis, and Kurdish leaders in the 1970s. It was startling to hear Doğan refer to them as "soft." Shamanism, as it is used here, indicates pre-Islamic Central Asian cultural and religious practices that, in the nationalist narrative, influenced Turkish Islam and accounted for its more egalitarian and liberal nature until it was polluted by Arab culture.

> The religious ones were called *Hilalci Bozkurtlar* [Gray Wolves with crescent moon, an Islamic symbol]. There was an argument over the flag, whether it should show a wolf or a crescent. The Hilalcis won. The fight still goes on from time to time; they've dragged it out.

From Doğan's account, I understood that together with religion (a distinctly Turkish Islam), the dominant basis for national subjectivity in the ultranationalist camp was Central Asian Turkic blood, for which Turks use the term *soy* (lineage, of the same blood) or, if being critical, *ırk* (race; as in *ırkçı*, racist). Doğan would likely agree with the military officer who took pains to explain to me that the MHP had hijacked the term *ülkücü* by incorporating racism, although the two men might have little else in common.

Over time the ultranationalists fractured along the lines of Turkish Islam, blood Turkism, and cultural pan-Turkism, with these elements of identity shifting and re-combining. A mixture of Turkist racism and Islam came to dominate the party and its adherents, many of whom were lower-class youth. The journalist Mustafa Akyol has called these religious ultranationalists "the Green Wolves." Akyol believes that the combination of Islam and a virulent anti-Western Green Wolf nationalism spread in the 1990s as a reaction against the more moderate and Western-friendly Islamic circles that were represented by the AKP.[21]

Turkish culture, as it was understood by Ziya Gökalp, incorporated forms of Cen-tral Asian Muslim values and Anatolian Sufi worship unique to Turks, which was not too different from the Turkish Islam promoted by the Green Wolves. For Gökalp, however, Islam was a set of cultural practices that could be shared and learned. Thus, a Muslim Turkish culture could unite the ethnically diverse children of empire if they learned to be Turks. For the MHP's Green Wolves, in contrast, Islam was associated with blood and defined national membership in an exclusion-ary and divisive manner.

The Green Wolves are part of an extremist ultranationalist fringe that brings to-gether pan-Turkic racism, potentially antisystem Islamism, and an anti-West stance. This fringe includes the *Alperen Ocakları* (Alperen Hearths), the youth branch of another ultranationalist party, the Grand Unity Party (*Büyük Birlik Partisi*), an off-shoot of MHP. The Alperen group was founded in 1997 under the name *Nizam-ı Alem Ocakları* and, like MHP's Green Wolves, emphasizes pan-Turkist racist nation-alism fused with conservative Islamic values. The Grand Unity Party is against Tur-key's joining the European Union and instead promotes an alliance in a region span-ning Central Asia to the Middle East, "based on common historic values."[22]

It is notable that after the death of Grand Unity Party leader Muhsin Yazıcıoğlu in a plane crash in April 2009, party officials worried openly that they would lose control of the Alperen Ocakları either to the MHP or to radical forces, by which was implied the forces of the "deep state" and Ergenekon, and that the youth would be-come involved in street skirmishes and violence.[23] Some of the suspects involved in the murder of Hrant Dink and other political assassinations are reportedly members of the Grand Unity Party and were previously affiliated with Nizam-ı Alem. In July 2009 the Alperenler tore down and burned posters announcing a classical music concert being held in Topkapı Palace, which is now a museum. They shouted *Allahu Akbar* (God is great) outside while the concert was going on, causing the celebrated international artists to escape out the back door after their performance. The Alp-erenler were protesting concertgoers' drinking wine at intermission in proximity to the sacred Islamic relics held in another part of the giant museum complex, and the misplaced levity of a musical program at a time when Turkic Uyghur Muslims in China were being repressed. While street activism by groups like the Alperenler appears regularly in the news, their views and confrontational practices cannot match the power of mainstream Muslim nationalism, spearheaded by AKP and the Gülen Movement, which are based on a very different understanding of the relation between Islam and national identity. In the present state of social and political tension, however, the possible function of groups like the Alperen Ocakları as provocateurs should not be minimized.

THE MANY FACES OF CONSERVATISM

Islamist, Kemalist, ulusalcı, ülkücü, milliyetçi—what do these categories tell us about their adherents' national subjectivities? The answers appear as a litany of convergences and divergences in the characteristics claimed by members of these groups. For instance, both Necmettin Erbakan and Ali Doğan consider themselves to be pious and conservative, but their understanding of what this description means and the consequences for national policy are quite different. The difference between the Islamist Erbakan's Milli Görüş conservatism and milliyetçi Doğan's liberal conservatism rests in whom they include in their definition of "us" and what role they believe religion should play in governance. To Doğan, Islam should stay out of politics, non-Muslim minorities are part of the nation ("I fought for minority rights."), and globalization means being open to the West as long as it is on Turkey's terms. When I asked him what he meant by conservatism, he responded, "It means globalization, but ours." Globalization, in other words, is eminently compatible with Islamic conservatism, as long as it is "ours," that, is led by Turkey and in Turkey's interest. For Erbakan, by contrast, Islam was the lens through which policy was defined. It tied Turkey to the formerly Ottoman Muslim world, rather than to the West, which he viewed with suspicion. In a remarkable convergence, Erbakan's Islamists and the Kemalist generals share this suspicion of the West.

One thing all nationalists agree on is that Turkish Islam differs from Islam tainted by Arab influence. Ali Doğan related a historical narrative that is often repeated in explanations of how Turks were arabized when Turkish Sufi elements were expelled from the Ottoman Empire and replaced by Arab religious scholars. "We have a Turkish Islamic sense different from Arabic," he explained.

In the time of Sultan Selim in 1514, Shah Ismail led the Turkish Alevis and they and the Bektaşis fled to Iran. This changed the population. That was when the Turkish understanding of religion changed. Sultan Selim brought three hundred [Arab] religious experts to Istanbul, and this led to a more Arab understanding of Islam. We think Arab customs are religion. Turkishness was lost.

Or as the Muslim theologian Ömer Özsoy put it, when reading the Quran, he sometimes wondered whether he was reading the word of God or about Arab culture.[24]

Referring to the hotly debated secularist claim that community pressure to obey Islamic behavioral norms was increasing, Doğan insisted that coercion came not from religion but from social pressure. "Religion isn't dangerous," he insisted. The implication was that uncomfortable social pressures arise not from "real" (Turkish) Islam but are remnants of foreign Arab customs, for example, the seclusion of women, that are neither Turkish nor truly Islamic. Judging by my conversations over the years, the idea that Turkish Islam has been tainted by Arab custom, a view that harks back to Gökalp, is widely shared.

Every nationalist, in whatever category, develops strategies of self-presentation containing particular forms of knowledge about Turkishness associated with historical narratives that "explain" Turkey and Turkishness. These basic components of Turkishness may contradict, overlap, and change over time as they are deployed within political communities by nationalist leaders and their followers. What is striking, however, is that the basic elements of Turkish national identity that are combined and recombined have remained remarkably consistent since the early Republic, at least until the challenge by unorthodox Muslim nationalism in the Third Republic. How has this continuity been maintained?

LEARNING TO BE THE NATION

If we consider blood, culture, language, Muslimness, secularity, and Westernness to be forms of knowledge that can be strategically implemented in discourse and practice to define oneself as a Turkish national subject, how are these learned? How do people come to know the elements of what it means to them to be Turkish? What accounts for the continuity between past and present in the basic components of identity, despite shifting configurations? The answer lies in schoolbooks, media, public rituals, the shared experience of compulsory military service, advertisements, cinema, popular culture, and word of mouth, which socialize national subjects and structure the reception of identity narratives by the public. I will focus primarily on education; other mechanisms of socialization are touched upon in future chapters.

Figure 3.1. Cover of a weekly political news magazine with the caption "How did the Turks become Muslim?" (Used with permission of *Nokta*.)

The most obvious source of knowledge about the nation and the characteristics expected of a member of that nation is the educational system. Teaching programs and schoolbooks until recently taught Kemalist nationalism as a security-conscious culture of fear and suspicion of others, especially non-Muslim others and outsiders. The ideal nation is homogenous and led by a militarist state that maintains order and unity. Cultural mixing and hybridity are perceived as threats to the state.

Since the Turkish-Islamic synthesis of the 1980s, the curriculum also has stressed an organic connection between Turkishness and Sunni Islam. This link is set within a framework of Turkey as a warrior nation stretching back to pre-Islamic Central Asia but culminating in the Ottoman *ghazi*, an ambiguous word that means one who fights on behalf of Islam, but is also a title given to Ataturk to honor him for his war exploits as an army officer, and today is used as a polite term for any war veteran. A soldier killed in battle is always referred to as a martyr (*şehit*), a term that blurs the boundary between a secular fallen soldier and the religious meaning of dying in battle for Islam.

In textbooks written after the Turkish-Islamic Synthesis, the state became sanctioned by Islam, and Islam became militarized.[25] Religion in the curriculum, like history, is in service to the state and to a restrictive vision of national unity. For instance, Alevis have complained that compulsory religious education in the ostensibly secular school system teaches only Sunni Muslim beliefs. In recent years, the AKP has increased the presence of Islam in the curriculum, but in ways that reflect Islam as faith rather than Islam as bastion of a unitary national culture. One result was the introduction of creationism;[26] another was the addition of other faiths, including Alevism, to the curriculum in 2011.

Until then, textbooks had presented a single ideal: national unity, togetherness and wholeness, that is, having a single voice. Raising different voices meant a society without order. Criticizing the state or the military was presented as the strategy of those wishing to divide Turkey. Kenan Çayır writes that the concept of nation in textbooks "does not include or tolerate differences." National culture "is framed as absolute, frozen, unchanging."[27] Education itself is narrowly defined as aiming to provide the consciousness needed to protect national culture and "to be alert to internal and external threats. . . . There is no room for any different points of view on any topic."[28]

Reporting on a project that analyzed 190 Turkish elementary and secondary education textbooks in 2003, Tanıl Bora concluded that "via the metaphor of language, a resistant, sterile national nucleus is depicted not only against ethnic assimilation and mixing/hybridity, but also against cultural interaction and differentiation."[29]

Teachers are instructed to inoculate children against the potentially deleterious heterogeneity outside the school environment. From a standard instruction manual for elementary school: "The teacher must draw the pupils' attention to the wrong and harmful traditions which they encounter in their families and persuade them to get rid of these traditions."[30] Sam Kaplan describes the language used by post-1980s Turkish educators and policy makers regarding the role of education as "immunizing children from the wrong knowledge." They used terms like germ warfare (*mikrop*), contagion, inoculation, and supplying the correct dose (*doz*) of knowledge. A ministerial directive, Kaplan writes, warned eighth-grade civics instructors against an "extreme 'dose' of examples taken from other subjects."[31]

TEACHING TO OBEY, LEARNING TO DIE

Security courses, mandatory for all high school students since 1926 and eliminated from the curriculum only in January 2012, were taught by active service or retired military officers appointed by the local garrison. The main framework for the security course texts and for discussion in the classrooms, which anthropologist Ayşe Gül Altınay observed in different areas of the country,[32] was the idea that Turkey had no friends, that no country in the world (including the European Union) wanted Turkey to be a strong country, and that therefore Turkey must always be a strong country. There was almost no discussion of peace, coexistence, dialogue or nonviolence.

In these courses, citizens that belong to a "different race" were presented as divisive internal elements supported by Turkey's enemies.[33] The only officially designated minorities in Turkey are non-Muslim. Such minorities, the students were taught, may be Turkish citizens but are not Turks. All dissent within Turkey was described as having an "external" origin and is "thus non-authentic, non-Turkish." Students were taught to fear all differences and to treat their non-Muslim friends as categorically different, "in fact, as non-Turkish."[34]

Bora suggests that the frequent use of the term "foreign" is a "frontier defining code" representative of the xenophobic discourse that dominates the books. The world is the "outside," a source of foreigners, enemy, and threat. "'Internal and external enemy' are always mentioned together as the categorical elements of a structure." I had long marveled at the strikingly similar language that Turks of all classes and professions used to speak of the nation—"internal and external enemy" was one set phrase that I encountered regularly. These analyses of Turkey's educational system gave me some insight into the origin of this language and to some extent the accompanying worldview.

"'Internal enemy' also bears the connotation of betrayal," Bora explains. External enemies mobilize internal enemies to divide Turkey, particularly targeting the young generation and intellectuals. Bora points out that in these texts, the Kurdish problem is never mentioned directly, but Greece and Greeks and Armenians are. Altınay poignantly describes the reactions of non-Muslim and Kurdish students, some living in the southeast, to the representation of minorities like them as potential betrayers and enemies of the nation. Some of the students withdrew psychologically, while others tried hard to win the favor of the officer teaching the course.[35]

Threat, Bora writes, is based on an assumption of existential enmity. A textbook states, "To demolish and destroy the Republic of Turkey is the great dream of internal and external powers."[36] This requires continual vigilance and alertness. The texts urge that the entire human potential of the country be directed toward this nationalist-Darwinian struggle. Only the strong survive.

The most frequently used term in high school history and social studies textbooks is "the state." In books about democracy and human rights, the word "right" appears on average 701 times, "the state" 678 times, and "democracy" 173 times. In three of four high school history texts, "the army" is the second most common term; in the fourth book it is "war." The military, Bora writes, is represented as the purest symbol of national identity. There is an idolization of Ataturk throughout the texts but also of a kind of "transcendental will" of the state. In a national security textbook, the national interest is defined as follows: "Issues which are deemed to be important for the survival of the nation by the decision-maker group within the state." Democracy is reduced to electoral politics and is not presented as participatory. Pluralism is defined as "the representation of different opinions by different political parties."[37]

The state is an entity beyond the politics of citizens, and the citizen is a passive recipient. Protection of democracy is the duty of the state, not its citizens.[38] Turkish nationalism is based on absolute loyalty to state authority, rather than on citizenship. In the textbooks, citizenship is portrayed as "martyrdom" and as "dying for the homeland," and civilian activities are devalued or co-opted.[39] The following is an excerpt from an eighth-grade Citizenship and Human Rights textbook:

> The state is the sovereign, organized, and superior force of a society.... There can be no force higher than the force of the state in governing the country. For example, the authority to make laws, to provide order and security in the country, to find and judge criminals, to determine the budget and provide education belongs to the state.[40]

Bora points out that there is no concern about accuracy of content, even of the "authenticity" of the nationalist mythology, which is presented in a contradictory manner. Instead, the books indulge in patriotic hyperbole with the common themes of enmity, violence, and kill or be killed. The aim, Bora writes, is "emotional depth, physical intensity, and verity." The militarism appeals to a "furious adolescent fanaticism," giving it a unique power of reference and legitimacy. The most frequently used words in high school texts about Turkish literature and language are death, war, and hero. In four of six books, death took first place. A poem about the flag that is chanted in primary schools goes like this:

> I will dig the grave
> of those who do not treat you like I do;
> I will destroy the nest
> of the bird that flies without saluting you . . . ,[41]

At age seven, students learn about the color red by drawing and painting the flag. The assignment is introduced with the following explanation: "Our ancestors have fought with the enemy and become martyrs. Our flag takes its red color from the blood of these martyrs."[42] It is a small step from this assignment to the Kırşehir students' making red flags out of their own blood to honor military martyrs. Second-grade pupils learn the meanings of words like struggle, martyr, and veteran. They learn that, if it is necessary, they should sacrifice their lives for their flag.

On February 21, 2011, the city of Bayburt celebrated the ninety-third anniversary of its liberation from Russian troops and Armenian irregulars that had occupied the city in World War I. As part of the ceremony, young boys dressed in period costume acted out the crucifixion of Turks by Armenians, and then the city's liberation. A photo of the ceremony in the newspaper showed preteen boys dressed as Turkish soldiers lying "dead" in a tangle of Turkish flags, clutching revolvers. The previous year, the same ceremony had drawn criticism for its use of animal blood to enhance authenticity. The ceremony was attended by the governor, mayor, AKP parliamentarians, and the commander of the local military garrison. The mayor oversaw the proceedings with civic pride and boosterism. The ceremony would improve the city's profile and attract new investment, he said, and make sure that "the youth doesn't forget."[43]

Every morning since 1933 primary school students have recited the pledge of allegiance: "I am a Turk, I am honest, I am a hard worker, and my principle is to love the elderly, protect those younger than me, and love my country more than myself. . . . I offer my existence to the Turkish nation as a gift." The students march, form "squads," and call their teachers "commanders." They shout out answers in clipped military cadences and bellow schoolyard speeches in the hectoring tone of generals and dictators. A 2008 television commercial for diapers featured babies in military uniform, digitally altered to appear to be standing. The officer baby sniffed around and asked in a threatening tone, "*Who* is the baby with the sweet-smelling diaper?" A baby in a plain, nonmilitary diaper sheepishly owned up.

Children are raw recruits, socialized to submit to state, community, and family; to have no independent desires; and to devote all their effort to serving and obeying others within these groups (nation, community, family, as modeled by their school) that provide the arenas for expressing Turkishness. Turks are educated to be a "we," rather than individuals. (A sweet-smelling civilian baby walks a fine line so as not to be suspected of disloyalty.) "Since the absolute truths are shaped on the basis of groups such as nations and people, and not on the basis of the individual, the good citizen becomes the person who has a single interest, who is involved in politics in a single direction," and who holds the interest of the country above his or her own interest.[44]

The national subject is shaped through an authoritarian educational culture in which teachers dictate lessons in a top-down manner, and common pedagogical techniques of rote memorization and repetition of stereotypes make available a single, ubiquitous vocabulary for expressing national identity. After the 1980 coup, many teachers were purged for their views, thereby reinforcing regimented teaching and learning. Military-like drills and chanting beginning in the earliest grades produce adults that physically embody the Kemalist nation's militarist ideals. Militarist learning, Altınay writes, involves "acceptance of violence as an appropriate means for resolving conflicts and the subsequent acceptance of 'the supreme sacrifice' of one's life for the nation."[45]

EU-LED EDUCATIONAL REFORMS

The educational system described above has shaped the current generation of Turks, but in 2004 EU-sponsored educational reform introduced "pupil-centered" curriculum programs for Turkish primary schools, based on critical thinking, problem solving, entrepreneurialism, and communication. After some pilot programs, in 2008, teachers were sent to implement these changes across the country. The anthropologist Müge Ayan Ceyhan observed a private, upper–middle class primary school in

Figure 3.2. Children wearing Ataturk masks during National Sovereignty and Children's Day celebrations in Bursa in 2008. (Used with permission of *Anadolu Ajansı*.)

Istanbul that was experimenting with this curriculum in the early stages of the project. Teachers, students, and parents, she noted, vacillated between the new principles that encouraged individualism, and the rigid obedience and conformity required by conventional practices based on a military model. These authoritarian qualities also characterize Turkish social life, Ceyhan observed, which gives priority to community and nation over the individual. As a result, at times parents and teachers did not comprehend or desire the new educational ideals. Teachers were unwilling to take risks; parents expected teachers to solve pupils' conflicts, reproducing their dependence on authority; and pupils did not acknowledge the individual rights of other pupils.[46]

The EU-backed initiative and a World Bank–funded project are working to expand the new model to secondary schools. The training of a nation of teachers in the new curriculum, however, remains a logistical challenge, and, as Ceyhan pointed out, acceptance of the new teaching methods will likely be hampered by cultural practices that promote a very different understanding of personhood widespread in the families and communities of teachers and their pupils. In 2009 the EU-funded project began to tackle the revision of textbooks. The leader of that project, a Finn, suggested making the texts more interactive but also changing content, particularly the strong nationalist discourse. To start with, the strident criticism of Greece has been modified, but further modifications undoubtedly will be controversial.[47] Ethnicity is still considered a dangerous source of contamination.

This view is made clear by the insistence that education be only in Turkish. In 2009, ten-year-old Medya Örmek in the eastern city of Diyarbakır turned a room in her family's home into a classroom and taught ten other children Kurdish. The little girl was responding to the Diyarbakır municipality's call to "turn every home into a learning place." Despite the mayor's support, Medya was investigated by the state prosecutor, and her parents were called in for questioning. While the AKP government's Kurdish Opening that same year allowed some universities to offer classes teaching the Kurdish language, education in Kurdish was still off limits. The charges against Medya were later dropped after her parents testified that it wasn't really a "course."[48]

MILITARY BONDING AND LEARNING TO FEAR

After a young man leaves school, his socialization continues during a year of compulsory military service. Induction into the military has become a well-developed ritual of manhood, with families and friends seeing the recruits off with elaborate festivities. A man generally is not expected to marry or begin a profession until he has returned from his stint in the army. Recruits are sent to parts of the country they have never seen and are thrown in with fellow recruits from everywhere. Men have told me that the friendships developed among recruits during this period are among the most enduring relationships in their lives. Personal networks developed in the army build a national subjectivity by supplementing local and family ties with enduring, highly affective ties forged under duress with men from other parts of the country and other walks of life.[49] Recruits are famously treated badly, although an officer in 2009 took harassment to a new level when he took the pin out of a grenade and ordered a recruit to hold it with his thumb on the mechanism as punishment for a minor infraction. The grenade exploded, killing the soldier.

In winter of 2008 I met with a teacher at Turkey's National Police Academy, a young man with a pleasant, open face, at a suburban cafe in Ankara. I had known him for several years, and we had had many conversations about his academic specialty. This time I was interested in his experiences at the police academy and his thoughts about the tensions I had noticed in Turkish society. After mulling my question over, he volunteered that he thought the army spread fear in society:

> The army really crushes [the recruits] in a brutal way. After military service, men see a soldier and they're afraid. If you take a poll and ask what is the most trusted institution, you'll find that most people will say "the army." But many will say that because they're afraid.

I mentioned that many people I knew, both pious and secular, told me they had voted for AKP in the 2007 election because it was an antiarmy vote. They were angry at the military's "cyber-memorandum" (or e-memorandum) that had appeared on its website at midnight on the day before parliament was to elect the country's president. The e-memorandum threatened unspecified action if Abdullah Gül was elected. The AKP responded by calling early elections. It did very well at the polls, and the army reluctantly accepted Gül's appointment.

Openly expressed anger at and criticism of the army was a relatively new phenomenon in Turkey. Did that mean people were less afraid, I asked him. If so, why was there such palpable tension in the streets and living rooms of the nation? What were people afraid of? I gave as an example the ubiquitous fear of missionaries and the subsequent killing of Hrant Dink in Istanbul, Reverend Santoro in Trabzon, and three Christian booksellers in Malatya. I did not say that I had begun to see the fear of missionaries, which made no rational sense given the small numbers of

Christians in Turkey, as a central metaphor for a more inchoate national feeling of threat. I wanted to know what the teacher, who is an excellent observer, made of the situation.

He thought about it, then responded:

A friend who had been in the military told me this story. When the soldiers got bored, they'd take a scorpion and put it on the ground and build a wall of vegetation and other trash around it, then set that on fire. The scorpion would turn and turn and, finding itself surrounded by fire, would eventually take its stinger and pierce itself. That is, it'll commit suicide. That's what this is, when people feel surrounded by enemies, that they're all alone and no one will help them. Then they do that sort of thing.

Turks have learned to be Turkish national subjects in a trial by fire—learning not only to become Turkish national subjects but to actually become the nation, to embody it. Thus, any threat to the nation is an existential threat. Likewise, the individual body is available for immolation for the sake of the nation. As Bedrettin Dalan warned his anthropological audience, and as school children learn daily, Turkey and Turkishness are under continual threat. The microbes of heterogeneity are widespread in the nonschool environment and threaten the health of the nation.

However, despite warnings and inoculations, Turks deploy a variety of strategies of self-presentation that refer to different forms of knowledge about Turkishness. These are associated with historical and cultural narratives that "explain" Turkey and Turkishness and so rely on certain basic components of Turkishness (blood, culture, language, Muslimness, secularity, and Westernness) that can be seen to endure but also contradict, overlap, and change in content over time. The ubiquity of these basic elements and their tweaking by the state, as in the Turkish-Islamic Synthesis, allows a semblance of order, the perception that if one could just get the boundaries of Turkishness right, the problem of heterogeneity could be controlled, and national unity safeguarded. I suggest, however, that on a national scale, competing narratives of Turkishness have diverged to such an extent that a sense of threat has become palpable, tripping the impulse to strike out or self-immolate. In the next chapter, I interrogate two key emblems of fear—the missionary and the headscarf—for insight into Turkey's social and political polarization.

CHAPTER 4

The Missionary and the Headscarf

TWO KEY METAPHORS that in popular discourse represent a perceived threat to Turkish society and nation are the missionary and the headscarf. There are other threats, such as armed attacks by the separatist Kurdish PKK, that elicit a fear of national disintegration and strong feelings of hostility toward the Kurdish minority. I focus here on the missionary and the headscarf because the threat they present is not as clear-cut as a PKK assault on an army camp but, rather, involve out-of-focus images of Turkey's becoming a Christian nation and Turkey's becoming Iran or Malaysia—each an extreme inversion of the other.

The Turkish army, state, and press have been very vocal in their concern about missionaries. Until recently, official websites for the army chief of staff and the state-run Directorate of Religious Affairs (Diyanet) listed missionary activity as one of the main threats facing Turkey. In 2001 the National Security Council announced that Protestant missionaries were the third largest threat to the nation.[1] A 2004 report by the Turkish armed forces claimed that Protestant missionaries aimed to pass out a million Bibles and to convert 10 percent of the Turkish population by 2020. The army believed that missionaries particularly targeted Kurds, who they believed were in a spiritual vacuum owing to terrorism and violence; Turkish youth unsettled by earthquakes and other natural disasters; Alevis; and others made vulnerable by a lack of (Islamic) religious knowledge. The report warned that there were 5,000 recent converts to non-Islamic religions (including Bahá'ís and Jehovah's Witnesses), with 185 persons converting to Christianity in the previous three years alone. The military urged cooperation with governors, mayors, and security and education personnel to counter this threat.[2]

Özyürek suggests that the antimissionary rhetoric was part of an anti–European Union campaign waged by radical nationalists of both Islamic and secular persuasion who, like the military officer I interviewed, opposed globalization in favor of an "absolutely independent Turkey." Their ranks generally did not include AKP supporters, who tended to be more internationalist and whom nationalists accused of

An earlier version of a portion of this chapter was published in *Current History* (White 2007).

opening the doors to foreign influence. To support their rejection of the European Union, radical nationalists promoted the idea that the former had sent missionaries to undermine Turkey. One of the key figures was Rahşan Ecevit, wife and close advisor of former Prime Minister Bülent Ecevit (d. 2006), a left-wing nationalist who had moved Turkey away from the European Economic Community to maintain Turkish independence. In 2005 Rahşan Ecevit began a campaign against missionaries, claiming that the European Union had begun a second Crusade against Turkey: "[O]ur citizens are being made into Christians, sometimes with persuasion and sometimes by providing them with material interests. . . . I want my country back."[3] It is only fitting, then, to find the village of Şimşirli in the Black Sea province of Rize in 2007 refusing 350,000 euros to build a sewage treatment facility because some of the villagers were suspicious and didn't want "EU money."[4]

In a 1999 article in its monthly magazine, the Diyanet warned that missionaries carried out their activities in private schools, hospitals, libraries, foreign language schools, shelters, orphanages, and pensions, where, under the guise of helping people, they pursued their aims to convert Muslims. Doctors, nurses, teachers, Peace Corps volunteers—anyone who came running to help—all might turn out to be missionaries. They particularly sought out Muslim countries (by implication, Turkey) where residents were cut off from their cultural and religious values, knew little about Islam, and were distanced from spiritual values. The Kurdish areas of east and southeast Turkey were considered to be particularly vulnerable to missionaries, who used "religion to support separatist interference." Missionaries, the article stated, distributed brochures and gave material support to "some of our citizens and those of our race (*soydaş*)" in return for changing their religion, getting them to "sell their conscience (*vicdan*) for money." To counter this, the article recommended revealing the missionaries' hidden agenda through television programs, written media, schools, and conferences. While the Turkish constitution guarantees freedom of religion and conscience, and Christian propagandizing is not illegal, the author continued, this should not be construed as allowing the spread of Christianity or its propaganda in a country whose population is 99 percent Muslim.[5] In 2005 the magazine published a warning that although missionaries wished their activities to appear as innocent religious work, in fact, they intended to divide the country and undermine its unity, and to lure its citizens into becoming tools of their dark ambitions. "Necessary precautions" should be taken, the author concluded.[6]

On the surface, this seems an unlikely concern. No more than 100,000 Christians remain in Turkey in a population of 74 million, and missionary activity is severely constrained by law and custom. The military's feared conversion of 10 percent of the population would mean more than 7 million converts, a number that vastly exceeds the size of present-day Turkish-speaking Protestant churches, only half of whose 3,000 members are converts from Islam.[7] Yet, a 2008 Pew poll found that unfavorable opinions about Christians in Turkey rose from 52 percent in 2004 to 74 percent in 2008, across all ages and levels of education. Only 10 percent of Turks had favorable views of Christians, slightly higher than of Jews, at 7 percent.[8] The continual antimissionary propaganda was accompanied by arrests of Turkish Protestant missionaries[9] and violence against Christians.

In 2006 the Italian Catholic priest Father Andrea Santoro was killed in his parish church in the Black Sea city of Trabzon by a nationalist teenager, who reportedly shouted "Allahu Akbar" as he fired his gun. People had whispered that Father Santoro was a missionary paying young Muslims to convert. The bishop of Anatolia responded that such a charge was groundless. For one thing, the struggling Christian community had no money, and the pews were demonstrably empty.[10] On December 16, 2007, a young man stabbed a Catholic priest in Izmir, claiming he had been inspired by the nationalist movie serial *Valley of the Wolves* (*Kurtlar Vadisi*), which had depicted missionaries as trying to take over Turkey. On April 18, 2007, one German and two Turkish Protestant converts in Malatya were murdered by five young Turks who said that they had been told the men were missionaries. The victims worked in a bookstore that had Bibles in stock. The attackers tied the men's hands and feet and tortured them for three hours, stabbed them hundreds of times, and finally slit their throats. They had come prepared with rope, bread knives, towels, and cell phones to film the murders. When interrogated, one of the men said, "We did this not for ourselves but for our religion. We are about to lose our nation right in front of our eyes."[11]

Foreign media and EU representatives expressed outrage and insisted that a Turkey destined to join the European Union first must show tolerance for different beliefs. During this period, prominent mention of the missionary threat disappeared from Turkish government websites.

In 2008 a number of videos circulating on YouTube captured these fears and their political context. Several had been commissioned by the Kemalist nationalist newspaper *Cumhuriyet* and shown on television. Others were amateur responses in the distinctive style of these ads. One of the latter begins with these words on the screen: "Are you aware of the danger?" It is filmed as seen through the eyes of someone pushing his way through a home toward a man uneasily asleep in his bed. Through the intruder's eyes, the viewer sees him lift a rolled-up copy of *Cumhuriyet* and beat the sleeping man with it. The man awakes, startled and defensive. The next screen warns:

"Because *they're* not sleeping." A subtle soundtrack throughout the clip plays ominous Christian-themed music, repeating the words "Jesu Christie" over and over.[12] Another version of the same ad shows the viewer as intruder looking in on a sleeping child first, with the implication that someone could harm the child because the parents are sleeping, before violently waking the father with the rolled-up newspaper.

That same year, Turkish villagers near the town of Midyat in southeastern Anatolia petitioned the government to reassign to their villages land that belonged to the 1,600-year-old Syriac Monastery of Mor Gabriel, complaining that the monks were missionaries. One of the petitions addressing the local officials rooted the village's right to the monastery's land in the 1453 Turkish conquest of Christian Byzantium: "You are the sons of Fatih the Conqueror, who once said 'I'll cut off the head of the one who cuts off a branch from my forest.' Don't cut off the head of a bishop but you must prevent his occupation and plunder."[13] The monks responded that they had been there for hundreds of years and had been paying taxes on this land to the Turkish state since 1938. The monastery won back some of the land in court but lost a substantial part to the state treasury.

Over the decades since the founding of the Republic, non-Muslim citizens have suffered discrimination, hostility, attacks, officially instigated pogroms, and a variety of restrictions. In June 1934 large numbers of Jews fled physical aggression and looting of their properties that eventually encompassed the entire region of Thrace. Authorities and the press showed little interest in stopping, reporting, or investigating the violence. The 1942 Wealth Tax law wiped out the livelihood of Turkey's Jewish population and led to mass out-migration. The declared purpose of the law was to tax speculators who had become wealthy under war conditions, but government statements made it clear that the real aim, as Prime Minister Şükrü Saraçoğlu explained in a closed meeting in parliament, was to "get rid of the foreigners who dominate our markets and give the Turkish market back to the Turks." The tax was imposed primarily on non-Muslim property and business owners, who were given fifteen days to pay or their properties would be confiscated and sold. Since the assessments were often greater than the value of their properties, many defaulted and were sent to the Aşkale forced-labor camp in Erzurum.[14]

On September 6 and 7, 1955, coordinated mobs attacked the Greek Orthodox population of Istanbul, raped dozens of women, and looted and destroyed thousands of shops and churches on the basis of a fabricated rumor that Ataturk's birth house in Salonica had been burned down as part of a "plot against Turkey." This violence occurred against the backdrop of deteriorating political conditions in Cyprus and a "Cyprus is Turkish" campaign that had ignited hatred against Turkey's Greek

(*Rum*) population. Student associations, drivers' associations, and trade unions brought in crowds of men; arms were distributed from central locations and bus stops; group leaders held lists of non-Muslim properties. Police and soldiers stood by or assisted the attackers until midnight, when military forces finally arrived to stop the mayhem. It later emerged that the rumor about Ataturk's house had been spread by nationalists to force Greeks to flee the country. The Republic's Turkification policies, whether realized through the legal system or by violence, largely succeeded in depriving non-Muslim citizens of their occupations, taking away their businesses, and initiating an exodus to Israel, Greece, and other havens abroad.[15]

The history of active distrust between the secular Turkish state and its non-Muslim citizens is rooted in World War I, when European powers backed the territorial ambitions of Christian Greece against the Ottoman Turks, and even earlier in the eighteenth and nineteenth centuries, when Europeans supported revolts by the Ottoman Empire's Christian minorities with the aim of acquiring control over these territories. Even the violent legacy of Christian Crusaders who rampaged through the region between the eleventh and thirteenth centuries to "win back the Holy Land" from the Muslim infidel still resonates in the region today and is used as a trope for presumed foreign imperial ambitions. In the post-1923 era of the Turkish nation-state, the missionary came to stand for all these predations and is emblematic of a continued perception of threat despite vastly changed international circumstances—Turkey is now a NATO member and a candidate for EU membership. The fear of conversion, I suggest, taps a deeper and more intimate vein: the loss of the national self rather than of territory.

LOCAL FOREIGNERS

In the official national imaginary, the authentic Turkish self is Muslim. The association of Turkish with Muslim in national discourse—for instance, as narrated in school books—means that non-Muslim Turkish citizens, including Turkey's small population of Jews, are not perceived by their fellow citizens to be part of the Turkish nation, which causes considerable distress to non-Muslim citizens who identify with Turkey.

Ishak Alaton is a successful Turkish industrialist and a well-known public figure. He is also Jewish and has deep roots in Istanbul.

> ALATON: [My family] has been here 520 years. Because sometimes on television some idiot asks me, I say, I've been here 520 years; how many years have *you* been here?

Alaton was forced to leave school after the eighth grade out of financial necessity when his father, Hayim Alaton, was bankrupted by the Wealth Tax and sent to the Aşkale labor camp. The young Alaton needed to support his family, so he found a job as an office boy. In 1948 when he was twenty-one, Alaton became Turkey's first non-Muslim reserve officer. Later he moved to Sweden, where he worked as a welder and attended night school to learn technical drawing. When he was twenty-six, he returned to Turkey and cofounded the Alarko company with Üzeyir Garih.[16] The company grew from a one-room office in 1954 to Alarko Holding, today one of Turkey's largest business conglomerates.

In an interview on the balcony of his office overlooking the Bosphorus on an unseasonably hot December day, he told me with unusual emotion, "Jenny, you can write this in your book, that the man you interviewed today, who has reached his eighty-second year, has never been given the feeling by this nation that I am part of it." He repeated the words, his voice cracking. A Turkish friend sitting with us pointed out that this was despite Alaton's having worked very hard at it. "Yes," he responded, "I thought very positively and I've experienced many positive things, but in terms of feelings, I've always remained a foreigner (*yabancı*) because they made me feel my foreignness every day." He had just told me the following story of an incident that he said had traumatized him.

> In the 1990s, during the [Welfare/Motherland Party] coalition . . . when Cemil Çiçek was Justice Minister, a new law was passed. The headline in the Official Gazette[17] was "Potential Saboteurs." That included: A. Foreign tourists; B. those who worked at foreign consulates and embassies, all of the workers; C, D, E, etcetera. Item F. Write this down carefully. *Yerli yabancılar* [local foreigners], including citizens of the Turkish Republic.

Alaton had learned about the new law when a journalist came and asked his opinion of it. It was against the constitution, he answered, which says that all are equal. The journalist went to Çiçek and delivered a message from Alaton that the minister should be ashamed of calling him a potential saboteur. Çiçek reportedly answered, "If Ishak Bey says something like that, it means he has a bad conscience and there's something to be suspicious of."

Alaton called Aydın Aybay, a law professor, who opened a case in the name of the Aybay Law Research Foundation. The trial lasted one and a half years, but he won; the court agreed that the new law was against the constitution. A few days later, Alaton relates, Internal Affairs Minister Ismet Sezgin wrote him a letter congratulating him for having saved Turkish justice from a bad law. Çiçek, Alaton pointed out, continued as justice minister, most recently in 2008:

It's a strange thing in Turkey, these things don't happen in daily life, they happen in the bureaucracy, in administration. That is, the Turkish Republic administration forcibly applies compulsory discrimination (*zoraki ayırımcılık*). A discriminatory, racist administration has always been at the head of the Turkish Republic. It was always there. It will always be there. . . . Until today, there has been no change. It's gotten worse.

Indeed, the bureaucratic divestiture of non-Muslim citizen rights and property is a continual theme throughout Republican history. During the Cyprus conflict in 1974, for instance, the Turkish Supreme Court of Appeal (*Yargıtay*) dispossessed non-Muslim foundations of any property they had acquired since 1934. In the ruling, non-Muslim citizens were referred to as *mukim yabancılar*, resident aliens.[18] Court challenges were deflected with the argument that "foreign nationals" were not allowed to own real estate in Turkey. When it was pointed out that the owners were non-Muslim Turkish citizens, the court acknowledged its mistake, but let the decision stand.[19] In 2008 a report on Turkey's non-Muslims was prepared by the Turkish Foreign Ministry, which caused the newspaper *Hürriyet* to remark, "How much stranger can it get than to have a report on citizens of the Turkish Republic living within the country's borders be prepared by the Foreign Ministry? A section of Turkish Republic citizens are treated 'like foreigners' just because they aren't Muslims."[20]

In conversations with Ishak Alaton in previous years, he had been more optimistic, seeing in the AKP and its outreach to non-Muslim minorities a chance to realize tolerance and the equal rights promised in the constitution. Since the 2008 Israeli attack on Gaza, however, Turkey has witnessed increasingly open anti-Semitic posters, billboards, and discourse, fueled by the AKP government's tacit approval. Most famously, on January 29, 2009, shortly after Israel's three-week-long invasion and bombing of Gaza in response to rocket attacks on Israel, Prime Minister Erdoğan told Shimon Peres at the Davos World Economic Forum that "You know how to kill well," before striding off the stage and out of the meeting. He received a hero's welcome at home and in the Arab world for standing up for embattled Gaza. While Erdoğan's criticism of Israel is shared by people in other parts of the world, in Turkey, where the powerful trope of the dangerous outsider frames all issues related to non-Muslims, anti-Israeli sentiment quickly turned into anti-Semitism. The Turkish Jewish community voiced its fear that the government was not doing enough to keep anti-Semitism from getting out of hand.[21]

In the dominant national narrative, non-Muslims are cast in the role of potentially traitorous agents for foreign powers, which poses a perennial danger of transition from prejudice to violent action.[22] The image of the missionary as threat to the nation and the national self unites nationalists of all types, since even secularists imagine Turkishness as Muslim, despite their rejection of Muslim practices, such as wearing the headscarf, that contradict the Kemalist tradition of a Muslim-Turkish nation with a secular lifestyle. "The rhetoric of the outsider unifies the nation," Mustafa Akyol pointed out. "There was a drama on TV during the 1980 coup. Between the ads they showed bread and two fists. Two fists right and left battle to get the bread. A dark hand comes and snatches the bread. In other words, a foreigner snatches it while Turks are fighting."

Adding to the tension is the elision of difference between non-Muslims who are considered a danger to the nation, whether Jews, Armenians, Greek Orthodox, or any of the smaller religious groups like the Assyrians, Protestants, Syrian Catholics, Chaldeans, and others that are not officially recognized by the Turkish state as minorities and thus enjoy no special international protection. Feeling stirred up against one switches on the well-oiled mechanism of blame and suspicion against all non-Turks.

In August 2009 the head of MHP, Devlet Bahçeli, warned party members that nationalists (*milliyetçiler* and *ülkücüler*) had their job cut out for them, that those with "dreams of the cross" would try to capture those dreams at their first opportunity after Sevres, and that this new colonialism would destroy national culture:

> Today the distance on the map between Washington, Brussels, London, Paris, Erivan, and Erbil isn't as far as it seems. Unfortunately, their representatives are among us on the pretext of working together, but are in places and offices that give direction to the population. They are workers in a factory, politicians in parliament. They are university professors, the trusted leader of the branch of a religious order. They are media owners, news column writers, state bureaucrats.

They are today's Trojan horse, he warned. "*Ülkücülük* and *milliyetçilik* aren't a marginal idea or a street movement. . . . But what I want defeatists to know is this . . . if the time comes, we would give our lives for this, Anatolia will be conquered anew."[23]

EMBLEM OF FEAR: THE HEADSCARF

The headscarf is another metacategory of threat that divides Turks, this time along lines of piety and secularity, but also over what it means to be Turkish (and by implication a Turkish Muslim and a Turkish woman). Along with the rise of the Islamist movement in the 1980s and the aspirations of the growing population of pious urban youth—many of them offspring of rural migrants—to be contemporary and modern, a distinctive, middle-class form of Islamic covering known as *tesettür* developed. (Secularists refer to this style of covering as *turban*.) Tesettür is a continually evolving form of modest but fashion-conscious dress consisting of a long coat or tunic matched with a silk or polyester scarf tightly wound around the head and neck, covering the hair entirely. It designates a way to be Turkish that directly contradicts the secularist national tradition, in which only peasants and the elderly cover their heads. Peasants are imagined in folkloric dress, with loose cotton *yemeni* scarves draped over their heads.

Urban secularists point to their grandmothers (and, on occasion, to the actress Gina Lollobrigida, although I was unable to find an image of this) wearing a kerchief that is loosely tied beneath the chin and reveals some hair. When a scarf is worn in this way, it is called an *eşarp*, from the French, and signals being culturally, but not politically, Muslim. The eşarp is brought up from time to time as a potential compromise that would allow women to cover without signaling Islamist political intent. Most recently, in August 2010, this idea was resurrected by the Republican People's Party as a solution that would allow covered women to attend university without breaking the law. The image of a campus full of Gina Lollobrigidas in fetching foulards, clutching their books, seemed to hold little appeal to young women who believed they should cover their hair to avoid attracting attention to their charms. They had been wearing wigs or bulky knit caps over their hair or even over their headscarves to get on campus, until these too were banned. (After all the political tension surrounding the issue, the situation was ameliorated, if not resolved, by a simple bureaucratic decision. In October 2010 the Higher Education Council indicated in a ruling on a particular case that under certain circumstances headscarves are permitted in university classrooms, thereby opening the door to individual universities to allow it.)

Despite the popular perception that tesettür is spreading, the proportion of women in Turkey who cover their heads actually declined between 1999, when 73 percent covered, and 2006, when only 64 percent did so. In this period, the popularity of the tesettür/turban style covering fell from 16 percent to 11 percent. (The rest of the women used a traditional covering like a yemeni.)[24] Tesettür has, however, become more visible as those who wear it—the upwardly mobile Islamic bourgeoisie—have left squatter homes, factory floors, and back-door house cleaning for universities, professional jobs, and other roles. They thus occupy urban public spaces, shops, and other venues (like the presidential palace) that had previously been taboo to covered lower-class women.

Feelings about tesettür resonate with deeply held beliefs about what qualifies as modern and contemporary. In conversations, women in tesettür expressed a desire to be modern, fashionable, and urban while expressing their Muslim faith.[25] Many secularists, in contrast, perceived the headscarf, particularly in its tesettür/turban form, to be a threat to the fundamentals of the Turkish nation and, as a symbol of political Islam, to its democratic state system. They disavowed it as Turkish. As with missionary conversion, a widely held belief among secularists is that women are being paid by Islamists to cover their heads and wear tesettür as a means of turning Turkey into Malaysia or Iran—in other words, into another nation. As Scott writes in regard to France, where Kemalism has historic roots and with which it shares a number of ideological assumptions regarding the role of the state, "the veil becomes a screen onto which were projected images of strangeness and fantasies of danger— danger to the fabric of French society and to the future of the republican nation."[26]

In 2008 several video advertisements used veiling to demonstrate the threat of Islam to the Republic. One shows a woman's eyes leaning forward to look into a ballot box, as seen from within the box. The woman's eyes remain framed by the slot, a visual reference to the face-veil. The voice-over says: "Do you see the danger in this ballot box? Consolidate your vote for a laicist and democratic Turkey. Protect your republic." *Republic* (*Cumhuriyet*) is also the name of the newspaper, and the term used for "protect" (*sahip çıkmak*) also means to "make your own," thus deftly turning a political warning into an advertisement for the newspaper.[27] In another ad, a woman dressed in a blouse is slowly being enveloped in black until only her face shows. She says, "Of course, I make my own decisions." Her voice, however, is that of a man.[28] In preparation for the September 12, 2010, referendum on the AKP government's proposed constitutional amendments, a similar video urged voters to reject the changes. The video graphically demonstrates a liberal but politically disengaged Turkish woman ("It's just a vote. What can change?") becoming immured in a black veil as Turkey turns to Iran around her.[29]

LOSING TURKISHNESS

What lies behind such an intense fear of losing one's national identity, especially in a nation like Turkey that has such a pronounced national particularity? For instance, why would the nation's military worry that large numbers of Turks, whose strong national consciousness is often and loudly proclaimed, would be susceptible to conversion to Christianity, an act that would, in effect, make them "enemies" of Turkey and no longer "Turks"? Worse, why would anyone fear that Turks would take such a vastly negative action in exchange for a few hundred liras? The same can be asked about the widespread secularist claim that women cover their heads in exchange for money in a national climate hostile to covering and at a time when the act of covering is actually decreasing.

One answer might be that individuals in Turkey can lose their national identity because national identity has been personalized and because the national subject is now a choosing subject. Proselytism by missionaries is about individual conversion, not collective conversion. The economic, political, and social revolution of the Third Republic has nurtured a new generation with greater freedom of choice that can be expressed through new media, civic activism, and consumerism. Individualism, however, is framed within a collective logic, so the emphasis on choice means that people, especially young people, are actively searching for arenas of belonging beyond social identities inherited from family, community, and the Kemalist nation. Islamic community networks, like those of the Gülen Movement, but also those of the Alperen Ocakları, have appealed to youth seeking to define themselves through alternative collectivities. These choices are unsettling to secular nationalists who see the nation's youth choosing unorthodox Islamic allegiances that undermine their loyalty to the Kemalist nation.

After almost a century of laicism, of state-defined Islam and the suppression of nonstate forms such as religious brotherhoods, has the Turkish-Muslim self become unmoored from religious authority? If so, then the fear described previously, which is not limited to secularists, is not about the invasion of Turkish territory by twenty-first-century Crusaders but about alienation from Turkishness by Turks themselves.

I would suggest that fear of missionaries is a widespread trope expressing this broader anxiety, one that goes beyond historic suspicion of Christians. The journalist Ayşe Önal[30] interviewed local Trabzon residents one month after the murder of Father Santoro. The gunman's mother told Önal that her son killed Santoro because he was a missionary, but when Önal asked what she meant by the term, the mother responded: "He was going to make him a Jew." In interviews in Malatya after the killings there, Önal encountered a similar displacement of meaning. People expressed fear that missionaries would make the country (*memleket*) "without religion" (*kafir* or *dinsiz*). Who were the missionaries? Answers included "the Jews" and "the Masons." Some mentioned Alevis as a threat to the nation because they were believed to be easier to convert.

Religious and ethno-religious categories are often used indiscriminately to express fear or to characterize someone as un-Turkish, an enemy. To smear President Abdullah Gül, an opposition politician announced that Gül's mother was of Armenian origin and that because of his "ethnic origins," Gül was unable to represent all Turks equally. In response, Gül made a public statement that the registered history of his family on both his mother's and father's side was "Muslim" and "Turk," and filed a lawsuit against the politician. The lawsuit petition states, "The defendant's claim, which is based on racism and discrimination, is a heavy assault on the client's personal and family values, honor and reputation." At the same time, Gül praised Turkey's diversity and reiterated the equality of all citizens under the constitution.[31]

Politicians and unsympathetic others have claimed that autopsies on PKK terrorists showed that some were uncircumcised, thus not Muslims, but Armenians.[32] The journalist Mustafa Akyol related the following:

> I went to a Kurdish village in the southeast, a village of village guards[33] that is loyal to the state. An old man said, "Armenians attacked us five times; we battled on that mountain. We also called them uncircumcised ones (*sünnetsizler*)." I realized he was talking about the PKK. Heathens (*gâvur*). Those people who attacked Kurds can't be Kurds, they must be heathens. . . .[34]

Bedrettin Dalan's calling Barack Obama Jewish was an elision of difference between non-Muslim faiths; it also called upon racism and an anti-Semitic association between the Jewish faith and international power (as in, Jews run the world).

This process can be seen in the fate of the Muslim convert community of Dönme introduced in chapter 1. The Dönme (Sabbateans) were Ottoman Jews who in the seventeenth century followed Sabbatai Sevi, a man they believed to be their Messiah, when he converted to Islam. His followers developed a syncretistic form of Muslim worship that combined Sufism and Kabbalah. They were a closed, traditional, and conservative society, based mostly in Salonica, but in public matters they were progressive and radically modern, promoting change, and introducing streetcars and a sewage system to the city. The Dönme were important actors in the Committee of Union and Progress, in the 1908 revolution against the sultan, and in the public sphere and proto-nation that became the Turkish Republic.

By the 1930s, influenced by European race theories, suspicious of Christian collusion with outside enemies, and driven by a desire to Turkify the economy, the Turkish government had relegated Gökalp's ethnicized cultural religiosity (Turkish Islam) to the private sphere and replaced it with racialized nationalism (Turkish blood) in the public arena. The Dönme, who as Muslims had forcibly been moved to Istanbul in the post–World War I population exchange with Greece, suddenly found themselves labeled as Jews, even though they were not accepted as such by the Jewish community.[35] People began to ask, "Who are these Dönme? Who are their ancestors?" Racial mixing or hybridity was believed to bring about degeneration, so maintaining purity and the distinction between insiders and outsiders came to be of supreme importance. Ottoman tolerance and pluralism were the problem; homogeneity and nationalism were the solution.[36] The cultural multiplicity of the well-traveled, cosmopolitan Dönme merchant families was antithetical to nationalism, and Dönme plans for globalizing Turkey's economy went counter to the state's plan for a protectionist "Turkey for the Turks" state-led economy. The Dönme were not accepted as Turks and, to the surprise of many Dönme who had been active collaborators in founding the Republic, were victimized by the 1942 Wealth Tax that was unequally applied to the country's Jewish and Christian rather than Muslim populations. It destroyed their wealth and the health of those who were sent to labor camps in the east when, despite having forfeited all their belongings, they were still unable to pay the exorbitant taxes. After this, Marc Baer writes, the Dönme ceased to exist as an identifiable community.

In 2010, after Israeli commandos killed nine Turks on board the MV *Mavi Marmara*, a ship that had attempted to break the Israeli blockade of Gaza, a Syriac church in Mardin province that was being used as a museum was vandalized with anti-Israel slogans. The 1,700-year-old Mor Jacob Syriac Orthodox Church was defaced with slogans like "Clear off, bastards"; "Clear off, Zionist dogs"; "Heretics, lay off"; "Zionist powers, clear off"; and "Prophet Muhammad, fight the infidels and hypocrites." [37] The slogans were directed against Zionism and infidels, not specifically Christians. This has been a pattern in antimissionary discourse in Turkey: it tends to be against anyone who is not Muslim (therefore not Turkish, and thus suspected of undermining the Turkish nation). The introduction of Zionism in these slogans can be seen as a result of the *Mavi Marmara* incident but also demonstrates how fluid the lines are among oppositional identities: Turkish Muslims versus Jews, Christians, Zionists, Masons, hypocrites, and generic infidels (who might well include Europeans and Americans), and foreign-led Islamists. The self-declared Kemalist author Ergun Poyraz wrote a book that accused Prime Minister Erdoğan and his AKP allies of being crypto-Jews, working hand-in-hand with Israel and the United States to transform Turkey from a secular into a "moderate Islamic republic" that, the book argues, would be easier for foreign powers to manipulate. The sensationalist book, which sold half a million copies, had images of the prime minister and his wife on the cover inside a six-pointed star.[38]

Mustafa Akyol points out, however, that Protestant evangelical missionaries are a particular source of fear because of their lack of ethnic roots:

What confuses us here is the existence of Turkish Protestants. When the Turkish Republic was founded, there were Turks (who were Muslims) and non-Muslims (Greeks, Armenians, Jews—they were an ethnic group, they spoke differently). The evangelicals are Turks exactly like us who are Christians. [That's why] there's so much hostility toward missionaries. A Greek can't convert a Turk into Greekness. But Protestants turn Turks into Christians. (Akyol interview, 2008)

Özyürek writes that,

unlike ethnic minorities, religious minorities have the potential to convert the members of the majority and thus threaten the assumed religious and cultural purity of the political unit. . . . [I]n the twenty-first century religious converts are the dangerous hybrids, polluting and challenging the cultural superiority and purity of the dominant group.[39]

A corollary explanation for this exaggerated fear of losing national identity is that Turkishness is an identity that, despite the powerful discourse about blood, has weak ethnic roots. The citizens of the new Republic were the remnants of an empire that at one point extended across southern Europe and North Africa. If you ask a Turk about his or her grandparents, more often than not they have a far-flung heritage, for instance, a grandmother from Aleppo and a grandfather from Sofia or Salonica. Very few Turks can point to Central Asian roots, which are lost in the mists of time. The parents of the artist and filmmaker Kerim Bora migrated to Turkey from Montenegro following World War II. In his primary school years, Bora said, "the teacher told us that we came from Central Asia. However, I knew that we were from Montenegro. I asked my father about it and he just laughed."[40]

The Republic also was founded on the basis of a shared language, Turkish, that was to some extent artificially constructed during the period of nationalist language reform.[41] Ataturk's words "How happy is he who calls himself a Turk" are inscribed on plaques and pedestals across the country, referring explicitly to language as a source of national identity and unity. The inscription appears particularly often and in large format in the Kurdish-speaking east, the state's not-so-subtle reminder that until recently speaking Kurdish was considered treason. If language is the national glue, then this explains the fear that speakers of a language besides Turkish, like Kurdish or Laz, might develop an alternative language-based identity that would undermine national unity. Literature and history also were enlisted in the early Republic to mold a Turkish national subject. Language, literature, and history alone, however, appear insufficient to hold the nation together. Özyürek discusses a 2001 debate on Turkish television about missionaries and nationalism. One of the participants was Zekeriya Beyaz, dean of the divinity school at Marmara University in Istanbul. According to Beyaz:

> Religion is the arch stone. When you pull it out everything else will crumble. Then you cannot have dedication to Turkish culture, patriotism, appreciation of historical heroes, or literary characters. When you become a member of the Anglican Church, you will be their man. You will read their literature.

In other words, only a Turk can appreciate Turkish literature and history. It is assumed that "once people step outside of their national culture and religion, they can no longer remain loyal to their country and their state."[42]

The fear of losing national identity and unity is exacerbated by a weak sense of citizenship. Turks have tended to revere the state as a father figure (*devlet baba*) but until recently have expressed little evidence of a relationship to their elected government based on mutual obligation—that is, as citizens who should pay taxes and can expect services. School textbooks, for instance, define proper citizenship in terms of "dying for the homeland," while devaluing civilian activities.[43]

In other words, individualization, or the emergence of the liberal individual as a marker of modernism, does not necessarily lead to more tolerance but, instead, can be destabilizing, leaving the individual national subject with nothing but the bitter gruel of political jockeying, impotent ideological categories, and nostalgia for an unself-conscious collectivity and the embrace of community. The rhetoric of fear implies that the state and parts of the population no longer trust in the inviolability of national boundaries, whether geographical or personal, and have stepped up boundary maintenance, pressure to conform, and demonization of the heterodox "other." The weakening of boundaries of Turkish identity has led not to a reveling in choice and creative self-definition, much less to increased tolerance, but rather to a defensive reinforcement of positions, a search for essential characteristics (blood, religion) and an aversion to mixing, and to heightened militarism.

Militarism is concerned with fears of weakness and boundary penetration.[44] These fears are kept at bay through purity rituals and taboos that focus intensely on objects that are "out of place" (for instance, the appearance of the headscarf in a public or middle-class space); on the purification of space through the placement of images (for example, busts of Ataturk or oversized Turkish flags);[45] on rehearsal of in-group/out-group membership in festivals and national holiday displays;[46] and on notions of purity of blood, custom, language, religious practice,[47] music, and even food. One might argue that it is the weakness of Turkish identity, particularly in its secular form, that leads to potentially destructive defensive behavior against enemies "within and without," such as attempted coups and antiminority violence. Identifying an enemy encourages the clarification of boundaries. As Neyzi put it, "Violence can be understood as a way of 'ensuring' the certainty of the categorical identity of the 'other,' and therefore of the self".[48]

Like Turkey, France attempts to maintain the unity of the nation by refusing to recognize difference. All individuals are assimilated to a singular culture—a shared language, history, and political ideology—and, as such, are formally equal before the law. National identity should have precedence over group identity, whether ethnic or religious: "One belongs either to a group or to the nation." Scott points out, however, that beneath France's cultural homogeneity one finds racism, postcolonial guilt, and fear, expressed as nationalism. By banning headscarves, the French attempt to define the boundary between East and West, between Islam and liberal values, and thereby the borders of Europe. But excluding Muslims from the public sphere and demonizing Muslim practices, Scott writes, are polemics that create their own reality of incompatible cultures and thereby sharpen divisions.[49]

Why ban headscarves at this moment in time? Because the nation-state is in crisis, which engenders a fear of difference and dissolution. In the case of France, national sovereignty is threatened by EU membership, and its domestic markets are weakened by globalization and cascading debt crises. Immigration, tourism, and global products have transformed the sight and sound of its human and cultural landscapes. Identifying a specific enemy as the anti-France brings "France" back into focus, an imagined nation that is racially and culturally homogenous, civilized, modern. Islam is the "dark counterpart" to France as an enduring, united, idealized republic. As in colonial times, the French state's civilizing mission is to liberate Muslims from "the grip of traditionalism." Getting rid of the veil means bringing modernity and thereby upholding "the mythology of the specialness and superiority of French republicanism."[50] For French nationalists, as for Kemalists, the veil is a clarifying boundary, the shadow that marks the location of the true Republican self.

The Muslim National Alternative

While not immune from militant nationalism, the Muslim definition of the Turkish nation appears to be less boundary- and less blood-driven than that held by Kemalist nationalists. Muslim nationalists consciously model their concept of the nation on the historical, flexibly bounded, and multidenominational Ottoman Empire, rather than solely on a defense of the present boundaries of the nation-state and a Central Asian bloodline. For instance, AKP has promoted rituals and monuments that celebrate the 1453 Conquest of Constantinople by the Turks over those celebrating the founding of the Republic in 1923.[51] It is no surprise that most government-sponsored international meetings are held in Istanbul rather than Ankara.

This "openness of boundaries" and focus on an Ottoman, rather than Republican, national narrative has given the AKP government license to develop relationships with countries in the Near East and the Balkans, as well as with Iran, which are viewed as "special friends" based on this historical connection. A Turkish withdrawal from Cyprus, long seen by secular nationalists as a treasonable surrender of Turkish land, becomes a solvable problem of jurisdiction under the Ottoman scenario. Muslim nationalists also have been inspired by the Ottoman model of ordering relations between Muslims and non-Muslims—the millet system—which integrated non-Muslims as separate and unequal, but tolerated, groups. This approach is mirrored in some advances in minority rights made under the AKP, such as allowing churches and synagogues to invest in repairing their buildings, something that had been banned throughout much of Republican history; returning some confiscated properties; and allowing occasional religious ceremonies to be held in historic Armenian churches and other places of worship that had been off limits or turned into museums.

It is apparent that the Ottoman Empire is used as a model for contemporary affairs uncritically, with no acknowledgment of inequalities between the Turkish center and non-Turkish peripheries and between Muslim and non-Muslim populations in Ottoman or present-day Turkey.[52] Foreign Minister Ahmet Davutoğlu, for instance, has proclaimed the unity of Turkey's timeless history in himself: "I am an Ottomanist; I am a Byzantinist; I am a Romanist. . . ."[53] Yet, reproductions of the moment of conquest of Christian Byzantium by the Turks are everywhere to be seen, reenacted in festivals, emblazoned upon subway station walls, "relived" in museums, fostered by the same Ottoman nostalgia that one finds in Davutoğlu's foreign policy. In September 2010 the Turkish pavilion at World Expo 2010 Shanghai attracted Chinese visitors with Turkish food (Iskender kebap, baklava, and Maraş ice cream) into a building decorated with designs found at the Neolithic site of Çatalhöyük in Anatolia, a nod to the Turkish History Thesis. A traditional Ottoman Janissary military band planned to march from the Turkish pavilion to the nearby Austrian pavilion to commemorate the eighteenth-century Ottoman siege of Vienna. "The band will play Beethoven's Turkish March, as well as Mozart's *Abduction from the Seraglio*.

The Austrian pavilion was in touch with the Austrian Consulate in Shanghai to find a female candidate that will be abducted by the band."[54] If we assume the absence of irony in these plans for entertainment in Shanghai, it is clear that the Turkish organizers did not consider the element of conquest (whether of a nation or a woman) as something that might be taken amiss by those (symbolically) conquered but, rather, as representing something essential about Turkish identity that should be celebrated in an international forum. It is also noteworthy that the nation was officially represented by pre-Islamic Anatolian archaeology and Ottoman (even Orientalist) themes, not by Islamic symbols. For Muslim nationalists, Islam—or, rather, Muslimhood—remains a personal attribute that accompanies a pious Muslim into daily life or public service as a moral and ethical guide, but faith in itself does not define his or her relation to the nation. Islam as an ethno-religious attribute does mark an individual as Turkish, but this is a personal boundary issue, not one to be acted out on a national stage in Shanghai.

Personhood and Community

Muslim nationalism is a collectivist national identity rooted in a specifically Turkish form of Islam with Sufi roots. It does not contradict the laicist state's Sunni Muslim definition of a Turk, but it uncouples that identity from state structures such as the Directorate of Religious Affairs, which governs mosques and Islamic instruction. This allows religiosity to become personalized within nonstate religious groups, such as the Nakşibendi Sufi order and Fethullah Gülen's religious movement, which operate through tight collective networks and provide powerful, if heterodox, Turkish identities not as susceptible to the fear of loss of the national self. The Muslim national tradition is based on a cultural Muslimhood, infused with a politico-historical Turkish/Ottoman identity, rather than a racialized or language-based Turkishness. In theory, this makes Muslim nationalists more open to negotiation with other identities, such as Turkey's non-Muslim minorities. In practice, negotiation of rights has been hampered by AKP's engagement in nationalist competition, focus on consolidation of power at the expense of rights, an uncritical authoritarian impulse, and the communalist nature of Turkish society, which at every level undermines implementation of decisions made on the basis of human and individual rights. (I revisit this subject in chapter 7.)

In contrast, secular nationalists appear increasingly to have migrated toward Turkish exceptionalism and isolationism, anti-Westernism, and the missionary/

Figure 4.1. Janissary band performing in the Istanbul district of Eyüp before an appearance by the AKP mayor, 2004.

threat script. A survey carried out by Ali Çarkoğlu in 2002, just before the AKP won its first national election, showed countrywide support for joining the European Union (64 percent), with little variation between low- or high-income earners, or by political party affiliation (except for Islamist Virtue Party supporters, who were less enthusiastic). Kurds, nationalists, and the highly religious all supported Turkey's EU membership. Çarkoğlu noted the puzzling fact that, despite this mass support, elites persistently resisted policy changes necessary for EU membership. Additionally, except for the AKP, pro-EU sentiment was not reflected in the parties' 2002 election rhetoric.[55] A national survey of high school seniors carried out in the same year also showed high levels of support (69 percent) for EU membership. In follow-up discussions with respondents, however, Küçükural noted that despite their support for the process, many of the students feared joining the European Union. They were deeply concerned about the moral degeneration of society that they assumed would follow, and the loss of Turkish customs and family values, especially in regard to male–female relations and reverence for the father, in their words, losing "one's honor in front of the community." They also feared that membership would open the door to foreign interference that would harm and humiliate Turkey. This fear was expressed in the form of conspiracy theories involving Turkey's "internal and external enemies" and losing Turkey's "dignity and pride."[56]

By 2007, after five years of AKP leadership, elite resistance to EU membership and popular fears about the consequences appeared to have gained the upper hand. A 2007 survey found that most respondents who identified as upper class and were CHP supporters said they opposed EU membership.[57] By 2009 popular support for EU membership had dropped to 46 percent.[58] Turkish support for NATO also dropped to 35 percent, with an equal percentage saying it was no longer essential.[59] Even more startling, in a 2009 study of Turkish youth, the majority of those who said they supported either the CHP or the Kurdish Democratic Society Party (*Demokratik Toplum Partisi*, DTP) admitted that they would like to leave the country, unlike other youth (like AKP supporters) who were happy to stay. For Kurdish youth, discrimination, poverty, and violence undoubtedly played a part in their desire to leave, but what explains the desire of CHP supporters to exit their country?[60]

Ali Bayramoğlu, in his study of religion and secularism in Turkey's democratization process, put his finger on the shift that seems to have occurred—or at least become apparent—in this period between 2002 and 2007. "The transformation of society," he writes, "resembles the accumulation of tension along fault lines. The energy is accumulated, and is then suddenly released. Transformation occurs more during the time of energy accumulation than at the moment of discharge. Even so the moment of discharge is when we perceive the transformation that has taken place." He is referring to a switch from the conflicts and politicization—a kind of survival of the fittest—of the 1980s that, he writes, took place under the umbrella of individualism, to a redefinition of the individual in terms of rights and liberties in the 1990s. The 2000s, by contrast, have seen the rise of a new social idea that Bayramoğlu calls "personalism." Unlike competitive individualism, personalism fosters a climate conducive to coexistence rather than mutual elimination. As middle-class members of secular and Islamic segments of society interact in newly pluralist social settings, they influence one another, leading to convergences in their ideas about democracy, freedom, and human rights.[61] Bayramoğlu believes that this has changed the way in which these actors perceive "the other," although he admits that while the *number* of "others" in society is thereby diminished, this transformation has failed to subdue the *perception* of "others" that continues unabated as a powerful "communal political reflex."[62] The identification and demonization of the Other, I would argue, is an outcome of the personalization of Turkish society exactly because differences between groups are disappearing in practice. Such mixing raises a primal fear—with which Turkey's youth is imprinted from childhood on— of losing the integrity of the family/nation, the authority of the father/state, one's honor before the community, and the dignity and pride of the nation before the world.

Open boundaries means that the definition of Turkishness is no longer clear, and the bloodline of the nation is no longer guaranteed to be pure. Kemalist claims that Turkish citizens can be paid to convert and to veil—that is, abandon their national identity (as secular Muslim Turks) for money—speak to a broader anxiety about loss of community and the corrosive effect of commercialization and globalization on group loyalty, whether that group is the family, the community, or the nation. The Kemalist sense of siege—and perhaps desire to exit—has been exacerbated by the rise of a highly collectivist Muslim national movement that is threatening not only because of its heterodox notions of Turkish national identity but also because it appears more stable and rooted than secular nationalism.

Any convergence between secular and Muslim nationalist discourses of human rights also can be perceived as a threat to Kemalist identity. Accordingly, Kemalists describe the AKP's interest in pursuing laws and a constitution based on individual human rights as duplicitous and as disguising the "Islamists'" true collectivist nature. A fear commonly expressed by secularists is that "eventually community pressure will make us all wear veils and then we'll become Iran." In some quarters, the response has been a heightening of essentialism, Turkey for the Turks, and an increased patrolling of boundaries for purity. Implicit in this discourse is the assumption that

Muslim nationalists are not Turkish but represent another form of the "enemy within." Their emblem is the headscarf, and like missionaries, they are working to destroy Turkey and replace it with a foreign (Christian or Islamic) state.

It is important to point out that, in fact, Muslim communal solidarity is self-consciously Turkish. Muslim nationalists do not envision the nation as Iran or Indonesia, and certainly not as Arab. Muslim nationalists, like their secular counterparts, patrol the national Muslim subject for purity, in this case against perceived inroads made by non-Turkish culture. The post-Ottoman model places Turkish Islam and Turks at the pinnacle; it does not envision Turkish participation in a transnational Islam that is not led and defined by Turks.

Conclusion

The basic building blocks of Turkish identity—history, blood, culture, language, Muslimness, and Westernness—have a continuous pedigree dating to the Republic's founding conversations, their emotional salience and role as touchstones for validity still intact today. The relative importance of these forms of knowledge for national subjectivity, however, are subject to dispute and change, even within the same nationalist "category" or political party. Muslim nationalists have introduced unorthodox definitions of national history based on Ottoman, rather than Republican, "founding moments,"[63] historical narratives, and commemorative rituals.

Certain assumptions are shared across categories, tying together parties that otherwise appear to have little in common in their understanding of what it means to be Turkish. To be Turkish means to be Muslim, a requirement with pronounced implications for non-Muslim citizens. Turkish Islam is different from and superior to Arab-infused Islam. The physical and cultural boundaries of the nation are understood by reference to cultural notions of honor and shame, with repercussions for women's place in the nation. Suspicion of the West cuts across Islamist and Kemalist lines, but Muslim nationalists and secular liberals are some of the biggest boosters of Western institutions and values. It is not surprising that fear of losing Turkey as a unitary state to foreign and minority mischief is widespread among a population socialized in Turkey's nationalist schools. The fear of losing Turkishness, however, seems more pronounced among Kemalists, whose subjectivity is bound up with Republican nationalism, than among Muslim nationalists, whose identities are rooted as much in expansive cultural notions of Ottoman Turkishness as in religious and community networks independent of the Republican project.

CHAPTER 5

No Mixing

AT A POLITICAL CONGRESS in 2009, Prime Minister Tayyip Erdoğan described Turkey as a mosaic. To illustrate his point that there was no room in Turkey for divisiveness, the prime minister listed fifteen names of poets, musicians, writers, Sufi religious leaders, and other historic figures that, he said, represented the unity of the Turkish nation. To the surprise of some, he included artists associated with the left, such as the writer Nâzim Hikmet and the satirist Aziz Nesin, who had been persecuted in their lifetimes (Hikmet spent most of his adult life behind bars or in exile; he died in 1963 in Moscow), and the Kurdish singer Ahmet Kaya.[1] The list occasioned great controversy, with opposition parties and pundits coming up with their own alternative lists. Oktay Vural, Deputy Group Chairman of the ultranationalist MHP, gave a press conference in which he denied vehemently that Turkey was a mosaic:

> We should ask the prime minister then, of what place are you prime minister? Are you prime minister of Mosaicstan? . . . [A nation's] wealth means being a whole, securing unity in society. We believe that the Turkish nation is not a mosaic, but a piece of marble.

The prime minister, Vural insisted, had no idea what the term nation meant if he thought like this. Vural then gave the names of several early Turkic heroes (Bilge Kağan, Alparslan) and Ataturk, who had not been on the prime minister's list. "This is who we are; we are one whole. A whole, not a mosaic. Everyone gives body (*vücüt*) to this whole, and a socioeconomic, a sociological identity is embodied within it."[2]

In this chapter I discuss Turkish identity as embodied in religion and race/bloodline as both of these are expressed in cultural aversion to mixing, coupled with anxiety that the boundaries that demarcate the border between "us" and "them" will become unclear. The aversion to mixing is in stark counterpoint to on-the-ground heterogeneity and increasing convergence between radically opposed identities, complicated by social class and gender divisions and the ongoing transformation of youthful subjectivities. What is actually being expressed in national and communal testing for purity and authenticity, I suggest, is not just a particular social or ideological content but, rather, two things:

1. the continued importance of the solidarity group for identity, safety, and survival, whether as family, community, or nation; and
2. an accompanying fear of dissolution by outside forces or betrayal by the enemy within.

Vural placed his metaphor of the marble nation squarely in the context of this enemy, "those in their Trojan horse who cannot conquer this nation from without, so wish to secure its conquest from within."[3] In the liberal environment of the Third Republic, anyone could be convinced or coerced to betray Turkishness and the nation, to blaspheme against what is sacred to its tradition, to assail boundaries that should be inviolable. As Kentel et al. put it, "Nationalisms appear as a series of discourses fostered by the fear of 'losing place/falling down' and are expressed in passionate forms."[4]

The sociologist Çağlar Keyder told me in 2008 that he had asked his students at the elite Bosphorus University what they feared they would lose if Turkey joined the European Union. They replied, nationalism. This surprised him, he said, because he had always thought of nationalism as something outside the individual, something you subscribed to, that disciplined you. But it seems, he concluded, that nationalism has become part of people's personal identity.[5] In other words, the national narrative brands a subject's perception of self, attributes of the body, and everyday practices with highly resonant markers of belonging. These guarantee the pleasurable and secure embrace of community, but they are also dangerous because they are subject to loss. In Turkey, the individual has become the nation, and the prospect of loss is immeasurably more inspiring of fear because it implies the loss of the "authentic" self. Charles Lindholm has suggested that the search for authenticity is a consequence of a modern loss of faith and meaning. Some seek authenticity through personal expression in art, musical performance, travel, or consumption, while others seek to anchor themselves in more collective forms (such as nationalism, religion, or minority identities) but also, on a smaller scale, in the construction of group identity around things like food and dance.[6]

In post-1980s Turkey, where almost half the population is under the age of thirty, urban young people with a high school education appear hesitant to link their subjective identities and lifestyles to a single national project, such as the Kemalist Republican ideals that shaped their parents, leading to accusations of selfishness by previous generations. Instead, young people are increasingly developing hybrid identities and expressing these through new media, civic activism, and consumerism, using "the language of the self and body."[7] They do so in a society that continues to be characterized by a collectivist culture that emphasizes values like obedience and conformity, and collective identity remains central to their construction of subjectivity.[8] The ability of the state to shape the identity of its youth, however, is increasingly challenged by rival authenticities. These may be powerfully rooted religious collectivities like the Gülen movement or solidarity groups built around subcultures, including environmentalists, feminists, gays, sports clubs, and street gangs. Both secular and Muslim bourgeoisie have developed their own enclaves within which distinction is gained through lifestyle, fashion, consumption, musical performance, and distinctive media and publishing realms.

The proliferation of collectivist subjectivities divorced from the state is exacerbated by the inability of young people to participate fully in public life. A lack of jobs keeps them economically dependent on an older generation. In 2007, almost 40 percent of young people between fifteen and twenty-four neither worked nor attended school but were simply "idle."[9] In 2010 the unemployment rate for young men outside of agriculture was 22 percent, and for young women, 29 percent.[10] Youth are also politically disenfranchised by what Neyzi has called a "political gerontocracy" that monopolizes the formal public sphere,[11] leaving youth to agitate at the political margins. The state and its institutions maintain a tight grip over the public activities of young people, in large part through bodily discipline. For instance, in 2010 in response to student protests about a variety of issues, police virtually locked down campuses, manhandling both male and female students while arresting them, and at times performing intrusive pat-downs of students entering campus. It is not uncommon for young people distributing leaflets to be arrested. Police in Ankara and Istanbul began to ask couples holding hands in public parks for their identification papers. High schools and even grade schools continue to carry out virginity checks (or pregnancy tests) on female students rumored to be "going with boys," leading to public humiliation and attempted suicides. (The issue of nation and control of the body, particularly as this affects women, is taken up in chapter 6.)

For the individual, survival depends on membership in a solidarity group. The family, while imposing its own mental, moral, and physical discipline, is a site of refuge from the unpredictable and uncontrolled power of the state. Kandiyoti has observed that "the role of primary groups and particularistic allegiances in mediating citizens' access to resources and services has remained critical."[12] "There's an Arab saying," the Turkish political scientist Soli Özel told me: "'Who escapes from the herd is carried off by wolves.' Without a family, you're basically a dog." In place of individualizing as a response to the spread of new forms of communication and self-production through commodities, Neyzi notes, Turkish youth seem "to be fragmenting into identity-based enclaves."[13]

"Individualism is a very Western thing," Özel told me over dinner with his family in his book-filled home on the upper Bosphorus. He spoke of the difficulties inherent in being an individual in Turkey, or a liberal, someone without the expected powerful affiliation to a group that identifies and protects you, and that demands all your loyalty and resources. "Everyone [in Turkey] wants more, but only for themselves," Özel lamented. For instance,

> you can't bring land together to benefit from economies of scale. This is just as true for textile owners. "Let it be small, let it be mine," (*küçük olsun, benim olsun*) is a scourge, a plague.... There is no conception of collective life. It's all about the state. People don't trust the state and they don't trust each other. The state serves as an intermediary between you and me. You can only trust your own. It's a predatory state. Its judicial system is not independent or impartial. Those you expect to be the most individualistic don't show those characteristics. It's a herd mentality. You know that if you had the power, you wouldn't let others breathe. You know others think the same, so you show you have power. You don't trust your state to be fair. Because there's no fair arbiter, I can't fundamentally trust you. It's too dangerous to be an individual unless you have a state you can trust.

This lack of interpersonal trust in Turkey has been well documented. A recent comparative survey of education and its social outcomes in OECD (Organisation for Economic Cooperation and Development) countries shows that a very small number (16 percent) of Turks with education below upper secondary level trust others, far below the OECD average of 34 percent. Unlike in other OECD countries, in which interpersonal trust increases substantially with higher education (42 percent among those with upper secondary, and 53 percent with tertiary level of education), in Turkey it declines even further, to 12 percent. In other words, the more educated an individual, the less trust they feel toward others. Turkey is alone among the twenty OECD countries in showing such a startling pattern.[14] In a 2007 poll, 39 percent of Turks agreed with the statement "Most people in this society are trustworthy" (compared with, say, 58 percent in the United States). Supporting Özel's observation that Turkey's lack of interpersonal trust is linked to a lack of trust in state institutions, the Pew survey found that in countries where people tend not to trust one another, concerns about political corruption also tend to be widespread.[15]

In a context of mutual suspicion and lack of confidence in the impartiality of refereeing institutions like the government, courts, police, and schools, other communities of belonging take on heightened importance. Protection and reliability are guaranteed by a community's established criteria of belonging and standards of loyalty. Özel, who is Jewish, talked about the importance in Turkey of the principle of loyalty to one's community. "I taught at a military academy," he told me. "They were anti-Semitic, but when I criticized Israel, I sensed they disliked me because I wasn't true to my people."

I also remembered that Halil, an Islamist friend in the working-class district of Ümraniye, used boundaries of affiliation and loyalty as criteria to judge a politician. We were discussing up-and-coming political actors like Mustafa Sarıgül, the mayor of Istanbul's Şişli district on the other side of the Bosphorus, who at that time was positioning himself to found a national political party of his own. Halil didn't like him. "He comes from everywhere," Halil complained. "He shows up at events everywhere, so he doesn't belong anywhere."

If you belong nowhere and your loyalties are not fixed, you have no soy, no recognizable social identity. Consequently, you are suspected of having no honor, a concept that speaks directly to your ability to uphold the standards of your family and community. Liberals, by the very nature of their willingness to cross boundaries and mix everything from ideas to food in fusion restaurants—not to mention the sexes—fall into this category. "What liberalism did," Özel explained, "it gave you combinatorial freedom. I don't have to like you to work with you because there's a common benefit. I don't judge you by your essential characteristics." But in the Turkish context, liberalism is not respected because it is *soysuz*, without a tribe. "The greatest enemy of the Republic was liberalism," Özel continued. "The greatest sin of the Jews was that they were cosmopolitan." People were afraid of cosmopolitanism because it was rootless, soysuz. People can change their minds, "sell their own." Liberals, in other words, have no allegiance, no hard-and-fast boundaries, no political, racial, or ethnic family, and thus no honor.

National Unmixing

Early twentieth-century nationalists abhorred cosmopolitanism. Baer writes that "New nations sought an imagined authenticity; cultural mixing was seen as negative and decadent, a threat to the purity of the nation."[16] After World War I and the Turkish war of liberation from European occupation, a peace treaty was signed at Lausanne on July 24, 1923, which recognized the Ankara government, rather than an imperial Ottoman government in Istanbul, as the representative of Turkey. The treaty also included a provision for a forcible exchange of populations, with 500,000 Greek Muslims moving to Turkey (including the Dönme of Salonika) and 1.2 million Orthodox Christians (Rum) to Greece. British Foreign Secretary Lord Curzon called this process "the unmixing of peoples."[17] In 1913, Christians constituted 20 percent of the population within the borders of what would become Turkey; in 1923, only 2.5 percent remained.[18] The peoples thus disentangled were not discrete populations to begin with but, rather, embodied the multiple customs and languages of their homeland, be it the empire or Greece. They were sent, often without the compensation promised them, to countries whose customs and languages were foreign to them and, perhaps more important, where they knew no one.

Unlike Ottoman policies that encouraged conversion as a means of social integration and advancement, a measure passed by the Turkish Grand National Assembly in 1923 forbade Christians and Jews from converting to Islam until their status as citizens had been clarified, presumably to prevent non-Muslims from avoiding deportation.[19] Baer argues that since this idea of nationhood was based on race, it did not tolerate the multiple identities that had existed in the plural society of the Ottoman Empire, nor did it allow for any "exit strategies such as cultural separateness."[20] In any case, conversion to Islam would not make a Christian or a Jew Turkish, as it did not convert blood and lineage. It is indicative of the racial conception of Islam that a Turk converting to Christianity, however, loses his or her Turkish identity.

As a consequence of such nationalist policies, the presence of mixed identities and ambiguous boundaries raised anxieties. In his discussion of the Dönme, Baer muses that in the early Republican era the unsettled nature of Dönme identity—Jew or Muslim, foreigner or Turk?—rendered their relationship with the majority population uncertain, unstable, and unpredictable.[21] Although they had been accepted as Muslims during Ottoman times, in the Republican era the Dönme were forced to abandon their religious identity for a secular Turkish identity, a "conversion" that was possible only if the Dönme ceased to exist as a recognizable community. Today's descendants are understandably reluctant to admit to Dönme ancestry. The specter of Dönme or Sabbateans as a cabal of "hidden Jews" or crypto-Jews indistinguishable among the ranks of Muslim Turks is regularly revisited in sensationalist books and film scenarios that accuse them of plotting to destroy Turkey from within.

Pressure to "unmix" Muslim Turkish from non-Muslim interests continued throughout Republican history. While Turkification policies were meant to unify the nation, they also aimed to create a Muslim-dominated economy. The draconian

Wealth Tax of 1942–44, discussed in the previous chapter, destroyed the livelihood of thousands of non-Muslims. The effect was to reduce non-Muslim participation in the economy and increase out-migration. In September 1955, Turkish nationalists carried out violent attacks on ethnic Greeks and other non-Muslim minorities living in Istanbul and their properties, including shops, homes, churches, and cemeteries. They were responding to a rumor broadcast by nationalist newspapers that the house in Thessalonica, Greece, in which Ataturk had been born had been bombed. Later, it emerged that the mob attacks had been orchestrated by the Turkish state to create pressure on remaining Greek Christians to leave the country. A nationalist pogrom against Jews in Thrace in 1934 caused a large part of the Jewish population to flee. The Princes' Islands just off the coast of Istanbul in the Sea of Marmara were once the summer refuge of Istanbul's Jews and Christians. Unable to sell their properties as they fled, many residents abandoned their latticed wooden houses set inside gardens. The stately old apartment buildings in Beyoğlu are riddled with apartments, some empty for decades, whose ownership is unknown or in dispute. Towns along the Aegean coast, like Ayvalık, still bear the physical scars of the Greek population's rapid flight—abandoned churches, their apses cracked like eggshells; churches repurposed as mosques; distinctive Greek-style houses renovated by Istanbuli vacationers. Further east in Van, until recent attempts to renovate them, Armenian churches like the elaborately carved tenth-century structure on Akdamar Island lay in ruins.[22] When I visited the remains of the fabled Varagavank (Seven Churches) monastery, it consisted of nothing more than a few brick vaults used to house goats amid a clutch of tumbledown Kurdish homes.

Turkification policies also targeted Kurds and Alevis. The Dersim massacre of 1937–38 in what is now the province of Tunceli killed tens of thousands of Alevi Kurds, including women and children, with artillery, air bombardment, and poison gas.[23] Many others were internally displaced. The massacres were sparked by resistance to the government's policy of mass resettlement and dispersal of the local population with the intention of assimilating them into Turkish culture. On November 23, 2011, Prime Minister Erdoğan formally apologized in the Grand National Assembly for the Dersim massacre, raising hopes among Armenians that this might herald willingness by the government to acknowledge and apologize for massacres of Christians. This seems unlikely at present.

Today's polls show an increasing rate of anti-Christian sentiment in Turkey, along with general intolerance against non-Turkish identities and nonconservative lifestyles, even among the youth. Unfavorable opinion of Jews went from 49 percent in 2004 to 76 percent in 2008, of Christians from 52 percent to 74 percent.[24] A number of studies, including a poll carried out by the Jewish community of Istanbul, demonstrate people's reluctance to live beside and mix socially with people different from themselves, particularly atheists, people who drink alcohol, homosexuals, Jews, Christians, Alevis, and foreigners.[25] The studies also suggest that religiosity has become a marker of trust and a standard for preferring people as partners, friends, neighbors, trade partners, landlords, and tenants.[26]

While young nationalists seem to differ from their elders in terms of political predictability, they are similar in their degree of alienation from the "other." Some of this homogeneity, as I discussed in chapter 3, derives from education and socialization in the nationalist trope of "the enemy within and the enemy without." In a 2009 study of elite Kemalist youth who consider themselves to be nationalist (ulusalcı), Üstel and Kaymaz found that although these young people didn't neatly fit given political categories in terms of their attitudes and voting patterns, they nevertheless exhibited a high incidence of nationalist and racist views, intolerance, and "othering." Toprak makes the case that a similar—and on some issues higher—level of intolerance characterizes the pious population.[27] The high school students in Küçükural's national study tended to support EU membership but at the same time expressed profound reservations about the effect of this on family values and relations between the sexes, areas in which the students expressed highly conservative views. They also feared harming Turkey by letting in the European "enemy without" and loosing the non-Muslim "enemy within."[28]

The conservative columnist Taha Akyol noted that Turkey was becoming a country of mutually intolerant and culturally gated communities.[29] In 2010, mainly Kurdish Diyarbakır province donated a fire truck to the Black Sea town of Çayırbaşı, which did not own one. Even though six fires had been put out by the truck in its first two months in the town, a bomb threat was made against it, and the issue divided the residents, one of whom objected, "They are not at peace with Turkish people. . . . The truck might extinguish fires, but they humiliate Turks. I do not want this truck to belong to our pure and clean village."[30]

The media has catered to and helped shape such attitudes. *Valley of the Wolves* (*Kurtlar Vadisi*) is a highly successful television series with plots torn from the headlines. Its hero, Polat Alemdar, is a patriotic Turkish undercover intelligence officer who infiltrates the mafia and becomes involved in shadowy affairs where rogue elements of the "deep state" intersect with organized crime. The series taps anti-Kurdish, anti-Israeli, and anti-American sentiment. In 2006 the series spawned a spin-off movie, Turkey's highest-grossing movie ever, in which the show's hero goes to Iraq to do battle with the U.S. military and to break up a Jewish plot to harvest organs. A television series called *Separation* (*Ayrılık*) began in 2009 with an opening scene that showed a group of Israeli soldiers mowing down civilians, then stalking a little Palestinian girl and shooting her at point-blank range. The plot of a more recent show had a large ship traveling to Gaza to break the blockade and being violently intercepted by Israeli soldiers, a scenario clearly inspired by the *Mavi Marmara* incident of May 2010.

Interpersonal Lamentations

The romanticization of ethnic identity and nostalgia for a shared communal past in such a climate of hostility to non-Muslim others is worthy of note. It is not uncommon to find older local residents who lament the loss of Istanbul's native Christian population in previously mixed neighborhoods like Kuzguncuk and Arnavutköy, where I have lived for extended periods. When I first moved to Arnavutköy in 1985, a vestige of Christian life was still discernible, although much reduced from earlier days. Many Orthodox Christians (Rum) left the area after the 1974 Cyprus crisis that nearly precipitated war between Turkey and Greece.[31] In 1985 a Rum bakery near the pier sold classic Turkish pastries and special bread at Easter. Christian residents sometimes invited their Muslim neighbors to attend part of the lengthy Easter service, during which people strolled about the marble floors of the spacious church, strewn with fragrant bay leaves, and chatted. Other worshipers made the rounds of the icons on the walls, or prayed in carved wooden pews designed for standing rather than sitting. At midnight a neighbor hurried over to warn me and a Muslim friend not to be alarmed just as what sounded like gunfire erupted above our heads: the arrival of the holiday marked by children shooting off noisemakers in the balcony. A popular taverna on the hill was frequented by working-class Rum as well as Muslim youth who spent weekend nights drinking rakı, dancing to Rum and Turkish tunes played on an electric keyboard by the village accountant, and smashing plates in a traditional expression of pleasure.

A decade later, the bakery and taverna had closed, and church services were much reduced as the Rum population dwindled. A Rum men's coffeehouse, no more than a room with a few plastic covered tables, was tucked discreetly under a stairway on a side street. There was no sign at the door. A family whose women wore the black, all-enveloping *çarşaf* moved into the neighborhood. The husband wore loose clothing and a white turban. Several long-time Muslim residents told me they were disturbed by the family's presence in the community, but their discomfort was tempered by the fact that the man's pharmacy was inexpensive and distributed free medicine to the poor.

A retired shopkeeper I had known for years, a dyed-in-the-wool nationalist who had on previous occasions railed against Greeks (*Yunanlı*, referring to Greek nationals) trying to undermine Turkey, lamented the departure of his Rum neighbors. The Rum made much better neighbors, he told me, than the "easterners" (by which I learned he meant rural Kurds and overtly pious Muslims) that had replaced them over the past two decades. When he was growing up, the shopkeeper reminisced, Muslim residents of Arnavutköy joined their Rum neighbors for holiday church services, and the Christians would refrain from smoking during Ramazan, the month of fasting, out of politeness for their observant Muslim neighbors, who were not permitted to smoke. Local residents, he said, had tried to protect their non-Muslim neighbors when mobs of outsiders came into the area and threatened them with violence.

Similar stories can be heard in Kuzguncuk on the Asian side, once a heavily Jewish neighborhood with a smaller population of Greek Christians and Armenians, of whom very few remain. A current Muslim resident described Easter in her youth as a time when all the local residents, Christian and Muslim alike, spread picnics in the streets and shared their food. Mills contrasts these narratives of multiethnic harmony—a "lost cosmopolitanism"—with the silence of Kuzguncuk's residents about the 1955 pogroms against the area's Christians.[32]

The loss that is lamented in these narratives arguably is not of religio-ethnic diversity but of a culture of urbanity and civility that had been shared by neighbors. Despite religious differences, old-time Muslim residents felt they had been more like their Christian neighbors than the uncivilized Muslim newcomers from rural areas and the east, and the unfamiliar Islamist turbaned men and their heavily veiled women. Easterners were described as single men "from who knows where" crammed into apartments meant for one family. "Who knows what they get up to." The word Kurd was not uttered, although clearly implied. The disturbing issue was not so much ethnic as cultural difference; lack of roots; unfamiliar customs; a lack of respect for the civilities of city living, specifically Istanbul living; and the intrinsic danger to the community posed by outsiders.

Üstel and Kaymaz found that nationalist youth, while essentializing non-Muslim minorities and Kurds, sometimes romanticized a Turkish past of Muslim–Christian togetherness,[33] and 5 percent of Turkish youth interviewed in a different national study considered their roots to be Armenian.[34] This interest in Armenian roots may be due to more open discussion of the 1915 massacres, acceptance of Armenians as an indigenous population (a series of exhibits in Istanbul over the past two years have documented the role of Armenians in Ottoman and Turkish history), and public discussion of a "secret history" of Armenian children who were taken by Turkish officers or by Muslim families during the massacres and raised as Muslims.

In a memoir, the liberal lawyer and writer Fethiye Çetin revealed that her grandmother, who she had thought was Muslim, was really an Armenian Christian who had been taken by a Turkish officer during the Armenian massacres. Turks called those children who survived the massacres "leftovers of the sword" or "those who have impure blood." Çetin's grandmother, whose given name was Heranush, was snatched from her mother's arms by a military police corporal who renamed her Seher and raised her as his daughter; his wife treated her as a servant. Seher eventually married the family's son. Unable to reconnect with her natal family, in her nineties she revealed her story to her startled granddaughter, who at Heranush's request tracked down her family in the United States. The book *My Grandmother: A Memoir* graphically describes Heranush's memories of the 1915 Turkish massacres in Armenian villages and the death march of women and children to Syria, which some members of her family survived.

The book, originally published in Turkish in 2004, has gone through many printings and began a public discussion of the "leftovers of the sword" and the 1915 massacres generally. This rise in public interest coincided with Turkish government moves to better relations with Armenia and encouragement for historians to examine and discuss the events of 1915, as long as the word "genocide" is not used. The official Turkish position is that both Armenians and Muslims died in the conflict and that the killings were a result of the fog of war. In comparison with the 1980s, when I remember that a tour guide in the Van region was arrested for telling foreign tourists that Armenians had once lived in the area, the atmosphere has lightened considerably, making public (and private) discussion of ethnic and religious issues more possible.

Alongside the AKP government's "Kurdish Opening," which wavers between increased liberties and repression for the Kurdish population in Turkey's eastern provinces, individuals have "outed" their mixed ancestry and revealed the public disapproval they or their families faced. In an interview in August 2009 the famous actress Hülya Avşar talked about being melez, a hybrid with Kurdish and Turkish parents who grew up partly in the Kurdish-speaking east. "On my mother's side there is Crete, there is nomadism. My father's side many ages ago was a Turkmen family that migrated from Kayseri" and mixed with Kurds, so became "Kurdified." She kept her Kurdish background to herself as a child; she understood that if it were known that her father, a banker, was Kurdish, it might cause problems. One day, when they lived in Ankara, she remembered, her father came home angry because he had been speaking Kurdish with someone on the bus and they were both made to get off.

In my conversations with pious Turks as well, I find an openness to Turkey's multiethnic, multidenominational past and present in principle. Yet paradoxically—as demonstrated in polls and in people's choices of lifestyle—many Turks appear to desire distance in their daily lives from those who are different. The space for lamentation and expression of sympathy with others appears to be a personally defined space—between author and reader, between neighbors—when what is shared can be experienced as a personal bond, which does not easily scale up to national categories.

Barth suggests that traditions of knowledge (like nationalism, Islam, democracy, modernity, Turkishness, urbanity), the internally coherent systems of thinking and practice that we learn and share and take for granted, exhibit plural forms when put into practice. Traditions of knowledge are nothing more than clusters of related ideas that are embedded in—and take their shape through—actual social relationships. People know different things and have different experiences, so although they may use the same nationalist discourse, their experience and expression of nationalism is always an interpretation of the nationalist tradition based on the context and particular framework of relations. Different settings, whether one is taking a poll or engaged in a neighborly conversation, bring into play different individual commitments and concerns that justify using one version of "truth" over another. As such, traditions of knowledge, while coherent and ordered, are continually constructed and reconstructed as people act them out.[35]

Starr, citing Anderson, defines cosmopolitanism as a "cultivated detachment from restrictive forms of identity," especially as these are represented by parochial allegiances to nation, state, and ethnos.[36] Cosmopolitanism in present-day Turkey is expressed either as a nostalgic longing for a lost golden age of coexistence or a liberal goal based on principles of individualism. In either case, "mixing" can become unmarked and nonthreatening only if Turkey denationalizes, that is, switches from an ethnic (or religio-racial) nationalism to a civic nationalism that defines the individual politically as a citizen, rather than on the basis of group membership. This may seem a daunting task. Ethnic and civic nationalisms represent substantially different traditions of knowledge—with competing "truths"—and, as we have seen, are deeply embedded in social relationships that reproduce them in everyday life. Yet, the very instability inherent in acting out nationalism in different contexts and relationships allows the tradition to be transformed. New knowledge can fundamentally change what individuals think they know, possibly causing a cascade of variation in systems of thinking and practice.[37] As Çetin said in an interview, "The 'enemy' can be in your family and can therefore never be the enemy; we are all human beings, that is the message of my book."[38]

Altınay and Türkyılmaz concluded their study of converted Armenian survivors by pointing out that their stories had opened up a "Pandora's box of national identity" and prompted new and difficult questions: "Who belongs to the Turkish nation? Who is an 'Armenian' and who is a 'Turk'? Whose lineage matters?" The most pressing question is whether the recent "coming out" of this group of survivors will "create new possibilities for mourning and reconciliation, or further ignite growing nationalist anxieties."[39]

The willingness to mix is central to liberal identity. At annual demonstrations to commemorate the assassination of Turkish Armenian journalist Hrant Dink, people held up signs saying, "*Hepimiz meleziz*" (We are all half-breeds) or "We are all Hrant Dink, We are all Armenian".[40] Yıldıray Oğur, a columnist for the newspaper *Taraf*, was inspired by Barack Obama's reference to himself in 2008 as a "mutt" to write a column entitled "Watch out! The *melezler* are coming!" In it, he argues against ideas of "blood purity" and points out that Turkey is *melez*-izing. "Types, species, categories, races are exploring each other." He mentions Alevis and Kurds, leftists and conservatives, Black Sea Turkish college women singing Kurdish songs, friendships between covered and uncovered women. Every day, he writes, he sees another wonderful example of this, especially among the youth. For now, though, Oğur admits, half-breeds will continue to have many enemies in a nation indoctrinated with racist ideas about purity. They will accuse them of "dirtying" Turkish blood and breaking the line of descent. "And the regime is most afraid of half-breeds because no rifle works against them."[41]

In a parody of the Dink signs, at an Istanbul demonstration on February 26, 2012, commemorating the 1992 Armenian massacre of Azerbaijani civilians at Khojali, some nationalist demonstrators held up signs stating, "You are all Armenians. You are all bastards." The Turkish term used was not melez (someone of mixed race), but *piç*, a derogatory word for illegitimate child, one that is not in any legitimate line of descent.[42]

POLLUTION AND THE LOST CITY

The theme of pollution by half-breeds who have lost their essential identity—people out of place—was reprised in the 1970s and 1980s by urbanites who objected to the

Figure 5.1. Crowd at a 2008 demonstration marking the anniversary of Hrant Dink's assassination. The sign reads, "We are all half-breeds."

"village-ification" (*köylaştırması*) and "otherization" (*ötekileştirması*) of their cities by migrants from Anatolia and the Black Sea coast looking for factory work in the cities and throwing up broad swaths of jury-rigged squatter houses around Turkey's cities. Their behavior was seen as an affront to civility and an offensive intrusion into urban life. Offenses ranged from women's wearing headscarves and men's wearing pajamas in the streets, to large families' picnicking in public parks, so that urbanites complained they were unable to use the parks themselves (because the space could not be shared between such disparate cultures.)

"Culture" is wielded here as a normative standard, associated with terms like "civilization" (*medeniyet*) and "modern living" (*çağdaş yaşamı*), and is evaluated hierarchically. Turkishness as civilization presumes the existence of a preexisting "folk culture" (*halk kültürü*) that maintains its characteristic "traditional" practices until its members are eventually assimilated into the mainstream and adopt the civilized normative standard. In Turkey, folk culture, associated with rural life, has been alternately manipulated, romanticized, and demonized by the state, the market, and the "modern" sector. Non-Muslim minority lifestyles or those of the urban poor, by contrast, are not considered to be folk culture but, rather, unassimilated and potentially threatening heterodox practices.

Village life has been romanticized as the original, unspoiled, authentic Turkey but also as an uncivilized lifestyle, rife with patriarchy and ignorance. For instance, some Turkish television advertisements show villagers in regional costume and speaking in regional dialects being surprised by modern technology (cell phones, prepared foods) that, a "modern" commentator implies, will improve their lives. Talk shows with audience participation sometimes put the spotlight on an older, motherly woman dressed in village clothes and *yemeni* (a light cotton headscarf common in villages), encouraging her to speak up loudly and volubly "from the heart" about her views of Turkish society. More often than not, the "village" woman is a foil for the offscreen urban "Islamist" woman who covers her head tightly in a large, modish tesettür scarf. The peasant mother is meant to represent the "true" Turkish peasant who is also a Muslim but exhibits Kemalist values, particularly the strength of women in society (with the unstated—or sometimes stated—assumption that "Islamist" women are oppressed). One might also see in this a coded reference to Ziya Gökalp's idea that Turkish Islam in its pure state has been preserved by the peasant, untainted by Arab custom in the Ottoman cities, and that it demonstrates the Turks' Central Asian legacy of gender equality.

The audience, often heavily populated by young secularists, appears surprised by the seeming contradiction of a "traditional, covered" woman expressing their own modern values, and applauds madly. In this way, culture is manipulated in the project of creating and keeping pure the definition of a "true" Turk and the ideal of a seamless national culture.

The yemeni is represented in movies and the media as authentic and as representative of a pure folkloric past. In the 1970s, though, squatter women began to wear polyester squares over their crochet-edged yemeni scarves, and skirts over their broad peasant trousers, a hybrid form that was neither urban nor rural. The adoption of the store-bought headscarf by migrant women blurred the boundary between peasants and secular urban women who had become pious in their later years, an acceptable life-cycle transformation among Kemalists signaling a withdrawal from sexual femininity. Until then, the store-bought eşarp with which these women covered their heads had differentiated them as modern, urban, and middle-class. The desire of migrants and their offspring to become urban and modern continued to drive a transformation of style and lifestyle over the next thirty years. By the 2000s, the yemeni was still worn indoors, but outside the home it was crowned by an elaborate confection of modish silk or polyester, the upscale tesettür fashion of the new pious bourgeoisie. As in the 1970s, the effect was of objects (a square of polyester, pajamas) out of place in an urban environment defined by a class-based culture in which those objects figured only in rural settings. Middle-class secular urbanites perceived the resulting ambiguity and blurred boundaries as threatening.

The term *arabesk* came to encompass the culture of squatter areas and migrants during this period—neither truly rural nor urban, belonging to no place, a mix of uncivilized cultural habits and lifestyles.[43] The term was coined in the late 1960s to describe an emerging musical genre, a mix of Western pop and Egyptian music, with rogue elements of Turkish folk music.[44] Strains of arabesk coiled from the windows of taxis, their dashboards decorated with lovingly hand-beaded dangles and plastic suction vases filled with cloth flowers. Dashboard and seats were covered in brilliant colors and in materials ranging from carpets to lustrous long-haired goatskins. The sinuous Arab sound and soulful lamentations about hard and unforgiving city life, homesickness, and the loss of love appealed to struggling migrants. Middle-class urbanites saw arabesk as uncivilized and threatening. Twice I witnessed conductors begin classical music concerts with diatribes against arabesk music, and once, a young man in the audience, moved by the attack on arabesk, rose to his feet and bore witness to his and his generation's devotion to the principles of Ataturk. He was rewarded with thunderous applause. Arabesk was banned from state radio and television, which oversaw the sanctity and purity of folk and classical Turkish music.[45]

As Öncü put it, "Arabesk came to denote impurity, hybridity, and bricolage, and soon acquired a wider chain of associations, denoting a musical genre, a film genre, as well as cultural habits and lifestyle of those who enjoyed them." To middle-class urban dwellers, it seemed that the Anatolian peasants in Istanbul had lost the purity and authenticity of their traditional folk heritage without acquiring the urbanity of cosmopolitan life and instead "had developed their own half-breed, pseudo-urban culture, which threatened to contaminate and pollute the entire city."[46] "Neither peasant nor urban, arabesk culture becomes a placeless phenomenon, both residual and marginal, but also dangerous, because its boundaries are ambiguous and margins confused."[47]

In the 1980s, a new epithet invented by a satirical magazine began to circulate in everyday speech: *maganda*—an aggressively vulgar type, usually depicted as an unkempt, hairy, bare-chested man wearing a gold necklace, who beats his wife, has too many children, and lives on the margins of the city but colonizes the urban centers to sexually harass women and engage in other uncivilized behavior. One of the graphic artists who coined the term *maganda* described the figure as "the animal in us . . . He is a stain which cannot be removed. . . . He is contagion, he infects."[48] The image is one of active male intrusion into the physical and moral boundaries of both the city and its women, the threat of cultural miscegenation made manifest. In 2009

Prime Minister Erdoğan sued opposition leader Deniz Baykal and a journalist for causing him "mental anguish" for referring to him in an interview as a maganda.

The sociologist Ferhat Kentel told me that modernization was a form of physical shame. "In school, you learn to feel shame at wearing pajamas to the store, to wear a scarf. You learn how to hold a knife and fork, how to correctly scratch your nose. Modernity and civilization teaches me to be ashamed. Then you learn to despise others who haven't passed that same test—those who still wear the scarf, Kurds who haven't learned Turkish properly and speak with a bad accent. I was tamed, domesticated, affected by that, while others rejected it." The elite, he said, don't speak the language of social class; they see only the cultural aspects, the Islamic aspects of movements from below, and see them as threats.[49]

One response by city authorities and residents themselves has been a process of "unmixing" through absorption, gentrification, urban planning, and suburbanization. In the 1970s and 1980s, municipalities reacted to illegal building by tearing down squatter homes, often to find them rebuilt the next day. However, in the run-up to elections, politicians found it expedient to pass out deeds to squatters to gain votes. Cities extended public services to squatter areas—electricity, sewage, bus lines.[50] As cities expanded and real estate values began to rise, squatter areas, often built on hillsides, became valuable for proximity to the city center and their views. Districts that had been settled and populated by poor rural migrants were absorbed by the city and gentrified, their poorer residents pushed to the outskirts into new housing projects, while others remained in nearly invisible pockets of poverty.

By the end of the millennium the term *gecekondu* (literally "placed there at night"), which had meant an identifiable area of illegal housing or squatter area, had been replaced in popular discourse by the term *varoş*, which derives from the Hungarian for the part of town outside the city walls. Varoş, like gecekondu, implies an entire universe of characteristics, from appearance to lifestyle and beliefs, but a varoş is not easily mapped or visually distinguished by location or architectural characteristics. It refers rather diffusely to any urban residential location of working-class and lower-middle-class pious residents, that is, the place of Black Turks.

Terms defining subjects by their poverty and rural origin, which can no longer convincingly be applied to the Islamic elite, have given way to markers of piety and lifestyle associated with certain distinctions of the body, like head covering for women and facial hair for men, and the refusal to ingest alcohol. Some Islamic men sported a distinctively shaped rounded beard and eschewed neckties as un-Islamic Western corruptions.[51] Even the mustache, Soner Cagaptay opined, has moved from being a sign of manhood to a marker of social class. "Until the early 1990s, almost all

Figure 5.2. New housing squeezes out the last squatter homes in Ümraniye.

Turkish men had one, whereas today the moustache belongs to those only in the lower-middle and working-class neighbourhoods known as varos [sic]."[52] He points to Prime Minister Erdoğan as an emblematic man from the varoş, despite his current wealth and position of power. That is, piety and certain bodily habits presented as characteristic of Black Turks are associated with lower-class status, regardless of the actual social position and wealth of the individual, allowing Kemalists and secular urbanists to draw a boundary between themselves and the threatening Other despite the increasing convergence of their location and characteristics.

Markers of difference among men would have been further erased by regulations being considered in 2009 by the Council of Higher Education (YÖK) that would have banned instructors from having beards and mustaches, and wearing sweaters that hid their ties. Beards and a refusal to wear ties were Islamist hallmarks, but today many men of the Islamic bourgeoisie have jettisoned both the mustache and the round Islamic beard and clothing distinctions in favor of the clean-shaven look of the global businessman, making them indistinguishable from secular Kemalist men. For some, this makes them—like the Dönme—a potentially threatening Trojan horse. Implementation of YÖK regulations was erratic, since they were rooted in multiple contradictory discourses that conflated male and female identity with bodily comportment, lifestyle, and religiosity. Instructors fought to keep their mustaches (which might signal regional or lower-class status, but also masculinity) and beards (depending on shape and length, beards might signal piety, a leftist identity, or masculine fashion—an unshaven "Miami Vice" look reflected in fashion ads and macho television heroes like Polat Alemdar in *Valley of the Wolves*). In some cases, male students were not allowed to attend class if their hair was long, undermining the national masculine ideal as incarnated in the popular Alemdar.

While young women until recently were banned from attending university with a headscarf, pious young men had no such impediment, as their piety is unmarked. Some professors complained to me that once on campus, "Islamist" men insisted that the university provide them with a prayer room, causing "disruption in the halls." Besides prayer, the only inviolable remaining marker that distinguishes a secular from a pious male subject is a willingness to drink alcohol, a practice given the status of a sacred tradition, intrinsically bound to the authority of Ataturk, himself a noted rakı enthusiast. The walls of numerous venerable fish restaurants, sites of alcohol consumption and emblems of urbanity, are crowded with framed portraits of Ataturk.[53] Many urban youth, however, have jettisoned the link between alcohol consumption and Kemalism. The hot new global clubs and eateries in the entertain-

Figure 5.3. Iconic fish restaurant with patrons drinking rakı under portraits of Ataturk.

ment districts of Turkey's major cities are decorated not with portraits of Ataturk but with emblems of global consumption.

DESACRALIZATION IN THE SUBURBS

As pious Muslim families, some of them offspring of migrants, became upwardly mobile in the globalized economy and the power politics of the AKP period, their lifestyles increasingly converged with those of the secular middle class. The New Turks live conservative lifestyles but compete with the old urban elite in consumerism and other markers of modernity, which requires greater efforts to distinguish the boundaries between them. Homogenous middle-class communities (*siteler*) have sprung up on the outskirts of the city, some populated by secularists, others by the pious, rarely if ever mixed. Prominent markers of difference are the presence of the headscarf in one and alcohol consumption in the other. Pious siteler are not dissimilar from the gated communities of the secular middle class, in that each is escaping from the ambiguities of the city and the continual offenses to the parameters of one's identity, to what one perceives as decent and necessary behavior and values.

Despite their grounding in Islamic or Kemalist doctrine, in practice, pious and secular siteler express visions of modernity and civility that are similar in their incorporation of Western styles and values and the importance of consumption for distinction, as well as in their expectations of family and women's concerns.[54] As Ayata points out in his analysis of secular siteler, discourse supporting sexual equality serves an important function in distinguishing secular middle-class residents from conservative traditionalists and from Islamists, who emphasize spiritual equality but believe in separate social roles and domains for men and women. By contrast, companionship in marriage is highly valued by the secular middle-class, and women are not excluded by definition from work and the public sphere. Nevertheless, Ayata writes, gender roles in the secular suburbs tend to be acted out within separate men's and women's domains. Women's home-based roles are reflected in their very low 2011 national labor force participation rate of 30 percent (compared with 73 percent for men)[55] and by the lack of women in formal politics.[56] Instead, Ayata observes, secular middle-class women act as (and are seen as) wives, mothers, homemakers, and managers of the house, in charge of provisioning, decoration, and the visual expression of "taste" that expresses a man's success.[57] In this realm, too, there is overlap between the Islamic and secular bourgeoisie. Traditions of knowledge like modernity and piety, when acted out in practice, converge around shared gender expectations, class hierarchies, and markers of distinction.

Aggressive marketing has created middle-class and elite Islamic styles that set themselves off against the "unconscious" veiling of the masses. In the 2000s the ideal "new Islamic woman" took part in previously male-dominated activities in the public sphere, whether political activism or shopping, which had been primarily a male activity in conservative communities. The private arena itself has been valorized by the market, resulting in a new bourgeois Islamic home environment marked by certain purchased commodities. This setting stands in contrast to an Islamic home marked primarily by religiously supported female virtues (like virginity, motherhood, housekeeping, and seclusion). A woman may move between being a "new Islamic woman" and being a secluded housewife, depending on her class and education. Both are legitimated with reference to Islamic doctrine. Veiling itself is a powerful and contradictory symbol both of pious women's right to act in public as well as their duty to remain secluded in the home.

In the 1990s and early 2000s, at the height of women's Islamist political activism, veiled activists from working-class backgrounds aspired to the well-publicized role of "new Islamic woman," dressing the part as prescribed by advertisements and Islamic magazines aimed at women. Eventually, however, many were forced by economic circumstances or community pressure to retreat into seclusion within the patriarchal family and the home, an arena set off in Islamist ideology as private in opposition to public. In addition, arenas for pious women's grassroots political activism narrowed with the disappearance of the Islamist movement and the AKP's consolidation of power as a hierarchical, cadre-based party. While women may work as activists, they generally remain outside the formal cadres of power. It is interesting to note that Islamism as a social movement created a space for women's political activism in the public sphere, while formal democratic politics narrowed their arena for participation. Nevertheless, some pious women have continued to push for higher education and professional jobs. When they were not allowed on college campuses with their heads covered, those who could afford to, went abroad for their education, while others earned professional certificates from private sector sources.

The development of an Islamic bourgeoisie, in other words, has created a situation similar to that described by Ayata for secular middle-class communities, where women's ideals may contradict women's actual "work," which is to raise children and to demonstrate and mirror their husbands' success through the exhibition of taste in fashion and furnishings. In pious middle-class homes, this aesthetic might take the form of less ostentation in order to highlight piety, coupled with the placement of Ottoman-referenced objets d'art. A friend knowledgeable about the Turkish art market told me that Ottoman calligraphies were in great demand by the wealthy pious sector. These buyers associate "Arabic" script with Islam regardless of what is actually written, which may be without any religious content—a poem, for instance, or an official decree. Owning a piece of Ottoman calligraphy, whatever the text, confers authentic roots, Islamic identity, and social capital.

Navaro-Yashin describes the fashion industry that has grown up around tesettür, a form of veiling that many secularists still associate with antisystem political Islam. At a tesettür fashion show, a woman watching the veiled models striding down the runway told Navaro-Yashin that she welcomed the elaboration of an explicitly middle-class form of veiling. She had recently begun to veil, she revealed, and the sales staff in her usual shops no longer recognized her, treating her as if she couldn't afford to shop there. If she wore couture tesettür, she reasoned, that wouldn't happen.[58]

The 1990s saw the spread of Islam as a form of personal expression, elite status, and lifestyle, including Islam-referenced gated communities and department stores. This development was reflected in articles and advertisements in self-consciously Islamic newspapers like *Zaman* and the television station Samanyolu, both associated with the Gülen movement. In one television ad a young man knocks on the door of a woman in tesettür hoping to woo her with flowers and then a box of chocolates, which he miraculously manages to shove under the door. The woman, whom we can see alone in the room on the other side of the door, remains uninterested and aloof until he pushes through a box in which she discovers a colorful headscarf of a particular brand. At that point, to my surprise, given common rules of comportment in the pious community, she opens the door and lets him in.

Kemalist expressions of Muslim identity similarly are referenced to lifestyle choices, the market, and various nonreligious sources of legitimacy. During Ramazan in November 2002, for instance, the special holiday pages in major Kemalist newspapers gave advice on such topics as whether sushi and lobster were permitted foods and how to take care of the skin while fasting. Subjects generally were approached from a pluralist angle, pointing out different Islamic interpretations and variations by region and country. Scientific explanations were amended to religious ones, for instance, explaining that research by veterinarians had revealed substances harmful to human beings in the flesh of animals like pigs, dogs, and lions.

The mammoth annual Fatih Book Fair that same year was held in the courtyard of the Sultan Ahmet Mosque. The book fair is self-consciously Islamic, and the crowds of patrons dressed the part. The book displays, however, sometimes presented surprising contrasts, with translations of Dostoyevsky, Gogol, Turgenev, and Jack London next to *The Big Islamic Catechism*, and Steinbeck and George Orwell sharing a shelf with *Islam's Smiling Face* and *Army and Commander in Islam*. One stand advertised a sale on Malcolm X, another a computer program for learning prayers in Arabic, a problem for most Turks, who do not understand Arabic. Shoppers, however, often reached over more esoteric offerings and picked up books like *Test Your Child's IQ* and slim, colorful volumes for children about Islam and prayer, including talking books that made the sounds of the Arabic alphabet.

The Mevlevi, or whirling dervishes, began appearing in popular music and video clips and on entertainment shows on television. This was a radical departure from their previous public performances, in which the public was told not to clap, since this was a religious ceremony, not a form of entertainment. On a late-night program on Show TV in 2002, the female host exchanged light banter with a sexy blond Turkish singer, both in low-cut evening gowns, then introduced a small group of young men dressed (and presented) as dervishes, along with a musician who played Sufi music to accompany them while they whirled for the cameras. One of the dervishes was a young boy of seven, the son of the musician. (Classic Mevlana performances often include at least one young apprentice dervish). When the whirling

Figure 5.4. Department store display for New Year's celebrations, with fir tree, tinsel, reindeer antlers, and Santa.

ended, the hostess asked the boy to announce, "Stay tuned. After the commercials, we'll be right back." This was still unusual enough to merit a lightly shocked article on the entertainment page of the newspaper *Sabah*, in which the journalist Yüksel Aytuğ criticized the show's host for asking the young dervish, "How long have you been turning?" Spinning tops "turn," the journalist admonished, but dervishes "whirl," and they do so in a ceremony with deep religious and philosophical meaning. They are not, he emphasized, dancers or entertainers.[59]

This desacralization of religious practices became another point of convergence between secular and pious, causing unease in some quarters. An article in the newspaper *Milliyet*, for instance, featured a musician who taught children Sufi whirling as a game and planned to put together a show around Sufi whirling and music by a South African singer.[60] A more Islamically oriented newspaper advised women to finger prayer beads to reduce stress.[61] Another newspaper showed an actress wearing a *muska*, or amulet, as a fashion accessory over a tight bathing suit. Cultural and musical syncretism is not new in Turkey, but the incorporation of religious practices into such risqué formats would have been thought highly inappropriate until recently and would have unleashed a negative reaction. Even more disturbing to some is the spread of Christian holiday customs among secularists. At year's end, Santa Claus greets shoppers at stores that display wreaths and other holiday decorations. People put up decorated fir trees (referred to as New Year's trees) in their homes, exchange gifts, and hold well-lubricated New Year's parties. The Santas have occasionally been attacked by knife-wielding assailants. I have heard conservative men and women in Ümraniye inveigh against the "*sosyete*" (high-society) types that engage in such dissolute behavior, associating Westernized behavior, Christian ritual, and alcohol consumption with the urban elite.

As Seufert pointed out, objects and practices associated with an Islamic (and Christian) identity came to be dislodged from their religious moorings. They became available, primarily via the marketplace and media, to those whose primary identity was not Islamic but who were interested in demonstrating that they were Muslim. Muslimhood has become fashionable and a means of self-expression. Seufert linked this to the development since the 1980s of a consumer society in which identity can be demonstrated through purchased goods, and items are advertised by playing on identities. This development implies a change in political focus as well. He argued that whereas in the past, Turks might have asked, What does an Islamic identity say about national identity? now they are asking, What does the nation mean for a Muslim? [62]

Muslimhood as Ethical Nostalgia

In other words, being Muslim was a cultural and ethical identity associated with being Turkish, but no longer with Kemalist nationalism. Official Kemalism did not provide many answers to the dilemmas faced by people trying to come up with a moral map for the post-1980 ferment in identities, opportunities, and challenges. The challenges included mass unemployment resulting from the privatization of Turkey's industries, as well as the financial and political rise of new sectors of the population, and the mixing of heretofore discrete social sectors and their expressive and performative qualities. For some people, the answers lay in reviving provincial modes of propriety that had been common even in cities. These norms and patterns of speech and behavior involved, among other things, rituals of cleanliness, distinct ideas of personal status and rights, and a focus on "intimacy, loyalty, interpersonal transparency and affection" and mutual support. These were anchored in a local and oral Islamic ethic.[63]

This widespread language and ethic, unacknowledged and even demonized by the Kemalists, served as a powerful foundation for Islamist politics. It is important to note that early Islamic parties, like the National Salvation Party (NSP) in the 1970s, did not do well in elections. Toprak suggests that this is because religion by itself was not a sufficient factor for mobilization.[64] It was not until the 1990s that an Islamic party began to organize and mobilize people on the basis of what Meeker calls a provincial "Islamic language of being" rather than just on the basis of local interests.[65] (The NSP catered to provincial small businessmen fearful of big business). That change allowed Islamic politics to expand beyond specific interests to attract people across a wide spectrum who perceived in the party a familiar and time-honored strategy for dealing with life's difficulties and change.

These developments were exacerbated by economic decline and privatization of state industries in the 1980s and 1990s. There was a perceptible nostalgia for traditional strategies and institutions that, in retrospect, seemed to provide solutions, a diffuse but discernible longing for a sheltering authority. In the early 2000s this sentiment was exemplified in the popularity of films and film series about rural landowning *aghas* who were gruff and demanding but who cared about their people, protected them, and met their needs. The Ottoman Empire, mothballed since 1923 by the Republic, has been dusted off to provide models for everything from tolerant multiculturalism to veiling styles and architectural models for summer resorts. The Welfare and Virtue parties that preceded AKP put forward Ottoman-inspired ideas ranging from a scheme for *millet*-style religious federalism to charity programs in which wealthy families "adopted" poor families. AKP was successful primarily because it organized and mobilized people on the basis of neighborhood networks built around the very characteristics described by Meeker's provincial propriety. The links between neighborhood networks, civic organizations, and political party—a powerful nexus I call "vernacular politics"[66]—created a broad, national movement that was flexible enough to incorporate a great variety of people. The masses, in effect, were mobilized on the basis of familiar personal ties and obligations, and their energies and interests were channeled into a national political program.

The rehabilitation of provincial modes of propriety as the bases for urban, modern Muslim identities and national political mobilization became possible with the development of an aggressive media. Television and radio were effectively deregulated in the 1980s as cable and satellite technology made the media impossible to control. The Turkish-Islamic synthesis of the 1980s meant that the government allowed a great variety of Islamic ideas and material to be published and broadcast, resulting in an explosion of new channels and publications. The newly opened economy of the 1980s brought wealth to conservative and provincial entrepreneurs. The Özal government brought them into the bureaucracy. All these factors led to the development of a new Islamist public culture, which almost immediately came into conflict with official public culture. Veiling developed a popular, chic style and began to appear in areas of the city, particularly middle-class areas, that were formerly the exclusive realm of secularists, and Islamic ideas were debated in the media.

Thus, there were multiple challenges to the Kemalist laicist definition of the boundaries and content of the public sphere, from media and market forces, from Muslim intellectuals and politicians, and from ordinary citizens looking for strategies for self-expression. Yet, there was simultaneous widespread concern about the social manifestations of other kinds of difference that were on the rise: an acceptance of lifestyle differences only if they were segregated; a politically unmoored and intolerant Muslimhood that divided people within the same social class, the same neighborhood. A middle-aged hotel clerk who has lived his entire life in Fatih, one of Istanbul's most religiously conservative neighborhoods, described a creeping division between residents who are more devout and those less observant. Whereas in the past they lived mixed together, he explained, now there is less tolerance. More religiously observant residents are disturbed by the more open clothing and lifestyles of their neighbors. They have, over time, become geographically segregated, so that those living behind the mosque tend to be more observant than those living in front of the mosque. Despite decades of convergence, paradoxically, the line between more and less pious has been drawn ever more starkly in geographic terms.

Kurds as "easterners" also are subject to geographic segregation, regardless of their actual location. They are associated in popular discourse and in the media with PKK violence and national disloyalty, with honor killings and petty crimes, with a lack of civilization—the Kurd as maganda and traitor. In the early Republic, Kurds were considered unassimilatable because of their tribal loyalties; in current times, for their assumed sympathy for the PKK. As Muslims, after all, it should be possible for them to marry into the national lineage and become "Turks." On a visit to Diyarbakır in 2010, Erdoğan listed Kurds among "our true [öz, biological] siblings."[67] To become the nation's damat (son-in-law), though, Kurds would have to give up their competing loyalties and lose the cultural characteristics that identify them as outsiders who lack the proper bodily habits, modes of propriety, piety, and cosmopolitan civility of the national subject.[68] Ideally, there should be no identifiably Kurdish neighborhoods. Those that are—like Istanbul's vibrant, but poor, Tarlabaşı—are being gentrified in such a way as to erase the Kurdish presence altogether.

CONSECRATING CLASS: GENTRIFICATION AND SUBURBANIZATION

Gentrification and suburbanization are spatial strategies for drawing new boundaries where convergences inside the global, capitalist remix sites have created ambiguity and anxiety. Istanbul as a global capital for music, art, and nightlife is a regular feature of the *New York Times* travel section, where reporters breathlessly describe the city's techno clubs; trendy shops and restaurants; art galleries and museums; jazz, blues, and reggae establishments; and the Istanbul Music Festival and jazz festivals. The city was chosen to be the 2010 European Culture Capital. But Potuoğlu-Cook points out that Turkey's rapid globalization is quite uneven, especially in Istanbul, and its vaunted cosmopolitanism is, as she put it, "cracked." Both secular and Islamic political leaders have used the Ottoman Empire as inspiration to gentrify the city and urban life. The city has in some cases torn down the existing historic urban fabric—displacing poor and ethnic residents—and built in its place an "upgrade" to an artificial reconstruction of a fictive Ottoman past. This fabrication is designed for tourist consumption as well as for Turkish elites, who also have become consumers of neo-Ottomania, a source of distinction and a remedy for nostalgia for a lost cosmopolitanism (now sanitized by standardization and the wholesale removal of any sources of class and ethnic pollution).

The Istanbul districts of Sulukule and Tarlabaşı are recent examples of municipal gentrification. Sulukule, beside the Byzantine city walls, had for hundreds of years been home to Istanbul's Roma population. The area was very poor, particularly since AKP had shut down Roma entertainment venues a few years earlier. The wooden housing stock was in bad shape; some balconies were leaning so far sideways that it was surprising women could hang their wash out without sliding off. In 2008 the municipality razed the entire neighborhood and moved the Roma residents to bleak apartment blocks on the outskirts of the city, where they were unable to make their traditional living as entertainers—indeed, unable to make a living at all—as there are no jobs in the area. Many were unable to pay the rent and the bus fare into the city. On the Sulukule site, the municipality built modern two-story villas with overhanging second stories in a faint architectural nod to Ottoman architecture. Tarlabaşı is an area at the base of Pera hill in Beyoğlu. Its ethnically mixed inhabitants, many of them Kurds, are being moved out in a similar manner, and most of the houses will be razed to make room for touristic hotels and shops.[69]

The population is riven by secular and pious factions, both of which desire the international acclaim and revenue of tourism and high-profile urban renewal, but at

Figure 5.5. Woman sitting in the window of an Istanbul restaurant rolling out dough. The restaurant advertises that it serves organic and authentic Turkish food. Behind her is an image of a traditional peasant woman, and stuffed donkeys before the window add ambiance. Similar restaurants that display "peasant" women preparing food in their windows dot the Westernized part of the city; one is called "*Otantik*" (Authentic).

the same time act within a highly class-divided and gendered economy where money clashes with honor. Commercialized modern veiling (tesettür) refers to the Ottoman past for legitimacy, as does belly dancing, which secular Turks use to represent authenticity to outsiders and to themselves, in a form of auto-Orientalism. Yet both practices, like gentrification, are rife with contradictions. Tesettür is a carrier of paradoxical symbolism, incorporating ideas about Islamic modernity in which women are educated and professionally and politically active while simultaneously denoting values like patriarchal hierarchy, gender segregation, and women's primary role as mothers whose place is in the home. I have found in my research on highly educated pious women that they experience great difficulty negotiating these contradictory expectations within their families.

Class- and gender-based contradictions are particularly evident in the practice of belly dancing. Potuoğlu-Cook observes that it not only lures tourists but also has become a fad among elite secular women, who attend classes for their own amusement and health benefits. It has become an elective dance form that, like urban gentrification, aims to upgrade the Ottoman past to create distinction and authenticity for elites, while its professional practitioners are low-paid, ill-used women whose appearance in public and participation in the labor market makes them morally suspect. Tesettür and belly dancing, what Potuoğlu-Cook calls the "fraternal twins" of Islamic and secular Turkey, are selectively chosen Ottoman elements, highly commodified and associated with social class status, their female practitioners hailed as authentically Turkish and modern, but also frowned upon and abused. Belly dancing and tesettür delineate what form of female presence is acceptable in the public sphere and are rife with contradictions as they "oscillate between abjection and sophistication."[70]

Urbanity, cosmopolitanism, and modernity are clusters of ideas that cohere in shared traditions of knowledge but that in practice become disordered and undetermined. What they are meant to express and what they are understood to mean varies when acted out by elite or lower-class women, by covered or secular women, and for a foreign or local audience. There is no "culture" clash per se, only clusters of cultural knowledge, values, skills, and orientations that are embedded in traditions of knowledge. These traditions become "true" only when acted out, through people's interpretation of them as they place them into the context of specific social relations. On the improvised stage of daily life, individual motives, class and gender expectations, and other individual subjective concerns twist and reorder the meanings of traditions whose content we believe to know.

This principle was starkly illustrated in a street battle between new residents and old-timers in the newly gentrifying Istanbul neighborhood of Tophane, in which both sides claimed superior urbanity, cosmopolitanism, and modernity. On September 21, 2010, mobs of local residents in the conservative neighborhood attacked the patrons of several art galleries, beating people with iron bars as they stood on sidewalks sipping sangria and strolling from gallery to gallery to view coordinated openings as part of an art walk. The men attacked the art patrons with knives, broken bottles, and pepper spray. Tophane is on the border of Beyoğlu, Istanbul's nightlife district, and is slowly gentrifying. Galleries had squeezed in beside butchers, grocers, and bakers. Trendy boutiques had opened beside men-only tea houses. Fifteen people were reported injured, including visitors from Europe, at least one of whom required stitches to close a head wound. Seven people were detained and then released. Initially, it was thought that local residents had been disturbed by some of the art on display, including an automobile hood ornament depicting a fallen winged Ataturk. But interviews with residents indicated that they were more worried about rising prices, the proliferation of bars and loud clubs, and lifestyle clashes with the new-comers, including perceived harassment of local women. They felt that the newcomers looked down on old-time residents because of their poorer clothing and habits that they perceived to be lower class. They were not against art or even development but were afraid of being squeezed out, as had happened in the officially designated "urban renewal areas" surrounding them. Many old-time residents spoke nostalgi-cally about a past when "everybody, Muslim and non-Muslim," lived together peace-fully in Tophane, respecting each other's traditions and religious sensitivities.[71] To-phane's Greeks, Armenians, and Jews had long ago been forced out in the often violent unmixing process described previously, but contemporary Muslim residents drew upon a romanticized civility of the past to reinforce their identities as rightful city dwellers, not migrants or Black Turks.

PURITY AND THE NATION

Michel Foucault has reminded us of the power of discourse to discipline and pro-duce the individual, in no small part by defining and regulating the subject's body[72]—giving meaning to blood, sex, gesture, and in Turkey everything from the color and visibility of a woman's hair to the shape of a man's beard.[73] Sheathed in the power of the state, discourse demarcates what is normal and right from what is abnormal and wrong and shapes the subject's conception of an appropriate self. This self, Stuart Hall has suggested, is "narrativized" within a story about belonging that is built upon resources of history, language, social class, and culture.[74] It is not only the subject that is positioned within a politically charged social field but also elements of culture itself—the categories of self and other, their representations, and the knowledge that makes them up. The press, media, market, home décor, clothing, body habits, and eating and leisure practices provide a continually transforming palette for individu-als to draw from in representing themselves. In Turkey, these elements are highly politicized and so, therefore, is any projected cultural identity. There is no neutral self. A sip of whisky, like a drop of blood, is a highly charged cultural marker of social class, lifestyle, and political values; it takes its power and meaning from the particu-lar national narrative and accompanying cultural tradition with which the individual identifies.

The kind of alcohol one drinks marks one's class and secular or pious lifestyle. "Rakı is barbaric. Whiskey is civilized," a lawyer once told me, brandishing her glass of scotch as we ordered dinner at a Chinese restaurant in Taksim Square. One could read from her statement that she was a secular Kemalist and that she disapproved of the customs of the lower classes, like drinking rakı, the national anise-flavored alcohol, or, even worse, not drinking alcohol at all, a marker of the pious Black Turk. She situated herself in an elite class through her choice of revealing clothing, appreciation of Chinese food, and choice of libation. Turkey's wine industry has flourished in the last two decades, and wine consumption now represents a new source of distinction. (Import taxes on alcoholic beverages are prohibitively high, so foreign wines are rarely available.) It is no coincidence that the AKP's continual encroachment on the legality of alcohol sales hits particularly hard at hard alcohol and wine, which are associated with Western lifestyles. The regulations cite public health and safety, especially the protection of young people. Cigarettes and luxury cars have come in for their own regulation and discouraging taxation. But opponents find in the alcohol regulations a stealthy attempt to regulate its consumption out of existence. Prime Minister Erdoğan reportedly has said he couldn't understand why people drank wine when they could just eat the grapes.[75]

Inspired by a colleague who works on food culture in Japan, I returned to Turkey, planning to inquire into the intersection of foreign and Turkish food cultures. But I discovered that outside of the fusion restaurants frequented by the global elite, Turkish food remained stubbornly "Turkish," and Schlotzsky's Deli on Baghdad Boulevard could have been dropped from anywhere in the United States. A friend told me of an argument she heard on a popular television cooking program that taught viewers to make Turkish food. One of the participants had made a sauce for her fish and was taken to task by the irate chef, who told her that she was supposed to be making *Turkish* food, and Turks don't put sauce on their fish. Indeed, Turkish menus outside of the tourist and elite areas seem untouched by experimentation or any admixture of foreign cuisine with the exception of "authentic" regional variations. An entrepreneurial woman in a Black Sea coast town appeared in the national news because she was serving "*hamsi* sushi" in her cafe. The "sushi" consisted of fresh anchovy, cooked, and rolled in rice—in essence the regional hamsi and rice specialty with a new name and in smaller portions. In recent years, Paşabahçe, Turkey's venerable glass producer, has offered variations on the classic Turkish tea glass shaped like a tulip, for instance, offering a model with a protruding glass bar that serves as a handle. Yet, people I know have scoffed at such abominations, commenting that tea must be served in the traditional glass for it to be "Turkish tea."

Purity of culture is linked to purity of lineage, both deemed essential to national integrity. A new law in 2010 banned assisted conception in Turkey unless donor and recipient are married. Women who go abroad and get pregnant via artificial insemination or egg donation face one to three years in jail. İrfan Şencan of the Health Ministry explained that the rationale behind the law was to "protect the ancestry (soy), to make the newborn's father and mother known. . . . It has nothing to do with race," she added defensively. Nevertheless, the ruling created controversy in Turkey as people debated whether indeed the law had roots in the nationalist understanding of soy or whether it was rooted in Islamic jurisprudence requiring the donors of egg and sperm to be married; otherwise the union is considered adulterous.[76] The sociologist Nilüfer Narlı insisted that the idea of a "pure race" was not part of Turkish culture. "Turks have been cosmopolitan in terms of their culture and genetic inheritance. Historically, Turks have been open to mixing with other people," she pointed out. "The Ottomans had the devşirme system [in which they captured or recruited boys from Christian families, raised them as Muslims, and trained them to take office in significant royal institutions], and sultans' wives were often foreigners."[77] One of the first women to be investigated under the new law was the sexy actress Sevda Demirel, who allegedly became pregnant after visiting a sperm bank in the United States. It was rumored in the press that she was bearing a mixed-race (black) child. Demirel later claimed she had made up the sperm bank story because she had no wish to reveal the identity of the father, a man who, she said, had wished her to veil in a çarşaf at the behest of his religious mother. Demirel claimed the Kemalist high ground and refused to veil, citing Ataturk's revolution. She also revealed that she had received threatening messages after the media publicity about her alleged visit to a foreign sperm bank.[78]

The emphasis on purity, especially purity of soy, is linked to Republican nationalism through a powerful threat paradigm—the fear that outsiders will undermine the integrity of the nation. Following the 1999 Kocaeli earthquake, which killed 17,000 people, Turkey's minister of health banned foreign blood donations from Greece from entering the country, citing concerns about protecting the integrity of Turkish blood. At times, this fear has taken on absurd proportions. In September 2010 the head of Turkey's Council of Higher Education (YÖK), Yusuf Ziya Özcan, gave a talk at a Turkish university on the importance of Turkey's universities' ramping up their own research capabilities. To support his argument, Özcan brought up the subject of tomato seeds, most of which, he claimed, were being imported from the United States and Israel, with dire consequences for Turkish eaters. "There is something called 'genetic programming.' They can implant a genetic mechanism into the tomatoes and we can eat it without even knowing. We can be infected with some diseases that we don't know anything about. In the meantime, you can destroy a whole nation." Forced to respond to Özcan's allegations, Turkey's Minister of Agriculture said that the country, in fact, imports only about 6 percent of its seeds from Israel.[79] The idea behind this example—the implicit threat of impure mixing and consequent annihilation of Turkishness—is so common that politicians as well as ordinary people on the street use it as a touchstone for truth.

Conclusion

All-encompassing narratives of identity, such as Kemalism, are fantasies of community that rely on difference to mark a frontier between *us* and *them*. Such fantasies require continual work to maintain boundaries between categories of people that often are more symbolic than real, either through physical and geographic "unmixing" or discursively. In the context of recent social transformations, these boundaries have become harder and harder to maintain as ostensibly opposite groups converge in their characteristics and practices, and as individual and group identities proliferate. Shared traditions of knowledge about what it means to be Turkish or Muslim or urban and modern are expressed in multiple variations when acted out by real people in real places. The disordering of cultural systems has occasioned uncertainty about what can be said to be properly Turkish, what is sacred to national identity, and what is malleable. Spirits are conjured from the past and used as talismans to ward off the anxiety of change, of the unknown path to the future. Kemalists place Ataturk's picture in the windows of their homes, facing out. Pious Muslim mayors invoke new rituals to counter old ones by hiring Ottoman-style marching bands and sponsoring reenactments of the Muslim conquest of Christian Byzantium in 1453 in place of Republican state rituals.

The maintenance of a national identity requires continual vigilance against the threat of forgetting, losing the coherence of the national narrative, and disappearing. It requires continual monitoring of boundaries against the incursion of impure elements (in language, ideas, cultural practices, and blood). In the next chapter I discuss the unending efforts to maintain continuity and purity, an attribute of both the nation and of women, and the effect of such practices on women's relation to the nation.

CHAPTER 6

Sex and the Nation

Veiled Identity

Ayşenur Bilgi Solak's cell phone pulsed on the desktop to a rumba beat with a sensual female voice singing "El Corazon" in Portuguese. Ayşenur is the thirty-three-year-old assistant to AKP's Istanbul provincial party leader. She attended grade school in Austria, then earned a BA in sociology at Bosphorus University in Istanbul. I was waiting in her office at party headquarters early one evening for her to finish her duties so we could talk.[1] The high-ceilinged room was bare of ornament, dominated by an enormous desk on which were arranged neat stacks of papers and three phones that rang on and off. Yellow sticky notes festooned a slim late-model computer next to a fax/printer. I lounged in the brown faux-leather easy chair before her desk and leafed through the latest issue of the glossy AKP-linked *Metropol* magazine. My eye was caught by an interview with the mayor of Tarsus, who explained proudly how his administration had brought organization to his city, tearing down thousands of stables and forbidding animal husbandry—instead, centralizing transport to villages—and replacing street peddlers with a city market.

Ayşenur strode in, her high heels clicking on the tile. She wore a matching red shirt with black-and-white polka dots under a black leather coat with white braiding. A headscarf with a design of big red roses was wound tightly around her head and neck. With her bright red lipstick, she appeared elegant, put-together, competent, no-nonsense.

We spent a few minutes discussing her work at AKP. She was involved, she told me, in the Union of Civilizations Project under former United Nations head Kofi Annan that was meant to counter Samuel Huntington's thesis about a "Clash of Civilizations." "We do outreach to the old Ottoman countries," she explained. Moving eventually to the topic of my visit, I asked her, "What is a national person (*milli insan*)?" "A national person is a Turk," she responded. "By Turk, I mean *Türkiyeli* or citizen. I was born here; my grandparents came from Bulgaria." Ayşenur used the unpopular neologism *Türkiyeli*, which downplays ethnic and religious differences. As Türkiyeli, your origin or blood makes no difference. When I probed her further about her identity, she said, "I would first say I'm a Muslim, then a woman, which means a mother, then a Turk, then married, then working, then a politician."

And what does nationalism mean to her? "A milliyetçi man, his family *looks* religious. Most milliyetçi are male. They have a horse, a woman, a gun, which they have in their house. They're hard, also in politics. They do politics with sharp boundaries. He wants his wife to cover because it's *namuslu* (honorable), even if he doesn't pray.... [N]ationalism means Turkish blood is the best." She parsed the various forms of nationalism:

> The CHP [the Kemalist Republican People's Party] is ulusalcı: the nation-state is turned inwards, the only friend we have is ourselves.... They are against the EU. In AKP's program, we don't accept this.... MHP [the ultranationalist Nationalist Action Party] is ülkücü, harder [*katı*, more severe] than the normal folk. Among the ülkücü, there are Islamic motifs, for instance [mention of] Allah. Their wives are covered. They tend not to let their daughters out of the house. They're marginal.

Ayşenur's description of nationalism, regardless of variety, is male and hard-edged without room for compromise. It is obsessed with an emphasis on boundaries of the nation, women's honor, and blood, and not concerned with the substance of religion. Islam appears rather as a motif. It is not an identity that she feels any kinship with. "Am I a nationalist (milliyetçi)? No, I'm someone who loves my nation.... I'm a citizen of the Turkish Republic."

When I asked other contemporary women about their place in the nation, to my surprise, only one, a middle-aged, educated, secular professor, mentioned Kemalist encouragement of women to participate in public life, and only after prompting on my part. Most women, whether pious or secular, described their relation to the nation in terms of citizenship or as Türkiyeli, the neologism that denotes a kind of *Leitkultur* in an attempt to free Turkish national subjectivity of its ethno-racial component. None of the women expressed a strong sense of nationalism.

On *Kurban Bayramı*, the sacrificial holiday, I visited friends in a village in the forest near the Black Sea that I had first come to know two decades earlier. Change has come slowly to this isolated settlement. The men's coffeehouse and the mosque flank the road as it enters the village. The village still has no store; bread and newspapers for the coffeehouse arrive every morning by truck. Daily life follows a predictable rhythm. During the day, men sit in the coffeehouse, do agricultural tasks, or cut wood in the forest for fuel and sale, a declining source of income as cities lay gas lines for heating. Boys hang out in groups and play soccer in the open space where the lanes cross. Women walk between the houses visiting, and girls work in the garden, help their mothers cook, and work on their trousseaux. The entire family gathers only to eat, men separate from women, who generally sit around a tray on the floor with their children.

I shared a room with Fevziye,[2] who is in her early thirties and divorced. Every morning before dawn her brother woke her to pray, then she went back to sleep. We filled the potbellied stove in the room with wood before going to sleep, but by morning the fire had gone out, leaving us to shiver as we rolled out from under our quilts. The women cook and clean and work in the fields, but during the holidays, which fell in winter that year, boredom set in, especially for family members visiting from Istanbul. The men sat around, the women sat around, waiting for visitors. Fevziye complained that she was bored. So did her brother-in-law, stretched out on the sofa. When I suggested that she bring some books to read on her next visit, she laughed. "If people here see you reading a book that's not the Quran, they'll laugh at you. Especially the women."

It was a relief and a source of excitement to set out on our own round of visits to the homes of relatives and friends. I knew many of the people we visited, but one home was new to me. We were met in a large central room by six women of various ages and their children. The women wore the long skirts or wide *şalvar* trousers common in the village, their hair draped with colorful yemeni gauze scarves. One was a college student; another, a grandmother; several were new mothers dandling babies. One told me matter-of-factly that she had conceived her child as a "tube baby." They were straightforward, fun, sparkling with ideas.

In the process of introducing me, my friend mentioned that I was doing research on nationalism. The women were immediately interested and insisted on contributing their opinions, leading to an animated, wide-ranging discussion without further prompting on my part. The women overlapped in their comments, so I was unable to put individual names to what they said. Trying to keep up, I scribbled furiously in my notebook. "Where's your tape recorder?" one of the women asked impatiently. For this research trip, I had finally replaced my bulky tape recorder with a sleek digital device the size of a cigarette lighter, but today for the first time I had left it behind at my friend's house. It was only five minutes away, but I didn't want to risk interrupting the conversation by going to get it.

In their discussion of nationalism, the women rejected the purity paradigm and, like Ayşenur Bilgi Solak, said they preferred a multiethnic, multidenominational so-

ciety in which Turkishness did not play a leading role. The tolerance that characterized the Ottoman period, one woman suggested, was undermined by nationalist
ideas that had entered Turkey from outside. Instead of referring to ethnic divisiveness of the kind that characterized state discourse about the Kurds, the women attributed Turkey's Kurdish problems to poverty in the east and overreliance on state
welfare. The women were particularly disturbed by the state's association of nationalism with Islam. They believed that the state's provocative nationalism distorted people's ability to live their Muslimness; that the state's grafting of Turkishness to Muslimness resulted in intolerance against non-Muslims/non-Turks and Alevis. This did
not, they argued, reflect the ideas of society, which are more tolerant. It especially
did not reflect the ideas of the younger generation to which many of them belonged.
Here's a stretch of the conversation, as caught by my pen.

WOMAN 1: I don't like Turkishness (*Türklük*). I believe in living humanely, a blessed life.
That is, I am Turkish, pure (*saf*), but it means nothing to me.

WOMAN 2 (the college student): There's provocation, but beneath that is a readiness to be
provoked that has accumulated over years. [For instance,] state politics against the
Kurds: There's only one flag. There have been two hundred years of Kurds! *Ulusal*
[nationalism] is passé.

WOMAN 3: You can't live like a human being [in the Kurdish east]. In Artvin there's a low
standard of living. Even in the *yayla* [nomadic mountain pastures] there's water,
telephone, electricity. But in the east there's nothing. It's their fault too. Black Sea coast
people are hard workers; Kurds are waiting [for the state]. . . .

WOMAN 2: Society and state have different meanings. People don't always tell the truth
in polls; they say what they think the questioner is asking. We're a country raised not
to express what we're thinking. Everything you say is punished. As a society we have
open ideas, but our speaking isn't open.

WOMAN 3: The ideas of the nation are very different from those of the state. People of the
folk are very different. They're from everywhere, they get along. The reason? The state
believes that behind every Kurd is a second state. I don't believe it. I have Kurdish
friends. [Fevziye, sitting beside me, agreed with this.] The Ottomans weren't
nationalist (milliyetçi). They weren't Turks. Nationalism came afterwards from the
outside. Nationalism is bound up with being Muslim.

FEVZIYE: They put pressure on Muslimness (*Müslümanlık*). You can't live as a Muslim the way you want to.

WOMAN 3: The differentiation between Laz and Kurd is new.

WOMAN 4: I read in the newspaper that while a Kurd was doing his army service, his mother phoned him and he couldn't talk to her. It was forbidden because the Kurd's mother couldn't speak Turkish.

WOMAN 2: Jewish—in Ottoman times you could speak that language. Not now. Without nationalism everything would be relaxed. Kurdish TV is a very good thing. That couldn't have been done before."

FEVZIYE: If it had been done earlier, maybe there wouldn't be Kurdish–Turkish enmity.

WOMAN 2: The new generation thinks like me, both men and women. The new generation mixes, has Alevi friends.

WOMAN 5: Me too.

WOMAN 2: Ninety-nine percent of my mother's generation thinks like that. They don't even take a sip of water in an Alevi's house. But we don't.

WOMAN 2: We need some young people in the state. Let them achieve something, become active.

Fevziye nudged me and told me that we had to leave, as we had more visits to perform. I did so reluctantly, having so enjoyed the conversation. When we were outside in the lane, I asked her, "Who are these women?"

"They're *çarşaflı*," she told me, referring to the black, all-enveloping veiled robe, which the women would have donned when they left the house. The only exception was the college student, who wore tesettür. "They're members of the Mahmut Efendi mosque in Istanbul," Fevziye explained. This mosque is known as the center of a highly conservative brotherhood affiliated with the Nakşibendi order. That I was surprised by this only highlighted my own ignorance and preconceptions; I hadn't expected women who wore the most conservative form of veiling in Turkey to be so intelligent, thoughtful, and politically engaged.

Later, back in our room, I asked Fevziye to help me fill in the details of some parts of the conversation I had only been able to sketch in my notes. Fevziye's evaluation of the conversation was that the women were saying, "I'm not happy about Turkishness. I feel no pride. We're not able to live Turkishness. We're hindered." Their goal of a "blessed life," Fevziye explained, "means citizenship isn't worth anything without humane feeling. . . . They look at things from an Islamic point of view. The girl, although she earned a diploma, couldn't find work except in interest-free banking because she's covered. Although she lives in Turkey, although she's a citizen, she isn't treated like one; she doesn't get the interest and attention she deserves."

The dual themes of women as alienated from Turkish nationalism and as lesser citizens were repeated in conversations with other pious women at different levels of education, both urban and rural. Havva, a young intern with a women's organization in Istanbul concerned with the rights of women who cover their heads, believes that women who cover their heads are put in the position of second-class citizens. She argues for a modern cosmopolitanism that has space for the acceptable as well as the "abnormal" fringe:

I was in Syria last summer. [In Turkey] we're modern, but people have more complexes here. In Syria, women are covered, but they go about their daily lives and relate to one another. They are *makbul* (acceptable) citizens. Here it's more complex. People have feelings of inferiority. . . . In 1923 [this country] lived through a traumatic period. They forgot their own history. . . . It was a new thing, not the announcement of the Republic, but what happened afterwards. Those with a religious identity were left outside the framework of Turkish, laicist, Sunni. . . . There's the *gerçek* (real) citizen and there's the rest, who are unimportant or [the state] has the right to hinder their lives. The Republic Meetings were held by actual (*aslı*) citizens. They said, "We'll choose the president of the Republic."

There's also a type of makbul woman, the Republican woman, an imaginary type manipulated by television to create a prototype of the uncovered woman, blond and modern, also honorable (namuslu), clean, sexually honorable (*iffetli*). Not spoiled, knows her stuff. Wears her skirt below the knees, self-assured, balanced. This is the Republican woman. Anything outside of this image is abnormal, pathological. For instance, women who wear top-to-toe black, black hair, like punks, some feminists, and women who cover [their heads] . . . It's the state's norm. The rest are second class, like U.S. blacks. Some cover in an extreme way having nothing to do with tesettür. But we're really a cosmopolitan people.

There are lots of migrant families. Istanbul has a larger population than Greece, so it's normal to see different things.

IDENTITY-CARD TURKS

In Ankara, I visited a group of pious women who belong to the Capitol City Women's Platform, a political interest group founded in 1995 by women inspired by their participation in the Fourth World Conference on Women in Beijing. The Platform lobbies parliament on women's issues. All the women are highly educated, several have master's degrees or PhDs in a variety of subjects from education to legal sociology. One young woman was studying for a PhD in political science in Malaysia. Hidayet Şefkatlı Tuksal, whose PhD is from Ankara University's prestigious School of Theology, is a founding member. Most of the women are pious and cover their heads, but none belong to an Islamic brotherhood. In my discussions with these women in previous years, they had expressed relief that I wasn't interested only in dissecting the headscarf issue. Turkish women have many more problems than just the headscarf, they pointed out. They see the Platform as a feminist organization working on women's issues, not as an Islamic organization concerned with the headscarf debate. As one woman put it, "I'm not in an Islamic movement, but Islam is our reference."

For this reason, they were often rudely received by secular ("çağdaş," modern) activists who would snub them at conferences, call out that people shouldn't listen to them, or get up and leave once they saw that their fellow speaker wore a headscarf. That has changed somewhat, Hidayet told me, and they now work together with some secular feminist and leftist women's groups on issues like lobbying for the new Penal Code that came into force in 2005. "They accept us because they find us modern women," she said, using the Turkish term *modern* instead of *çağdaş*. The Platform members expressed similar frustration with pious scholars and activists, as well as with representatives of an alternative politics movement, who the Platform members complained did not see it as a problem that only a handful of women were invited to their conferences amid a hundred men. "They listen, but how much do they pay attention?" I have heard elite pious women (some in the Platform, others in high-profile media positions) complain about this with regard to their own husbands and male colleagues, among whom number some well-known Islamic intellectuals. Referring to the AKP, one woman scoffed, "Anyway, there they generally just have women appointed to the display window." Newspapers, Hidayet complained, write about them as "'two headscarved speakers of the symposium'. . . . When they see a woman with headscarf, they only see the headscarf, nothing else."

The Platform stands against what its members see as using Islam to legitimate abuse of women's rights, like polygyny or different rights to inheritance for men and women specified in the Quran. Some people insist that shari'a law is necessary, Hidayet said, but many women are just confused about which system they should prefer—the secular one that appears to give them more rights or the one that follows Allah's word. The Platform wants equal rights in Turkey, not shari'a law, on the principle that Allah's opinion would have been on the side of equality, and what was expressed in the Quran was suited to the conditions of that particular historic period. In a heated conversation a few years ago, a Platform member said of male Islamic intellectuals that "They use religion to get advantage for themselves," like taking second "wives" through religious ceremonies, and refusing to discuss women's problems except within a religious context. The men, the Platform women complained, referred everything to the "headscarf problem" and were not interested in other kinds of women's rights. In other words, pious women activists feel doubly silenced—by secular feminists and by pious men. Their silence is reinforced by male domination of the sphere of intellectual Islamic discourse and by foreign scholarship that bothers little with educated pious women's voices. The domain of Islamic intellectuals in Turkey is a closed circle.

One chilly autumn evening in 2008 about ten women—some familiar, others new to me—gathered in the Ankara apartment that serves as the Platform's headquarters. Another freewheeling discussion about the individual and the nation ensued, and this time I was able to tape it. Here I reproduce segments of a conversation that went on for hours and ranged over a wide variety of topics. Were I to try to summarize their positions, it would not capture the extent and complexity of their ideas. Instead, I dip into the flow of dialogue to give the reader a sense of the range of the women's views.

I began our discussion of the nation and nationalism by asking them who they were. One woman noted that they were struggling between two warring forms of self-presentation. In more conservative circles, the ideal woman sat at home and watched the children. But the Platform women wanted to be in politics. "I always put politics first, education, work. We're a women's group that struggles together with other women whose heads are uncovered to do politics."

Hidayet nudged her and clarified, "She's asking about how you represent yourself on a personal level."

WOMAN 1: "On a personal level, I'm someone who lives in Turkey; there's that thing about genes. But they say that nationalism is quite remote from all Middle Eastern peoples (*kavimler*, tribes, sects). I'm a Turk, of course, because I'm from Turkey. . . . I don't see being a Turk any other way."

[At this point in the Turkish transcript of the interview, I found an interjection in English by the woman I hired to transcribe the tapes, whom I knew to be a strong Kemalist: Jenny, you see this is the whole problem; they don't see themselves like Turk, they prefer to be Muslim, they can be Arab or Turk or Sudanese, it doesn't make any difference for them.]

WOMAN 1, CONTINUED: "A Turk living in Turkey. Religion, reason, universal (*evrensel*), an assemblage. I live in Turkey, so I'm a Turk. My mother's language is *Rumca* [Istanbul Greek]."

WOMAN 2: "I'm of the world. It's mixed. Being a Turk doesn't mean that much to me. I could live anywhere."

WOMAN 3: "It was my choice—at university I became religious. It was something I researched and found by myself, an identity that I chose and wanted. I didn't choose to be a Turk; it might not be my preference."

WOMAN 4: "I think differently from [Woman 3]. A feeling of belonging is important to me. Of course first of all we're all Muslim, but besides being Muslim, Turkish identity—not racialism, but in terms of a feeling of belonging—that makes me very happy. I've never been abroad, but our family ties are extremely strong; we have a lifestyle in which we are continually acting in solidarity, so relatives to the second, third, fourth degree are still strongly tied together." She gave an example of relatives' choosing to go on trips and holidays together. "For this reason, living in this country, being a Turk makes me happy."

WOMAN 5: "That could come from *hemşerilik* [fellow countryman, citizen] ties, from their being so strong and widespread. When you live in Turkey, you can't be alienated in any way. It's not so important to be a Turk because we live in Turkey, so we're all Turks."

WOMAN 6: "There are citizens who aren't Turks. We have neighbors who aren't Turks, well, those of another race like Kurds, Laz, Circassians, and so on. We have so many relationships with them that, how shall I say it, race, being Turkish, being Circassian makes no difference, because though there are small differences here and there and even separations, we all live under normal circumstances, in the same circumstances, in the same country, in the same social circle."

WOMAN 7: "In a situation like this, nationalism isn't so important for us, although it's found front and center on Turkey's agenda and some things are continually being aggravated. From the moment you start going to funerals [of martyred soldiers], nationalism, and so on—who knows what else—comes out into the open. These aren't normal relationships, but [there are those who] try to shape them according to the country's agenda, who have started to come to people's doors, to the funerals of their sons along with their coffins. So then people start saying 'No, I'm a Kurd,' 'No, I'm Circassian,' 'No, I'm Armenian.'"

WOMAN 8: "Normally I don't introduce myself to anyone or anywhere by saying 'I'm a Turk.' You don't need to, but when you go abroad . . . your nationality gains importance, so then you introduce yourself as "I'm from Turkey (*Türkiyeliyim*), I'm a Turk or something like that."

WOMAN 7: "[National] identity card information."

WOMAN 8: "But not in the sense of race."

[At this point several women began to speak at once, so the speakers could not be identified individually.]

WOMAN: "Unlike other [countries] this conception of nation, this idea of race, hasn't managed to get established."

WOMAN: "That probably has something to do with religion."

WOMAN: "It's in your genes."

WOMAN: "You, foreigners (*acemi,* Persians), Arabs—none has superiority [over the other]. Your belief [*ihlas,* sincerity of heart] is important. Your superiority is in your ihlas."

WOMAN: "It's the same thing with the example of men and women. Every sort of superiority is from the devil."

One woman pointed out that there were people in more conservative circles who thought differently about Turkishness than the Platform women. Another woman disagreed and pointed out that, as far as she could see, for all of them intellectual presence was more important than "being a Turk or coming from A nation or B nation." Several women chimed in and agreed that this was indeed what characterized their platform.

WOMAN: "Our husbands are like that too."

This comment led to some introspective debate. Several women agreed; others didn't.

HIDAYET: "They're more nationalist than we are."

WOMAN: "Our not being nationalist means [we're seen as] simple, naive, female."

WOMAN 3: "[The men are] clear-cut in that regard, more rational, see things in black and white. We see more gray."

Several women suggested that seeing things in black and white was more suited to the male character, as men were not emotional. Another added that perhaps doing their army service had something to do with it.

WOMAN 3 DISAGREED: "[He was like that] before he went to the army." When they sat at home and discussed these issues, she added, her three sons' opinions were significantly closer to their father's than to hers.

The women debated whether greater interest in and participation in politics, especially during the fraught postcoup years after 1980, had made men more sharp-edged in their views.

Hidayet suggested another reason: "We've worked with Kurds. We carried out joint projects with our leftist friends, with feminists. I mean, we've come together with a lot of people who don't think like us and with whom we don't have much opportunity to get together. But our husbands don't have this kind of opportunity." Hidayet made an exception for *Mazlumder* [the Islamic Human Rights Organization]. "Admittedly there are a lot of types in there that haven't changed, but there's a young generation of men that think like us." She named some of the younger men in

Mazlumder but then added that even among their own women's networks, there were differences, with some women more nationalist than others. They attended different conferences than did the Platform women and were weak in developing relations with other groups. "This lack of relations is the reason why [people think that] it's better to remain in the same place one is standing on." Television, she added, contributes to nationalist divisiveness. "Television these days broadcasts completely nationalist programs. While we watch TV with some knowledge and a critical stance, other viewers don't have this critical view, and this creates a collectivity in which normal Muslim people who used to belong to an umma [have become] a nationalist conservative sector that is characterized by a strange enmity against Kurds."

The women continued to debate the role of biological differences between men and women and whether women, with their capacity for relationships, broader and more inclusive views, and greater objectivity, would make better political leaders. Not everyone was convinced. Some suggested that only "women who thought like men" would be successful in politics. Hidayet disagreed strongly with that view, arguing that when it came to the decision-making mechanisms in politics, one shouldn't have to suddenly change one's sex.

WOMAN: "I don't think any of this will change under the present male dominance."

WOMAN: "In any case, women who think like men are already entering the decision-making mechanisms."

WOMAN: "Oh, they [women in the government] are just required to do that; I think it's a disadvantage."

WOMAN: "There aren't a lot anyway; women are generally very uninterested in politics."

WOMAN: "[Government minister] Nimet Çubukçu is just a pawn. . . . I mean, her areas of responsibility are 'women and family.'"

Some women disagreed about the minister's status as pawn, but the consensus appeared to be that since the political rules were made by men, women had to become like men to be players.[3]

The women were critical of the government's anti-Kurdish rhetoric and a statement made by Defense Minister Vecdi Gönul denying that any Armenian deportations or post–World War I forced population exchanges had occurred. Gönül, they said, had also blamed the entire Kurdish movement on Armenians and claimed that PKK fighters were uncircumcised [and thus Christian]. One Platform member said she met with two highly placed women in government to ask the government to apologize to the Armenian community. Another member, who had spoken with Gönül, was appalled when he told her that all the wealth in Izmir was in Rum [Greek-speaking Christian] hands. Despite their activism, the women felt generally disempowered and frustrated at their inability to have their voices heard. "Besides Mazlumder and one MP no one said anything about this. Because women have no collectivity, they aren't able to speak out in any way. Men, although they've unified, [are divided by] their own circles, the wealthy, and so on." The term for collectivity (*birikim*) has the additional meaning of accumulation, and one of the women spoke directly to this problem: "If you look, you see that women only own 1 percent of property and capital."[4]

In other words, women lack strength in accumulation of capital and social capital, and consequently have no voice in politics. One woman gave the example of a university where the directives of women in the administration were not followed. Men, too, are divided, but they occupy the mechanisms of power and make the rules. The women also differentiate between their own educated critical stance and the more gullible populace, which is easily led by television propaganda. As one woman put it, "*Vatan* (fatherland) is a village concept." Their own notion of national unity was based on solidarity groups like kinship, family, and soil-based *hemşeri* networks among those from the same village, town, city, province, even region. Turkishness itself is, in this sense, a form of soil-based solidarity: We are Turkish because we live in Turkey.

The Platform women saw no direct link between religion and nationalism, pointing to differences within the pious community in the extent of people's nationalist feeling. The women did identify a pronounced difference between men and women in nationalist thinking, particularly in regard to antiminority stances, and debated the source of this difference in biology, in the different life experiences of men and women, or in the constraints of patriarchal social and political institutions. They saw nationalism, like women, used as a pawn in a political game. The Platform women, like Havva and the women in the village, were concerned with issues of social justice for women and for minorities that at times brought them into contact with people of different beliefs and lifestyles, and into conflict with nationalist and state-supported ethnic and gender-based hierarchies.

Not all women, pious or secular, have opportunities for mixing with those of different views, lifestyles, and "races," nor does such contact necessarily lead to more tolerance. This is particularly the case when the populations are competing over jobs, housing, status, and power in the community. The Arnavutköy resident mentioned in chapter 5 was tolerant toward and nostalgic about his now-gone Christian Rum neighbors but railed against the culturally unfamiliar Kurds who had taken their place and who, he claimed, were destabilizing the neighborhood. By contrast, the Nakşibendi women discussed previously would have had little opportunity to come into contact with Kurds in the village or in their relatively circumscribed lives in an ultraconservative community in Istanbul. Their husbands, however, might well find themselves in economic competition with other urban groups. Nevertheless, given the high rate of intolerance shown by both men and women in recent polls, I found pious women's openness toward difference and their rejection of nationalist definitions of unity striking. This openness was understood as a natural attribute of women, while men's understanding of the world was characterized by clear-cut boundaries and sharp divisions. The women interpreted Islamic beliefs about equality to apply to minorities and women equally, but admitted that men were inclined to a different view. They saw nationalist discourse as promoting artificial divisions and hierarchies in society that they felt did not define them, so they opted out of national subjectivity in favor of other forms of solidarity.

Nevertheless, despite pious women's rejection of nationalism as an alien state-promoted set of ideas that does not define them, their society, or their generation, women and sex remain central elements of nationalist discourse, linked to cultural notions of honor that in everyday practice shape these same women's lives.

THE BORDER IS HONOR

In October 2008 a PKK attack over the Iraqi border on a Turkish army outpost in Aktütün in the eastern province of Hakkari left fifteen Turkish soldiers dead and more than twenty wounded. There was public outrage over what was perceived to be the army's incompetence in failing to act on intelligence indicating an attack was imminent and over the flimsy protections afforded their soldiers on the border. This anger was significant as a sign of the public's increasing willingness to challenge the military and resulted in significant media coverage, but what caught my attention was a photo from a Facebook site set up by soldiers after the attack, showing scenes of the Aktütün base. In one image, a soldier had laid out stones on a hillside beneath a sandbagged bunker to spell out *Hudut Namustur* (the border is honor), a sickle moon and star to designate the Turkish flag, and the soldier's first name.

There are different words for honor in Turkish, each with its own repertoire of meanings: *namus, onur, şeref, iffet, ırz. Onur* refers to a man's dignity and self-respect. *Şeref* is pride based on distinction and glory; rakı drinkers toast each other's şeref. But a person's *namus* is a critical evaluation of one's good name by society and one's peers. While both men and women are perceived to have namus, the designation is closely associated with pride, especially masculine pride. A *namuslu* person obeys society's moral norms, doesn't steal or lie, and obeys society's sexual rules. Women are alone in being judged by their *iffet*, a characteristic of their person (unlike namus, which relies on the social evaluation of others) that refers explicitly to their sexual honor (chastity and innocence). Even rumors about loss of a family member's iffet destroys a man's (and by extension, his family's) namus. A man whose namus has been destroyed through public disapproval has lost the right to hold his head up in society, and in traditional communities a man without namus may lose his social identity and even be shunned, along with his entire family. No one will do business with him; no one will marry his children.

To "clean" one's namus might require an extreme act, such as an "honor" killing, in which a family designates one member, often an underage teenage boy—who will receive a less severe jail sentence—to kill the female relative whose iffet has been stained, thus restoring the family's honor within the community.[5] The related term *ırz* (chastity) is used specifically to refer to dishonor though intercourse. To "spoil" (*bozmak*) someone's ırz means to deflower a virgin. To rape, *ırzına geçmek*, means literally to move into and thereby despoil purity. It is interesting to note that both uses of the term mean to dishonor the woman, regardless of whether the sexual act is part of marriage or outside of social norms, implying that being penetrated in and of itself undermines honor, regardless of the social legitimacy of the act. A bride after the wedding night carries with her the shame of having been penetrated, an act that defines her as vulnerable, needing protection, and as quintessentially female. Similarly, a male's honor is defiled by being penetrated but is never affected by the act of penetration. This incongruity is nowhere more clearly delineated than by the classic regional definition of homosexual as a man who is penetrated by another man, making him "like a woman." The derogatory term *ibne* refers only to the passive partner in a sexual encounter between men.[6] When I asked some of my (male) informants about this, they shrugged and said that the active partner was simply being a man. To be a man means to penetrate, it doesn't matter what.

The journalist Ayşe Önal, who has written a book about "honor" killings, talked about the use of these terms in popular discourse. Önal has hosted a number of political talk shows on television, including a cooking show on which she interviewed guests while they ate the food she cooked. "On a food program," she told me, "you can talk about *Arnavutciğeri* [Albanian liver, an appetizer], but you can't say '*Rum* food*'* because it will corrupt honor [*namus bozar*]." She once heard someone say in this context, "Don't dishonor the kitchen." [*Mutfağın ırzına geçme*; literally, don't rape the kitchen.] The term for sexual purity is used for forbidding the mixing of not only food nationalities but also national identities. Önal, who has lived on and off in Europe, complained that "The Iranians in England assimilate, but for Turks to adjust to Germany means being raped (*ırzına geçmek*). Erdoğan said, 'All of the immorality [*ahlaksızlık*], we've taken from the West.' He wasn't referring to robbing a house, murdering your mother, or stealing taxes, but to women's immorality." Önal also sees a clear link between sexual purity and national honor. If a man's namus has been tainted, it means the woman at home has been "sold," she explained. "In films, you see a woman yelling to her son, 'You're selling my purity/honor; you're selling military service to the enemy.'" (*Sen benim ırzımı satıyorsun, düşmana askerliği satıyorsun.*) The soldier's mother is accusing him of dishonor for selling out his country along with her sexual purity. Put another way, at least in popular discourse, serving a foreign enemy army is equivalent to allowing your mother to be violated.

In May 2009 CHP Izmir MP Canan Arıtman, like many of her colleagues in the Grand National Assembly, reacted heatedly to a draft law that would have permitted private foreign companies to compete for the job of clearing the Turkish-Syrian border of mines planted there in the 1950s. The law provided a lucrative incentive: In lieu of de-mining costs, the Turkish government would lease the de-mined land for forty-four years to the company that won the bid. Arıtman pointed out that soldiers doing their civic duty at the border are taught by military officials that "the border is honor" (*sınır namustur*). "If we turn over our border lands to foreigners as part of a Build-Operate model, how can we ask our Little Mehmets [soldiers] to guard the border with their lives? If the border is honor, can one trade in [and profit by] honor?"[7] "Selling" one's honor is the ultimate betrayal, opening the inviolable boundaries of communal and national identity to enemy penetration. "Selling" or "selling out" a female member's sexual purity or one's military loyalty, much like converting to Christianity or covering one's head in return for money, can be understood as the ultimate selfish act that alienates a subject from his or her community.

What does it mean, then, for a soldier to associate the nation and its boundary with namus? National purity, I suggest in this chapter, is associated with sexual purity in that both represent the possibility of illegitimate penetration of essential boundaries, whether by a PKK incursion, by the Trojan horse of "the enemy within," or by "hidden Jews" like the Dönme, a term that also has a slang meaning of transsexual, someone with an ambiguous identity, a sexual trickster.

Violating its boundaries shatters the honor of the nation, as it does the honor of the family on which the nation is modeled, and requires a purifying response. It is no surprise, then, that the term *honor* (namus) is ubiquitous in political discussions and nationalist discourse. Where the boundary is vulnerable, the difference between insider and outsider can be hair thin, resulting in renewed—even frenzied—attention to boundary maintenance. This is nowhere more clear than in the discursive association between the penetrability of national boundaries, female sexual vulnerability, and male sexual agency.

A topic brought up continually to this day by politicians and military personnel as well as by ordinary people is something called the "hooding incident," which occurred almost a decade ago but has severely damaged Turkish attitudes toward the United States. On July 4, 2003, dozens of U.S. soldiers raided an office used by the Turkish Special Forces in the northern Iraqi city of Sulaimaniya and took eleven Turkish soldiers into custody over allegations that they were planning to assassinate the governor of Kirkuk. The Americans covered the Turkish soldiers' heads with hoods and led them out of their headquarters at gunpoint. They were taken south, interrogated, and released after forty-eight hours. In an analysis of U.S.–Turkey relations reported in the press in 2009, Turkish Retired Major Erdal Sipahi revealed that the "hooding incident" almost led Turkey to go to war with U.S. forces in Iraq.[8] As Çarkoğlu and Kalaycıoğlu put it, "the 'hood incident' was a major milestone in the development of anti-Americanism in Turkey because people from all walks of life and covering the entire gamut of political ideologies, except perhaps for Kurdish nationalists, became united in condemning the U.S. military for what they considered to be humiliating treatment of the Turkish soldiers." It was "an affront to the pride of the Turkish army and nation."[9] Five years after it happened, a hip young Istanbul shopkeeper who wished to explain to me the difference between Turkish and U.S. culture found the best example to be that the United States had hooded Turkish officers. "*We* don't do that," he exclaimed. "It shamed us to the world." In the first episode of the immensely popular nationalist film series *Valley of the Wolves: Iraq*, a Turkish commando team goes to Iraq to track down the U.S. military commander responsible for the hooding and get revenge, thus purifying Turkey's honor and presiding over a national catharsis among viewers.

It is significant that in popular discourse, it is the hooding—the humiliation of Turkish soldiers—that is always mentioned as the unacceptable act, not the arrests, which were short-lived and for which the United States apologized. What is it about hooding that makes this incident so powerful and so long-lived? Clearly, the manner of the arrest is perceived as dishonoring Turkish soldiers. That is, the soldiers were blinded in a humiliating manner and made vulnerable, rather than being arrested like men. Önal explained that "old women after forty don't have sex and in secular families cover their heads to show this, that they've become mothers. . . . When the soldiers were hooded, the sack meant 'fuck your mother.' It broke the border of self, made the soldier a woman."

The betrayal of a Turkish soldier's manhood is a betrayal of the Turkish nation. For this, America has never been forgiven. Vulnerability is unacceptable in a soldier not only because he is a man, but because he *is* the nation; vulnerability undermines both manhood and national honor. In 2008, eight soldiers disappeared during a battle on the Iraqi border, captured by PKK forces. Days later they were released, but returned to Turkey to accusations of betrayal in the media: Why were you not killed? A Turkish soldier doesn't allow himself to be captured. You should have fought to the death. The soldiers were accused of allowing themselves to be taken; perhaps they were in league with the PKK since they accepted their hospitality. Eventually some were convicted of a variety of crimes, including dereliction of duty, incitement to disobedience of orders, and supporting propaganda of a splittist terror group, with punishments between one and two years in jail. The court decision read in part, "It's impossible for a soldier to leave his weapon and give himself up."[10]

Sometimes, implicit associations slip into explicit discourse. In 2008 the journalist Fatih Altaylı, known for his crude references to women, wrote an Internet column criticizing a television discussion program that featured Gülay Göktürk, a female journalist from the *Bugün* daily. In his article, which was roundly condemned by women's rights activists, Altaylı addressed Göktürk: "Lady, maybe you are not aware of the fact that the Turkish army is also protecting what is between a woman's legs. The Turkish army protects the borders of Turkey, and this border lies between a woman's legs."[11]

In the dual discourse of honor and nation, the nation, like a family or tribe, depends for its honor on the chastity (iffet) of its women. Women's sexual vulnerability endangers the integrity of the family and, in the shadow discourse of the nation, the integrity of the national lineage, or soy. Soldiers can be made "like" women and dirty the honor of the nation. Women's boundaries, like those of the nation, must be protected, and their behavior, like those of a nation's subjects, must be demonstrably pure.[12] Women and national subjects maintain this purity under the *himaye*, the protection and control, of the male/state.

This underlying mirroring of family and state explains the state's interest in clinically verifying the virginity of girls and women through officially mandated virginity tests. Until 2002 the Penal Code authorized prosecutors to demand examinations to determine if the hymen was intact or ruptured in cases of rape, prostitution, and accusations of extramarital relations in order to decide whether intercourse had taken place. In addition, the Law on Duties and Powers of the Police gave the police extensive authority for overseeing public morality, which led to arbitrary virginity examinations ordered by school officials in cases of truancy, by administrators of state-run orphanages, by vocational high schools and prisons, and by the police for women whose actions were considered "socially inappropriate," an ill-defined standard that has included sitting in a park with male company and walking or driving alone at night. Virginity testing was banned in 2002 following the attempted suicide of five schoolgirls who were being threatened with forcible examination. The practice continues, however, with women "voluntarily" undergoing the examinations. In a 2003 study of Turkish nurses and midwives, more than 80 percent said they had been present during a virginity exam, and just over half believed that virginity was important, and disapproved of premarital sexual relations.[13] In fall 2010, young couples holding hands or sitting together on benches in a public park in the elite Çankaya district of Ankara, not far from the presidential palace, were singled out by police for immoral behavior and asked for their identification cards. Although no orders for virginity tests were reported in the press, young people, surely aware of the risk, left the park quickly upon seeing the police van. In April 2011, school officials pulled a thirteen-year-old girl out of class and subjected her to a pregnancy test in the bathroom because it had been rumored that she "went around with men." The girl, publicly humiliated and accused of prostitution, reportedly attempted suicide.[14]

The anthropologist Ayşe Parla interprets "the state's routinized intrusion into women's bodies" to be "a fundamental facet of its sovereign claim over social relations in the name of the nation." Following Foucault, she sees virginity examinations as the state's attempt to create docile citizen bodies through a form of surveillance and documentation that makes it possible for the state to classify and punish individuals. In other words, Parla argues, state control of women's bodies is not a traditional lapse in Turkey's modernity but, rather, constitutes a specifically modern, objectifying form of power that, in the Turkish case, reflects a cultural preoccupation with women's sexual purity and Ataturk's nationalist vision of the virtuous asexual woman citizen. Far from dying out with modernization, traditional codes of honor and shame were given new life by the nationalists who attributed to them new meanings and significance.[15]

Figure 6.1. Postcard showing a man and his mother, typical of photomontage souvenirs created for men going off to military service. The men wear rented uniforms and provide pictures of their mothers or wives to include in the photograph. The photographer might add other elements, such as an image of military jets streaking across the background. The men give the postcards as souvenirs to their families before they leave. (My gratitude to Chantal Zakari and Mike Mandel for use of this image from their collection.)

Mothers of the Nation

Roles made available to women under Kemalist nationalism were

1. the virtuous asexual woman, modern and self-controlled, a product of education, so chaste that her sexuality became irrelevant;
2. mothers of martyrs; and
3. as depicted in nationalist novels, the entirely Westernized woman who was immoral and loose.

The nation as imagined by Ataturk and his circle, under the tutelage of the sociologist Ziya Gökalp, encouraged educated, professional women to participate in the common work of the nation but downplayed sexuality, romance, and any expression of individualism that might compete with loyalty to the nation and threaten the biological and ideological reproduction of the nation. This policy created the *makbul* (acceptable) woman that Havva described previously, the prototype for the makbul citizen. Marriage and childbearing were presented as national duties, regardless of a woman's education or profession. "As far as the founding fathers were concerned, the woman question was resolved once women were formally proclaimed citizens."[16]

This degendered notion of citizenship masked discrimination beneath an illusion of unity. Early female members of the Grand National Assembly wore boxy clothing and long skirts that hid their femininity. It was only in July 2011 that parliament seriously debated altering regulations that required female deputies to wear skirts and allow them for the first time to don trousers.[17] The desexualized, virtuous woman provided a nonthreatening public image in a society that for the most part still believed that women should remain in the home. When urban elite women raised their voices in public, they spoke as modern, patriotic citizens in the guise of asexual female civil servants or "mothers and martyr-heroines." The Republican woman with her severe suit and bare face was mirrored by the *bacı*, symbolic sister or sexually unavailable female comrade, of the Turkish Left in the 1960s and 1970s.[18] By contrast, the veil powerfully confirms a woman's femaleness by forbidding access.

For the Kemalists, as for pious conservatives, the highest duty of woman was motherhood. But Kemalists in the early Republic rearticulated motherhood within nationalist discourse to make it consistent with the degendered notion of citizenship. The traditional ideal of "mother of sons" who would support their family became the nationalist ideal of "mother of martyrs," bearer of sons whose blood nourished the nation-state. Mothers supported national integrity by bearing and nurturing sons who became soldiers and, in turn, nourished the nation with their blood. As every schoolchild learns, their highest calling is to shed blood for their nation. The blood of martyrs *becomes* the flag (see chapter 1) and gives Turks the right to be masters of the nation. "We are all soldiers" can be amended to include "All soldiers have mothers."

School textbooks focus almost entirely on Ataturk's mother, Zübeyde; his father and sister are rarely mentioned. His wife, Lâtife, to whom he was married between 1923 and 1925, is never mentioned; many Turks have no idea Ataturk was ever married. When I looked for her house in Istanbul's Beyoğlu district, I found that it had been razed. Textbooks demonstrate Ataturk's family life using a single motif— Ataturk as a school child or adult statesman, kissing his mother's hand. Most often she is depicted as a smiling elderly woman wearing metal-rimmed glasses and a large headscarf."[19]

A mother's substance—of which breast milk is a powerful cultural marker—is transubstantiated into a martyr's blood that nourishes the national body. Kaplan, in his ethnography of a village in southern Turkey, describes the townspeople's belief that semen flows through a man's veins, having originated in his mother's breast milk, which is believed to derive from menstrual blood not shed during pregnancy.[20] Most women claimed to nurse sons longer than daughters, arguing that "because mother's milk is sinless, pure, and clean, it contributed to their son's virility and, hence, military heroism." Even seventh-grade pupils were able to tell Kaplan that mother's milk gave strength to Turkish soldiers. As the village youth going off to do military service boarded the bus taking them to the induction center, "townswomen shouted out to their departing sons, 'My lion, my child, may the milk and goodness I have given you bring you good luck.'"[21]

The moral obligation between mother and child is expressed in a common verbal idiom as an unrepayable "milk debt" (*süt hakkı*), a lifelong debt of service and support in return for the nurturance, labor, and sacrifice a mother has expended in raising a child. This debt is particularly expected to bind sons to their mothers, as daughters generally move to their husband's household after marriage; most women must depend on their sons and their in-marrying brides for support in old age. This dependence sets up a structural conflict between sons' mothers and their wives, who often find themselves on the losing end of a battle over loyalty and love,[22] a pattern that is repeated in their relation to the masculine nation. A mother can curse a son or daughter for disobedience in a serious matter by saying she will never forgive the milk debt: "*hakkımı helal etmem*," a curse that is never used lightly. The moral obligation between mother and son, imagined as a bond based on milk, is repeated in the moral obligation of citizen-child to the state—their bond is based on blood and expressed as *vatan borcu*, military service as a "debt to the nation."

Being the mother of an adult male is a powerful category in part because it is constructed as asexual and thus neither threatening nor threatened, unlike the vulnerable position of young wife and daughter. The threat to "fuck your mother" is thus the most dire not only because it soils a mother's sexual honor (and thus the man's *namus*) but because it denies the asexual status that gives motherhood such emblematic force. In contrast, pregnancy is a condition of heightened vulnerability and an outward sign of sexual activity (the dishonor of sexual penetration) that may occasion embarrassment if mentioned in mixed company. Thus, while soldiers must worry about the iffet of their sexually active wives, they are free to worship their mothers, who have nurtured them with their essential substance, just as they will nurture the nation with their blood.

An American businessman who lives in Turkey told me about a puzzling scene he had witnessed on a vacation to the Mediterranean coast. He was visiting a ruined castle at the top of a hill. As he climbed the steep, grassy incline, he observed a dozen Turkish soldiers making many trips up and down the hill, each time climbing back up clutching handfuls of pink flowers. When he got to the courtyard of the castle, he saw that the soldiers had arranged masses of flowers on the ground in the shape of a large heart, at the center of which flowers spelled out the word *anne* (mother). The soldiers had laid their rifles to the side and were posing one at a time inside the heart while another soldier took their photograph. The American, who was gay, was amused at what he saw as the sentimental feminine behavior of the soldiers. I was struck by the fact that they were not posing romantically for their sweethearts or wives, but for their mothers, whose adoration was encouraged as an admirable, masculine, nationalist trait.

The linkages among a mother's body as a nurturing physical medium, her ability and willingness to bear and raise martyrs, a woman's rights as a citizen, and her identity as a national subject were crassly illustrated in a criminal case filed against the popular transsexual singer and actress Bülent Ersoy. In 2008 she was taken to court for criticizing the Turkish army's cross-border operations into Northern Iraq against the PKK in which dozens of soldiers and hundreds of PKK fighters reportedly lost their lives. Ersoy, while acting as a judge on a national pop star competition "Popstar Alaturka," said on live television:

I cannot know exactly what it means to have a child. I am not a mother and will never be able to be one. But I am a human being; and as a human being, to bury them . . . I may not know how these mother's hearts are breaking, but mothers understand. . . . This is not a war under normal conditions. It is written down and people are forced to play along.

Another judge, the singer Ebru Gündeş, answered, "Let Allah grant everyone the happiness of being a soldier's mother. May I have a glorious son and send him to the military," to which Ersoy replied, "and then you get his dead body back."

Gündeş responded with a well-worn nationalist slogan, "Martyrs don't die, the country can't be [divided]."

> ERSOY: "Always the same clichéd words. . . . Children go, bloody tears, funerals. . . . I don't share your opinion. Why do we take part in the game? All right, the country can't be separated, but . . . should all mothers just give birth and bury their children, is that it?"

Ersoy was charged with turning the public against military service, which is a crime. The prosecutor, citing the slogan "All Turks are born as soldiers," demanded three years' imprisonment. Ersoy was acquitted, but the prosecutor filed an appeal. His rationale was that Ersoy's medical inability to bear children was an insult to Turkish mothers. "It would be naïve to evaluate as goodwill and freedom of expression," he reportedly said, "the words uttered by a person who is medically unable to bear children and who is thus arguably provoking Turkish mothers." *Bianet*, a liberal news website that reported on the case, used this header, "If you cannot give birth, you had better shut up!"[23]

Altınay points out that national security textbooks used for both male and female students in Turkish schools contain no mention of women. Instead, the textbooks teach that proper citizenship means martyrdom and dying for the homeland, while civilian activities are devalued. Civilian life is presented as properly based on military values of obedience, acceptance of violence as an appropriate means of resolving conflicts, and obedience to the state. Turkey does not recognize conscientious objector status, so men who refuse military service are forced to join their units or are incarcerated. Without a document proving military service, a man is unable to get work in the legal job market, may not undertake common legal transactions like buying and selling property, apply for a driver's license or passport, or open a bank account. He would have a very hard time getting married under such circumstances. In other words, if he is not a soldier, he is not a man. If students are "soldiers," and citizenship means martyrdom, what roles can be played by women? The association of men and masculinity with military service in effect marginalizes women as citizens because they do not do military service.[24] And a woman who cannot and will not give birth to martyrs, like a man who refuses to be a soldier, has no honorable place in the nation.

Cultural associations of women's physicality with nurturance, and men with lineage identity, also contribute to women's marginalization as national subjects. A Turkish friend pointed out to me that the stories of a rediscovered Armenian heritage related in chapter 5 tended to be told by women. Men would be less likely to "come out" with a Christian identity, because their offspring would be haunted by a mixed-blood identity in a way that Christian women's offspring are not. Women's identity has always been more malleable. It was permitted for a Muslim to marry a Christian woman as long as their children were raised as Muslims, while it would have been (and often still is) unacceptable for a Muslim woman to marry a Christian man. The man literally and figuratively plants the seed of identity in the soil of the woman's body. The metaphor of seed and soil is common enough to be encountered in folk sayings, religious sermons, and in daily conversation.[25] A man's blood is the source of his children's identity, while the mother supplies a nurturing medium. This cultural attribute of women makes them "weak" carriers of national identity incapable of instantiating—only of nurturing—Turkish national identity.

The secular Kemalist military use of the religious term *martyr* to refer to its dead soldiers marks the men's sacrifice to a sacred ideal, the unity and integrity of the state. The red Turkish flag represents the state and the blood of martyrs that flowed to keep it safe. Martyr's blood is a sanctified substance, the most desirable transubstantiation of mother's milk, and blood from the fingers of schoolchildren, all willing to nurture death. The sociologist Ferhat Kentel, discussing the link between masculinity, martyrdom, and religion, said, "When [soldiers] die, that is become martyred, covered mothers and women who wouldn't be allowed to appear at their [son's or husband's military] oath ceremonies, go to the funeral and use Islamic language, calling the fallen soldier a martyr."[26] Martyrs' funerals are a perfect storm of nationalism. They are emotion-laden and often televised public rituals that exhibit the unity of Turkish blood, Muslim identity, and the highest masculine ideal, which is to give one's life for the nation. The martyrs' women, their sexuality veiled by headscarves, represent the vulnerable nation weeping over the coffin, often along with a national audience. Kentel points out the irony that the presence of covered women, though permitted at a soldier's private funeral, would be illegal at any formal military event.

In her review of gender and sexuality in the making of nations, Joanne Nagel observes that the national state is essentially a masculine institution characterized by a nationalist culture that articulates with the "microculture" of masculinity in everyday life. Nationalists the world over have tended to liken the nation to a family in which men and women have "natural" roles to play.[27] Women occupy an important symbolic place as "Mothers of the Nation" who are assigned the role of biologically and culturally reproducing the nation but are often thereby distanced from political participation as citizens. Berkovitch, for instance, describes laws passed in the first years of the State of Israel that continue to define women's relation to the state as mother and wife, and not as individual or citizen. Motherhood is a significant "national mission" through which women are incorporated into the Israeli state.[28] In contrast, masculinity is identified with the masculinity of the Jewish combat soldier and perceived to represent good citizenship. Women in the Israeli army simply structure their gender roles and national identity according to the masculine model during their service without challenging the differentiated structure of citizenship that otherwise defines them.[29]

Individual women, particularly from elite families, have used the role of mother of the nation to claim entry into the public arena. "Indira Ghandi, Winnie Mandela, and Safiyya Zaghlul (1876–1946) became known respectively, as the mothers of India, South Africa, and Egypt, which gave them great political clout."[30] But for the rest, cross-cultural comparisons point to an inverse relationship between the prominence of women in allegories of the nation and their access to state politics. Historically, women's activism in nationalist movements tends to be suppressed or forgotten, while female symbols endure. Beth Baron begins her book *Egypt as a Woman* with a depiction of a big public ceremony arranged by the Egyptian government in 1928 for the unveiling of a statue, *Nahdat Misr* (the Awakening of Egypt), that depicts the newly independent modern nation as a woman. With only a few exceptions, women—who had played an active role in the independence movement—were explicitly barred from the ceremony.[31]

In addition to their idealized role as mothers of the nation, women also represent national vulnerability. They embody both family and national honor, so their purity must be impeccable. "Women's shame is the family's shame, the nation's shame, the man's shame."[32] The microculture of militarized masculinity, in turn, is highly sexualized with discourse and imagery of rape, penetration, and sexual conquest, with women portrayed as victims, whores, or legitimate targets of rape. European fantasies of conquest were figured as sexual conquests, and the imperial project had deeply erotic overtones. France's "subjugation of Algeria was often depicted by metaphors of disrobing, unveiling, and penetration."[33]

Baron describes women nationalist writers in 1920s Egypt using the rhetoric of national honor in such a way as to desexualize it and disassociate it from female purity. But they were up against powerful ideals of nationalist masculinity that were explicitly based in codes of honor and honed on the battlefield of revolution and war. At the critical moment when the nationalists seized power, Baron writes, real women (as opposed to their symbolic representations) were cut out of power.[34] Nagel muses, "According to a Southern African Tswana proverb, 'a woman has no tribe.' . . . I wonder whether it might not also be true that a woman has no nation, or that for many women the nation does not 'feel' the same as it does to many men."[35]

CHAPTER 7

Choice and Community

THE GIRL WITH BLUE HAIR

HAVVA IS A FRESH-FACED YOUNG WOMAN of twenty-two with a shy but self-confident manner. She works as an intern at a women's rights association. When she was sixteen, Havva read four books that changed her life: *Mavi Saçlı Kız* (*The Girl with Blue Hair*) by Burçak Çerezcioğlu, *Sophie's World* by the Norwegian writer Jostein Gaarder, and *The Alchemist* and *Veronika Decides to Die* by the Brazilian writer Paulo Coelho, translated into Turkish. These books caused her to start reading the Quran. "It slowly moved to a place in my head," she explained about the Quran. She also began to wear a headscarf.

> Veronika looks out the window and wonders about modern life. . . . I was lightly depressed. For instance, every day I'd watch TV, which I found meaningless—the meaning given to brand names, the injustices. When the U.S. attacked Afghanistan I found that very saddening. I started reading the Quran about it, for instance, the life of the Prophet. I tried to understand why pain occurs. No one can say no [to it]. . . . My father particularly wanted me to go to university. It was my dream. I loved studying. I wanted to live a regular future, to find work, to move upwards. I wanted to study psychology then, although now I'm more interested in sociology and politics. I wanted to go abroad to study. I thought about studying philosophy in France.

In her spare time, Havva volunteered in a youth club. She marked the moment she became politically active as when she joined a petition drive to get the AKP to listen to covered women's other problems, besides the headscarf issue. What problems? I asked her. "Article 301 of the Penal Code that makes it illegal to insult Turkishness; [issues with] Kurds, minorities, the Alevi." She said she realized that "the source of our problems is a culture of forbidding."

Then she read *The Girl with Blue Hair*, the diary of a sixteen-year-old girl who died of cancer. "It's a real story," Havva explained. "She was very happy. She lived a modern, luxurious life, but something was missing. She spent summers with friends on vacation. They went to discos. [A life like that] looks great on the surface, but it has no meaning." *Sophie's World,* too, is about a search for meaning. In the book, a fifteen-year-old girl, Sophie, receives a letter from a mysterious philosopher who, in their correspondence, undertakes to educate her in philosophy. The book alternates discussions of pre-Socratics, Plato, and St. Augustine with Sophie's relations with her parents and a mystery involving another young girl, Hilde, that Sophie must solve using her new knowledge. *The Alchemist* is a fable about an Andalusian shepherd boy who travels to Egypt to find a treasure about which he has had a dream. Along the way, he meets spiritual mentors, including an alchemist. "My heart is afraid that it will have to suffer," the boy confides to the alchemist one night. "Tell your heart that the fear of suffering is worse than the suffering itself," the alchemist replies. "And that no heart has ever suffered when it goes in search of its dreams, because every second of the search is a second's encounter with God and with eternity."

In *Veronika Decides to Die*, the title character is young and attractive, with boyfriends, a job, and a loving family. But one day she tries to kill herself with an overdose of sleeping pills. She wakes up in a mental hospital under the care of a psychiatrist. When Veronika is told that she has only a few days to live, she begins to question her ideas about the meaning of life. All these books are about a young person's coming to the end of what had been tethering them to a perhaps comfortable, but ultimately meaningless, life. All find their path through surrender of the past, of previous pleasures and goals; an acknowledgment of their frailty; and a recommitment to life on new terms, often with the guidance of a (male) spiritual guide, freely chosen.

At sixteen, inspired to try to find meaning in life, Havva covered her head. "I wasn't religious. I had a traditional understanding of religion, but I didn't say prayers. I fasted only during Ramazan, and didn't read the Quran. I thought, read, wrote, but in a more interpersonal way. Religion was part of my everyday life." She had to leave high school when she put on the scarf but managed to finish school by taking an exam. What does Islam bring her? "Meaningless things are pushed away. [It gives me] another world. To reach that world, there's this world. Even if things are bad, I feel calm within." Her thirst for justice led her to politics, even before she found Islam. Both her piety and her politics are *şuurlu*, consciously chosen, based on thought, reflection, and learning. As such, they are distinct elements of Havva's subjectivity and do not necessarily operate in tandem. Havva's political choices are not derived from her faith but are based on a distinctly modern, literature-inspired philosophical stance that motivates both her piety and her politics. Havva voted for the first time in 2007 when she was eighteen. She gave her vote to AKP not because it was Islamic but because it represented justice. "It was the first time a party had stood up against the army. No other government has done this. With the other coups, they've always tipped their hats and moved on. I thought about voting for independents, but giving the vote to AKP was more of a direct answer."

Not all young women's choices to cover or uncover are based on reading or philosophy. I visited a pious working-class family I know quite well in Ümraniye on a day that three sisters and their children were together in the apartment. All the women covered their heads, even at home. One of the children, a young girl of eighteen named Rabia, sat on the floor leaning against the sofa, her face framed by raven-black hair in a blunt cut. When someone asked what she had done to her hair, she announced nonchalantly that she had dyed it. One of her aunts leaned over and confided in me that a month earlier, Rabia had decided to uncover her head. Rabia's mother stood in the middle of the room, pointed at her daughter and screeched, "Look at her. I told her she was ugly like that, but she doesn't listen to me. Tell her." She appealed to the room for support. A couple of the women told Rabia mildly, "You'd look nicer covered." One asked what her father had to say about it. The mother shrugged disparagingly, and I had the impression that her husband didn't pay much attention to his family. She turned to me and asked me what I thought. I pointed to my uncovered hair and said, "Look at me. What do you think I think? I think you should leave her alone. She's an adult and should be able to make up her own mind." My reply was taken like anyone else's comment, causing no commotion.

Rabia herself looked unperturbed. She leaned back with a slight smile, following the conversation and simultaneously texting on her cell phone. Her younger sister squatted on the carpet beside her, also texting. She, too, was uncovered but, being younger, did not face the same extent of her mother's wrath. The issue flared up several times during the evening, but Rabia seemed unconcerned. She told me she wanted to be an accountant and was studying for the university exams. She'd also like to be a grade school teacher, but she also admires theater and acting. Although she didn't explicitly say so, for all these plans, the headscarf stands in her way. When I asked her why she had uncovered, she responded, "I've never liked covering," but it was clear that there was no special reason, just "I wanted to."

The balance between individual choice and community loyalty is being tested and renegotiated. Conscious Islam answers not to the authority of a sheikh or imam but to the authority of the conscience and desire, which are both increasingly being shaped by the media and the market that teach young people what it can mean to be Muslim and Turkish in a manner that entertains choice. Yet, Havva's ability to choose did not loose her from the need or desire for community. Indeed, it was the emotional desert and moral emptiness of consumer society and the media that led her to seek meaning by choosing to live a life of piety and political activism. These are not the lonely pursuits of individuals. Havva's chosen path led her to solidarity groups of like-minded people outside of her family, such as political interest groups and civic organizations. Similarly, Rabia has decided to try to gain a foothold on the path to professional development even at the risk of alienation from her extended family, whose women all cover. She may find tolerance among her aunts, or she may develop an alternative solidarity group (whom was she texting?), or in a few years she might succumb to pressure from her husband's family to stop working after what is likely to be an arranged marriage. Unlike her mother's generation, though, whose desires for education and professions were inevitably choked off when they married, young women of Rabia's age have more opportunities for development within their cultural milieu, in part financed by pious businesses and foundations that set up training and hiring programs and segregated dormitories for women from pious or conservative backgrounds. Rabia faces more hurdles than Havva because of their social class and educational differences. Each will encounter levels of friction and resistance in her respective environment as a result of her choices.

One reason for the decline of Kemalism as a form of identity and affiliation for young people like Havva may be its inability to create sustained community. Çarkoğlu and Kalaycıoğlu observed that "the relatively modernized minority in Turkey seems to have severed their ties with the rural society and culture, yet they have not been able to create a new social context rich in social capital that in turn would allow them to construct a countervailing political force to those of the primordial patronage groups." Instead, Kemalists seem to be leading a highly individualistic lifestyle, with little in the way of social capital, that is, durable networks based on generalized trust and mutually supportive relations. "So far, all that such individualism has been able to do is take part in mass rallies organized by political parties, trade unions, and a few non-primordial interest associations." These rallies take the form of protests, an uproar against some sensitive issue that produces intense, yet short-lived, public reactions. The authors cite the Republican Meetings as examples, pointing out that such collective action draws attention to the issues but does not produce long-term forms of sustained commitment. Primordial patronage groups, they suggest, just have to wait out these "one-time, one-shot protest rallies," then go on with their business of clientelism within firmly emplaced associational networks.[1] The Kemalist nation does create powerful masculine bonds through the trope of the soldier and imbues men with a national ideal that they can embody but provides few obvious roles for women like Havva and Rabia in national solidarity groups.

Havva's affiliations of choice were not religious networks, or hemşeri relations based on common soil, or shared ethnic, racial, and national blood. Hers was a modern choice of affiliation based on rational thought and moral judgment, but one that did not result in a secularist lifestyle or Kemalist nationalism—to the contrary. It is necessary, perhaps, to add an individual/moral dimension of communality to Çarkoğlu and Kalaycıoğlu's "primordial patronage groups," important as these remain, to fill in the ground between the ideal typical concepts of the lonely secular individualist and the citizen embedded in "primordial" networks (based on faith, soil, or blood). Individual/moral solidarity groups can take civic or religious forms that are voluntary and changing rather than dyed-in-the-wool identities.

Identity is in flux, shaped by reading, media, life experiences, and the exigencies of daily negotiations with family, community, and the state over what is possible. Duties are balanced against desires. Commodities and style are sites for uninhibited identity experimentation, now possible even with veiling. A young woman I observed on the street in Beyoğlu paired a pop-art headscarf with a matching poodle skirt and red high-top sneakers. A mother in Üsküdar strolling with her husband and two toddlers combined a headscarf wound into a high cone with a tightly fitted colorful tunic. She wore makeup and teetered on open-toed high-heeled sandals that showed off her red toenails. Conscious Islam may be shaped as much by the market and personal desire as by thought and reflection on more philosophical issues.

In their search for social justice and women's empowerment, female activists in Turkey's Islamist movement in the 1980s and 1990s became powerful political brokers who delivered votes for Islamist parties. Women in the Gülen movement are motivated by a commitment to justice and make a conscious choice to serve others. They are the oil that makes the many Gülen schools and programs across the globe run like clockwork. This process is not unique to Turkey. In her book on Shi'i women's participation in the Islamist Hezbollah organization in the southern suburbs of Beirut, Lara Deeb argues that these women have made rational choices to join the Islamist movement in order to stand up against social and political injustice. The women consider themselves to be completely modern and cosmopolitan, as well as pious.[2]

However, although Gülenist women would be the first to describe themselves as actively choosing subjects, they do not participate in central decision-making in Gülenist foundations. The movement's emphasis on conservative communal and gender values, backed by reference to patriarchal interpretations of Islam, have kept women out of positions of authority except in their own complementary female networks. In the case of Turkish women's activism in support of Islamist parties, their expecta-

Figure 7.1. Young woman in fashionable *tesettür* with jeans coat and unconventional semi-transparent headscarf.

tions for central party authority and participation were not met once the parties came to power. Nevertheless, women are highly visible symbols of Islamist success and remain in the public arena, prominently displayed in the "shop window" of public piety to mobilize followers. Turam notes that despite its progressive discourse, the Gülen movement incorporates women into the public sphere without actually intending to empower them.[3]

Is the inspiring feeling of being a modern, choosing Muslim woman an illusion? The possibilities of freely chosen actions are narrowed when others—the family, the community—define the parameters of one's being, as is inevitably the case for women in patriarchal, communalist societies. Saba Mahmood argues, however, that even in such restrictive circumstances, women can be actors in their own lives. When women subordinate themselves *willingly* to an ethically valued cultural and political formation, she writes, this is a form of agency, much like that expressed by a slave who upon being freed chooses to continue being a slave. Mahmood studied women who voluntarily participated in a grassroots women's piety movement in Cairo that involved community service but also a difficult self-negating personal regimen that the women strove to carry out as a means toward self-perfection. Mahmood argues against implicit feminist assumptions that whenever women's actions are constrained, the women are oppressed, and the scholar's duty becomes one of identifying forms of resistance. Mahmood maintains that in struggling to enact the ideals and codes of this difficult tradition and by measuring herself against these codes, a woman comes into being as an authentic self. Rather than the passive acceptance one might assume, subordination instead requires continual effort and struggle to attain mastery over the requirements of the desired identity.[4]

Could this explanation apply to the cheerful Gülen women who are the first to tell you that they are fulfilled by their many activities and don't need to be in the boardroom? To the Turkish Islamist activists who may be soured by their experiences with the male-dominated party structure but have thrown themselves into civic organizing, circumventing and sometimes countering the party? To the Hezbollah women marching in Beirut, setting up clinics, distributing relief supplies? To Havva's route to justice and piety through Paul Coelho and *The Girl with Blue Hair*? To Rabia's flat-out refusal under pressure?

Attempts by scholars like Deeb and Mahmood to dispel stereotypes about anti-modern Islam and the subjugated Muslim woman are important corrections, but they run the risk of muting the voices of the women themselves, their sometimes contradictory ways of being in the world, and their complaints about the very organizations, communities, and families that enfold them. Women uphold the rules of comportment for reasons of piety and propriety but at the same time may chafe at them.[5] A woman I know in Ümraniye has subjected herself to a difficult home-based course to learn Arabic so that she can eventually read the Quran. She hopes someday to attend a school of theology. Her husband, a pious Islamist, forbids her to leave their home, even to go to the nearby open market with his mother and sisters-in-law. Her actions are willed, and, as a pious woman, she values her goal very highly, even though the communal context is unlikely to permit her to progress all the way to a degree. Yet there is more to her story than willing subordination. There is a steely resolve to strike out along a path of her own making that has nothing or everything to do with piety. There are also constraints to which her consent is irrelevant. She is not a freed slave choosing to remain in thrall, but rather, she remains embedded in a society in which community, family, and their attendant norms are not only valued but necessary for survival. As Soli Özel put it, "Who escapes from the herd is carried off by wolves." In other words, a woman's subjectivity as a pious individual and her actions as a public Muslim originate in multiple motivations, only some of which can be attributed to piety and will.

Not all the women I described in this chapter came to public piety through organizations or groups but, rather, through exposure to a variety of influences untethered to any particular place or even religious practice. I have suggested that in the context of globalization and commercialization, Islamic ideas, practices, and identities have become personalized and unmoored from formal groups that claim to represent them. Like magpies picking gold from the flotsam of ideas, opportunities, and products carried in by the global tide, the women line their paths with motivations and justifications of their own devising. They are moving less toward religiously defined self-perfection, ritual, and doctrine, or even service for the sake of religion, but rather, toward a better understanding of what justice and life mean to them and where this self-realization can take them. The line between religion and secularity is wafer thin. Piety is not the goad or the goal, but the journey.

In his analysis of themes in "Islamist fiction" genres, Kenan Çayır writes that since the 1990s the books have commonly included narratives of self-transformation. But whereas earlier fiction for the pious market featured characters discovering Islamic ideals and, in some cases, a militant Islamic cause, recent novels focus on ordinary pious individuals discovering meaning in life, sometimes in opposition to the dictates of the Islamic establishment. For instance, the characters speak against the "Jacobin" nature of Islamism that aims to control standards of what it means to be Muslim, and, instead, support secular democracy. They critically reexamine the concept of the "Golden Age" of the Prophet Muhammad; female characters censure actors in the Islamic past for being patriarchal. In the novels, pious women criticize male Islamist characters, employing a human rights discourse. There is an evident disillusionment with Islamic politics.[6]

I can envision young men and women making individual choices to affiliate with others over a wide range of moral and ethical issues, not bound by their parents' hidebound categories of religiosity, ideology, or nationalism. Such diversity is possible because the impetus for affiliation is individual—Havva's books, for instance, or Rabia's desires. Another point of departure is a particular life experience that leads to a search for social justice or meaning or a particular goal. The lawyer Fatma Benli directs AK-DER (*Ayrımcılığa Karşı Kadın Hakları Derneği*, Association for Women's Rights Against Discrimination), an association dedicated to the rights of covered and uncovered women. She describes her seminal moment of choice:

> I wrote an MA thesis, but I couldn't finish. There was a half-hour presentation. The scarf ban had just started, so I couldn't finish. Some women wore hats or wigs. They allowed you to take the exam with a wig. I tried. It's just half an hour, I told myself. The jury arrived. But I thought, it's too artificial for me. I couldn't do it. I started to cry and left. I know it's just hair, but it means me.

Today AK-DER holds public seminars for women, explaining their rights and how to use them; its members lobby judges and parliament. AK-DER was one of the women's organizations that pushed successfully to change the Penal Code.

Choice is not new for women or for youth, who struggle and strategize around the constrictions of age, class, and gender in their daily lives. Women continually engage in large or small acts of independence. A very poor working-class woman I know tells her stingy husband that she is visiting a friend when in fact she is cleaning houses. She uses the money to purchase basic necessities and trousseau items for her four daughters, but one day she announced proudly (and a little shamefacedly) that she had bought herself two leather jackets as well. A well-educated member of the Capital City Women's Platform told the group about how her husband's relatives refused to send her to a private hospital to have her first baby, insisting that it was a waste of money and that she should go to a public hospital. She refused and paid for the hospital with gold bracelets she had received at her wedding. About this incident, she commented, "The feeling of being independent is something you probably don't forget all your life." Many of these everyday strategies involve women's acquisition or disposition of strategic resources, something that has been well documented.[7]

What is new perhaps is that young people, and young women in particular, are able to make choices that affect their subjectivity, their sense of who they are in the world; that they are influenced and guided in these choices in nontraditional ways; and that some are able to act out these identities as modern hybrid lifestyles that combine elements of globalism, secularism, Islamic piety, consumerism, work, professional engagement, and political activism. These unpredictable and perhaps unstable subjectivities find a place within the market economy, civil society, and pious

Figure 7.2. Shoes belonging to different generations before the door of a conservative, working-class home in Ümraniye. (It is customary to remove shoes before entering a living space.)

organizations like the Gülen movement that appear to focus on networks and social engagement, rather than rules. Women in the Gülen movement, for instance, are active in all these areas, although their status in the movement does not extend to decision-making roles. The availability of choice doesn't mean a rejection of community but simply that the individual has more options for solidarity. Likewise, choice in the elements of one's subjective relation to the world doesn't guarantee the emancipation of youth or women from the demands of community.

Traditions of knowledge about being Turkish or being Muslim, for instance, including the importance of solidarity groups and conceptions of community, are acted out in the context of specific social relations. These relations are shaped by class and gender expectations and other characteristics, including personal variations, which produce different experiences and interpretations of the cluster of ideas that make up a tradition of knowledge. In other words, even though a tradition is a coherent system of thinking and practice that one has learned, the outcome is always unpredictable, because people act out traditions (their identification as Turks, Muslims, and so on) based on individual desires and concerns. People bring a vast range and confluence of cultural materials and experiences to bear in any circumstance in which they act out Turkishness or Muslimness. Barth would say that change happens from within, simply as a result of individual variation.

Peter Mandaville writes that

> Muslim politics today is about the individualisation of religious belief and practice . . . , embodying the ethics of a shared conception of the good life. Their communion exists not through common membership in tight, hierarchically organised social movement organisations, [although the Gülen movement still contains elements of this model] but rather through shared patterns of consumption (listening, reading, shopping) and forms of everyday life.

Contemporary Islamic activism "is premised on the idea that social vision is expressed through the everyday activities that characterize a particular way of 'being in the world,' rather than through external organization towards achievement of political power or a national consciousness." Islamic norms are mediated and reconfigured not only by the structural force of the state but also through neoliberal norms (like consumerism) and structures (globalized markets).[8]

Choice and community are not contradictory desires. Having chosen a manner of being in the world, the individual seeks out forms of solidarity. The Capital City Women's Platform leader, Hidayet Şefkatlı Tuksal, reflected that when people don't feel the need for mutuality and become individuals, they enter "a state that is against human nature—the city person who is alone." After a while, people try to revive the values of community, for instance, through neighborly ties. But even urban networks are breaking down in Turkey's burgeoning metropolises. "You used to be able to go to anyone's door," an old woman in Ümraniye complained to me, "and you'd be asked in for tea. Now neighbors don't know each other." While older residents may lament the loss of traditional forms of neighborhood solidarity, younger people are experimenting with new visions of community.

COMMUNITY AND CHANGE

I do not wish to represent youthful subjectivity and experimentation as the norm but, rather, as an aspect of Turkish society, especially in the cities,[9] that marks an important trend away from "preformed" identities like Kemalism and Islamism. But as Çarkoğlu and Kalaycıoğlu learned from their study of conservatism in Turkey, "religion, soil, and blood relations continue to provide the foundation of major associational ties in Turkey," particularly in ensuring basic survival needs and opportunities. "It is the familiar, traditional, religious, and the newly conservative values and lifestyles promoted and resurrected by such primordial associations and ties that provide the new city dwellers with families, jobs, neighborhoods, credit, and contacts. Such ties, bonds, and contacts are then mobilized to create political associations, relations, and careers based on religious brotherhood, soil-based solidarity, and even tribal or lineage solidarity."[10]

These ties create a special type of bonding that recaptures nostalgia for mutual assistance, neighborliness, face-to-face relations, for an idealized Islamic community. Capitalist relations and patron-client systems, like relations between citizen and state, are represented as economies of affection based on family, neighborly and Islamic "love" (*sevgi*) and service (*hizmet*), terms that appear frequently in Islamist, Gülenist, and AKP discourse.[11] "People relations" appear to drive everything, disguising structural constraints and allowing a feeling of control when the contours of life may be well outside the individual's control. This feeling has extended even to the citizen's relation with Ataturk, whose image, once imposed by the state on public arenas and ubiquitous in shops, has been privatized and brought into homes, where it is ensconced in small shrines. The range of available Ataturk portraits, previously dominated by severe images of the leader in uniform or formal dress, has expanded to include snapshots of the leader in his bathing suit and other informal poses. The relationship with Ataturk's image (and his ideas) has thus been made to appear a personal, rather than state-imposed, choice.[12]

A 1998 national study of Turkish youth between the ages of fifteen and twenty-seven showed that the world shaping young people remained primarily the parental home—on which many remain dependent—and school, through which students imbibe the values of the state. The main sources of information about what to believe were family—which taught personal characteristics like honesty, traditional values, and piety—and the state, which taught technical knowledge and nationalism. Küçükural's 2005 study of high school students showed a high degree of conservatism, particularly with regard to the sacrosanct authority of the father and the inappropriateness of male–female contact (60 percent thought that young people kissing in a public space should be warned).

Idealism and consciousness of citizenship, subjective areas that develop independently of family and state, were little in evidence in the 1998 report. When asked to characterize themselves using multiple designations, respondents identified primarily as religious/traditional or nationalist, followed in much smaller proportions by Kemalist and pluralist. What is most interesting, however, is that, pictured as a column, each "identity" contained layers of the other designations as well. Self-designation as religious/traditional or nationalist was often followed in second and third place by pluralist, Kemalist, and left.[13] A 2009 study that asked youth about their political identities found even stronger evidence that Turkish youth don't see identity as an either-or proposition but, rather, have multiple levels of self-identification that combine Islam, Kemalism, conservatism, and secularism. This combination is reflected in their voting behavior, with 38 percent of those voting for AKP identifying themselves as Kemalist. As the author of the study, psychologist Selçuk Şirin, noted, "In the context of Turkey, where we have political parties or political groups that only explain or describe their own identity in opposition to others, it is very difficult to find people who have multiple identities." This makes his findings that young people in Turkey do have multiple identities and creatively combine arenas of belonging all the more notable.[14]

Neither conservatism nor adherence to traditional values means a rejection of change. The paradox of Turkish conservatism is that while old customs and traditions are generally respected, beyond a limited scope for women's rights, there is no support for maintaining the status quo. Indeed, contrary to what one might expect, conservatives in Turkey seem to be least attracted to maintaining the status quo, compared with secular centrists, who tend to be more dogmatic. Çarkoğlu and Kalaycıoğlu believe that conservatives wish "to return to the good old days, to a myth of a comfortable setting of customs and traditions that Turkish society once had, with their current affluence intact."[15] And for that to happen, society has to change.

Their study shows that the majority of conservatives hold positions that are at odds with some aspect of the status quo. There is very little support for punishing women according to "so-called customs" like honor killing. About 52 percent support women's rights and allowing women to attend university wearing a headscarf. Birth control is supported by both rural and urban respondents, with 48 percent wanting to make it easier to obtain. At the same time, there is little public support for making either divorce or abortion easier. Indeed, a quarter of respondents wish to make divorce harder to obtain. Forty-seven percent are in favor of making cohabitation of different cultures easier (nearly as many as for cohabitation of different ethnicities), but 42 percent also support increased political action to protect national interests, presumably against the familiar enemies "within" and "without." "Most people seem to favor some kind of coexistence of differences," the authors write, "but the specific basis for such an arrangement is not clear in their minds."[16] Interestingly, none of this support is correlated with AKP membership, because the party has become too heterogeneous to typecast. There is, however, a class difference, with lower-class respondents showing less tolerance for liberalizing gender relations, especially sexual norms.[17]

The AKP exhibits the same kind of category-bending heterogeneity that characterizes Turkish youth. The AKP government, a behemoth of national, local, and individual interests, benefits from the status quo while radically changing elements of it. The AKP speaks the language of "love" (*sevgi*) and fellowship, mutual assistance, neighborliness, and face-to-face relations. It projects the values of an idealized Muslim community set within a democratic, secular (but not laicist) system of governance that provides the mechanism for change in the direction of a conservative "golden age" in which affluence and morality can coexist. The post-imperial Ottoman desire for a global leadership role adds another layer of complexity.

The road to this end is a system of liberal laws based on individual human rights that will ensure that the state will no longer be able to infringe on freedom of religion. With the wind of EU accession requirements at its back, the AKP government has enacted a number of legal changes on that basis and is at present pushing for a new constitution that, many hope, will enshrine these values. After intensive lobbying by women's rights activists, a new Penal Code was approved by parliament in 2004 initiating legal changes that protect women as individuals rather than defining women's rights primarily on the basis of their status as family and community members. Previously, attacks on a man's body constituted a breach of individual rights, but a sexual attack on a woman's body was not considered a violation of her individual rights. Rather, it was a crime against public decency and the family order. According to this logic, a rapist was not liable if he married the woman he had deflowered, since the basic principle of the law was to ensure the continuity and intactness of the family. Until 1987, jail terms were reduced if the woman raped or abducted was already married or a prostitute (that is, not a virgin). Other AKP initiatives have supported women's rights. For example, government incentives encouraged parents to send their daughters to school, and female illiteracy dropped from 28 percent in 1990 to 10 percent in 2010.

These liberal interventions have been contradicted in practice by a lack of implementation, especially in regard to the rights of women. The newspapers are full of stories of women who are threatened by their spouse or family and who seek the protection of police or courts, now legally mandated to protect them, only to be returned to their persecutors because the judge or policeman considers it to be a family matter or has nowhere to send the woman.[18] AKP municipalities have been consistently unfriendly toward women's shelters. In 2008 the World Economic Forum ranked Turkey an embarrassing 127th of 140 nations in status of women in society. Party leaders, including the prime minister, have reinforced traditional gender norms by emphasizing that women are valued—but not equal—and that their proper role is taking care of home and children, and by encouraging women to have at least three children. The number of women in political office has remained extremely low for both secular and conservative parties. The AKP is against a quota system that would bring more women into politics. Turkey in 2009 had the lowest share of women in the workforce in Europe, 22 percent (30 percent in 2011), a number that has actually decreased substantially over the past decade. By comparison, the average in OECD countries was 62 percent and in developing countries, 33 percent.[19]

The conservative view of women as embedded in society continues to stand in the way of implementation of new liberal practices. In this view, a person's rights derive from their family and community status, so women are never individuals, as the new laws established them to be. Additionally, she must be a member in good standing of her family and community, that is, an honorable woman under the himaye (protection, control) of honorable men. Family and communal claims on women and women's honor are deeply embedded not only in conservatism (which is open to change, but not in matters of gender) but also in the conceptual structure of nation and nationalism. In 2011, to the consternation of women's activists, AKP changed the name of the State Ministry for Women's Issues and Women's Status to Ministry of Family and Social Politics (*Aile ve Sosyal Politikalar Bakanlığı*), thus changing the focus of the ministry from "women" to "family," and from a concern with women's status to a focus on social welfare. The ministry was given a 25 billion TL budget and made a main arm of the government's antipoverty campaign.[20] Feminists complained that women now "have no name" in government,[21] that is, have disappeared as a government issue and become reembedded in family and community.

Residual Citizenship

Kandiyoti has observed that women in the Muslim world "have not emerged as full-fledged citizens but often remained members of religious/ethnic collectivities whose control is relinquished by the state to the patriarchal interests of their communities."[22] This understanding of women's rights as rooted in their community status, rather than in their humanity, is reinforced not only by the statements and practices of government figures that model and legitimate this view for the populace, but also by state institutions such as the police and the judiciary. It is mirrored in the conceptual structure of nation and nationalism, which sets up "the nation" as a vulnerable female, with the nationalist as the protective male whose honor reflects that of the entire national family and ensures the continuity of the national lineage.[23]

Nationalism implies control—of the body, of national boundaries, and of boundaries of the body.[24] The discourse of nationalism uses the same language and imagery as that of sexual honor.[25] That is, the shame brought about by a penetration of sexual boundaries is parallel to the loss of honor due to a penetration of the nation's borders. In a Religious Affairs Directorate article warning of the danger posed by missionaries within Turkey, the author illustrated his point by connecting a bloody attack against Muslims in Kosovo with a threat to the Turkish motherland and, in the same breath, connecting it to an assault against women's sexual honor, indeed, to the entire cultural arsenal of honor: "These are "attacks against *ırz* [chastity, purity, honor], *namus* [good name, honor], *iffet* [chastity, innocence], *haysiyet* [personal dignity, honor], and *şeref* [honor, distinction]. . . . We have a debt of loyalty and honor [*namus*] to those who put this motherland [*vatan*] under our protection [*emanet*, in our care]."[26]

Such highly sexualized and gendered discourse positions men and women differently in the national imaginary and is reflected in men's and women's everyday understandings of their relation to the nation. Although women are displayed as part of the national ideal, they are not constructed—nor, as reflected in my discussions, do they generally view themselves—as active players. In Turkey and other militaristic societies, women enter nationalist discourse as providers of sons for the military, and this function is expressed in a worship of mothers, especially mothers of martyrs, as fallen soldiers are called.[27] The participation of women in public life that is a hallmark of Kemalist nationalism was mentioned only once by one of my interlocutors, a secular professional woman, as part of her national identity—and only as an afterthought—pointing to a disconnect between Kemalist ideology and national subjectivity.

Instead, women tended to see their relation to the nation in terms of citizenship. "Citizenship is a weak category," the sociologist Ferhat Kentel told me. You use it when you say, "The folk (*halk*) took over the beaches; the citizen (*vatandaş*) couldn't get into the sea." But citizen is also a good term, Kentel added, because it refers to a person who is obedient. The journalist Mustafa Akyol gave a similar definition:[28]

Citizen is used to refer to a man who is a little ignorant. A citizen is someone who waits in a line and tries to get his papers signed. It's a passive thing to be a citizen. It's lower middle class. A director/administrator (*müdür*) isn't a citizen. He's the state, so he's above the citizen. The citizen waits at the door. If you are the niece of a politician, then you knock on the door and go right in. Citizens are expected to be passive and obedient. People with some privilege are above the citizen. For instance, a friend drove through a red light. He [just] showed the police the traffic director's calling card.

Kentel's and Akyol's observations mesh with Aydın's finding, based on a study of attitudes toward citizenship and the state, that the relationship between citizen and state is primarily characterized by fear:

> The state is viewed as an almost "holy," unchanging/unchangeable body whose existence is "naturalized." . . . [It] is perceived and conceptualized as a body mimicking the role of the patriarch (or, in Turkish, *aile reisi*). Many citizens also view the state as a body that needs protection from "threats," including those internal, ideological ones.

The government, by contrast, is perceived as a more functional locus riddled with petty politics and clientilistic relations.[29]

A Turkish man (if he is not a conscientious objector) can be a full citizen, a soldier and protector (whether or not he is a producer), whereas a woman is a ranked or "residual" citizen. Her vulnerable physicality puts her under the emanet (protection and control) of men and the state. Pious women experience a further divide between what Havva called the "*makbul*" (acceptable) citizen in the Kemalist mold, and the residual citizen of the covered woman. The lowest rank of citizen is the non-Muslim who is considered to be the "inside outsider," a non-Turkish citizen of suspect loyalty.

In a convergence with Kemalist nationalism, the Muslim nationalist narrative likewise excludes women, who appear as passive figures on national display, not active in the work force or in politics, and as vulnerable, socially embedded beings whose physical integrity and honor must be protected through social control (rather than as free individuals). Secularist and Muslim nationalists are united in their fear of losing honor by allowing their defenses to be penetrated. For Muslim nationalists, this anxiety focuses on women; geographic and to some extent ethnic and religious borders are potentially open. For Kemalists, by contrast, the physical borders of the nation are a major source of honor (namus), along with jealously guarded cultural and racial boundaries. Some Kemalists favor slamming the door shut on the world entirely, as with a kind of national chastity belt that will allow Turkey to retain its ethno-racial purity. As one high-ranking officer told me, as a nationalist he believes Turkey should disconnect from the European Union, the United States, NATO, and the world market. "Turkishness is enough," he insisted.

The cluster of ideas that links family to nation, and women's sexual honor to national integrity, continually reinforces family and communal claims on women in society. Choice, hybridity, and experimentation with roles are thereby constrained for women in ways they are not for men. Nevertheless, the continual acting out of traditions in new and unexpected ways—influenced by books, media, globalization, the market, and new opportunities—inevitably shapes traditions to allow for new "truths" about what it means to be Muslim and Turkish.

CHAPTER 8

Conclusion

IN THE PREVIOUS CHAPTERS, I have explored the origins of polarization and social tension around certain key issues in contemporary Turkey, such as the headscarf and a fear of missionary conversion. These have become markers of belonging within the Turkish national community but also represent competing narratives about what it means to be Turkish and what it means to be Muslim. To all appearances, there appears to be a standoff between secularism and Islam, with one side accusing the other of heavy-handed imposition of its own values and practices on Turkish society as a whole.

For secularists, the national tradition is heavily bound up with Kemalism, that is, Ataturk's model for society, a secular lifestyle, and an emphasis on cultural, linguistic, and racial purity. Some fear disappearing as a nation altogether if these markers of Turkishness are further eroded by the tsunami of outside influences and subversive freedoms generated by globalization and the process of EU alignment that they believe have unleashed Islamic fundamentalism. Evidence for this is AKP's creeping conservatism, its campaign to limit alcohol consumption, and attempts to change laws that make it illegal for covered women to appear in certain key public spaces. Conversely, pious Muslims object to the Kemalist laicist stranglehold over religious discourse and practice that has been in place since the founding of the Republic. Kemalist dominance has been maintained through coups, the banning of elected parties, education, and national mass ceremonies. Muslim nationalists wish to replace Kemalist laicism with secularism that would allow freedom of religious expression for Muslims and to some extent for non-Muslims, although suspicion of non-Muslim citizens and outsiders is deeply entrenched in the population as a whole.[1] To this end, Muslim nationalists have undercut the power of the army, reorganized the judicial system, changed laws, and added their own Ottoman-themed national rituals. The lines of social tension appear to be drawn largely along these parameters.

Yet, these seemingly discrete "categories" of secular and Islamic—and the social and political positions implied by these terms—break down on closer examination.

Secular Kemalism, for instance, has become sacralized to the extent that it has taken on elements of religion, replete with veneration of Ataturk's image, mystical appearances, rituals of worship, and assertions of truth taken on faith. At the same time, Islam has arguably become personalized and to some extent commercialized as the post-1980s Muslim bourgeoisie has developed a market for Muslim leisure and fashion, literature, music, and lifestyle—not all religion-referenced. Political Islamism has been replaced by cultural Muslimhood. Being a "conscious" Muslim, that is, freely choosing one's Muslim path and accompanying lifestyle, has become a marker of modernity, even if that choice leads one to a solidarity group rather than to an individualistic lifestyle. Modern Muslims want the right to choose to be Muslim in the way they desire. Their influence has spread through enough of the capillaries of power that they have been able to provide a credible Muslim alternative vision of the nation and what it means to be Turkish—a Muslim nationalism that is challenging the Kemalist tradition.

Scaled up to the national level, these developments lead to the counterintuitive observation that many socially conservative, pious Turkish Muslims support globalization, a liberal economy, and laws based on individual rights (rather than casting the individual as subordinate to state or community), while some socially liberal Kemalists oppose them.[2] Muslim nationalists see in these policies a means to gain freedom of religious expression within Turkey and a chance to reclaim the country's prominence as a former empire through global political and economic integration. Kemalists see the same policies as a threat to Turkey's national integrity because they allow the proliferation of divisive ideas and practices, such as those supporting religious and ethnic rights. They also undermine safeguards that until now had given the Kemalist state and its guardian military a semblance of control over national social and political processes. For instance, the EU integration process has curtailed the representation of military officers on the National Security Council and has led to changes in the law that allow military personnel to be tried in civilian courts. Citizens have begun to file cases in courts across the nation against the leaders of the 1980 coup. The army is no longer untouchable and thus is unable to steer a straying nation back toward Kemalist unity, away from the impure mixing of tradition, blood/race, language, and custom that Kemalists fear will destroy Turkishness and the Turkish nation. This danger has led some Kemalists to call for Turkey to disconnect from the wider world altogether and create a pure, unadulterated "Turkey for the Turks." Placards at Republic Meetings read, "Army, do your duty," expressing nostalgia for a strongman able and willing to carry out a coup.

Another area in which assumptions about a secular/Islamic divide break down is the hybridity on the ground of both Turkish and Muslim identities. National subjectivities are better described by delineating the processes by which people develop them, rather than as categories to label them. This is particularly true for Turkish youth, whose identities no longer predict their politics and who seem less and less linked to a state project despite heavy Kemalist indoctrination in school. Instead, they exhibit simultaneous layers of sometimes contradictory views and values and sport multiple labels.

Turkishness is as much a product of the media and market as of the educational system. For instance, post-Ottomanism or Ottomania, as some call it, has now infected all sectors of society, pious and secular alike. Some participate in an "Ottoman" national identity by purchasing genuine antiques for their homes or modern art with Ottoman references. Others make do with Oriental-style knickknacks, not infrequently made in China. A television soap opera about the life of Sultan Suleiman the Magnificent has become so popular that shopping malls have set up stands where customers can dress up as "Ottoman characters" like the sultan's wife, Hürrem, and have their pictures taken. Demand for Ottoman-style costumes is exceeding the ability of ateliers to produce them.[3] It won't be long before brides and grooms begin to don Ottoman court dress for their wedding photos. An individual's understanding of national tradition might also incorporate the ideas of solidarity groups, ranging from environmentalist NGOs or rocker culture to the Gülen movement. Social class and gender add further variables that position individuals differently vis-à-vis the nation. Turkishness has become a work in progress and its expression context-dependent.

Muslim and secular nationalisms also share a number of basic assumptions. One is the embodied nature of Turkish identity, whether demonstrated by a flag made of children's blood or a tattoo of Ataturk's signature on one's arm; martial training of the body in the service of the state from kindergarten through military service; or the belief that a citizen's life blood belongs to the state, and the highest expression of patriotism is to shed that blood. There is a masculinist cast to nationalism, a division of labor between male martyrs for the nation and mothers who have produced the male soldier's body that is to be sacrificed. Sexually active women play a different role. They are cast as vulnerable females whose physical boundaries can be breached and thus must be controlled, much as the nation's borders must be guarded against foreign penetration. Either act brings impurity to the bloodline and dishonor to the (national) family. Thus, the state and its institutions have a vested interest in controlling the sexuality of girls and women, for instance, through officially mandated virginity tests and patrolling of public spaces for "immoral" behavior.

Control of the body is acted out at many levels of society, within the hierarchies of the patriarchal family, as a consequence of unequal social relations, and in relations between citizen and state. The institutions of family, society, and nation-state serve as discursive and functional metonyms for one another. This fractal repetition of the highly sexualized themes of martyr's mother and victim at different levels of experience hinders women from developing a national subjectivity beyond these roles. Instead, women identify with the problematic and weak category of citizen. Covered women are doubly alienated from the masculine state-centered nation as residual citizens whose heterodox feminine identity does not align with the acceptable image of the (already alienated) Kemalist citizen woman. Both Muslim and secular nationalists share this highly gendered understanding of the nation that limits women's role in what are essentially masculinist and militarist configurations of national identity. This complex of ideas about women as national subjects is reflected in their extraordinarily low participation in political and economic life.

Nevertheless, in periods of revolutionary transformation in Turkey and elsewhere, women have found openings to pursue their own goals in the public arena. A variety of Islamist movements have provided pious women such opportunities, for example, as demonstrated by their remarkable political activism in Turkey's Islamist movement in the 1980s and 1990s. During this same period, at a time of great existential threat after Israel invaded Lebanon and bombed Beirut, Shi'i women joined Lebanon's Hezbollah. Women's participation in Jordan's Islamic Action Front (IAF) and Yemen's Islah Party increased in the 1990s when intraparty disputes and external challenges opened windows of opportunity for women to become active.[4] The 2011 Nobel Peace Prize was awarded to Tawakkul Karman, who played a leading role in the opposition protests in Yemen that started after revolts in Tunisia and Egypt that year sparked a series of uprisings across the Arab world against entrenched illiberal governments in what has come to be known as the Arab Spring.

Yet, once the AKP won elections and consolidated its power, Islamist activist women were locked out of meaningful participation in political decision-making. Despite social liberalization and women's increasing participation in civil society in Jordan and Yemen, neither the IAF nor Islah consistently supported women's activism; instead, they continued to criticize and slander women in prominent positions. Once strife ended and conditions normalized, the window of opportunity for women closed. It remains to be seen what role Ms. Karwan will play in Yemeni politics now that the existing government has been overthrown and new parties are coming to power. The indications from Egypt and Libya are not positive. In Egypt, women participated equally in the Tahrir Square protests but were pushed to the sidelines in the formation of new political parties in preparation for the first post-Mubarak elections, and found scant representation in the new government. Many Libyan women were dismayed when transitional leader Mustafa Abdul Jalil celebrated Liberation Day in November 2011 not by explaining his party's plans for rebuilding the country's economy or setting up democratic elections but by announcing that in the new post-Gaddafi Libya he wanted men to be allowed to marry up to four wives without getting permission from their existing wives, as required by Gaddafi-era law. As activists and parties consolidate power and are absorbed into male-dominated political systems, women's revolutionary role becomes less important if not outright forgotten. It is rapidly replaced by nationalist discourse and imagery that represents women as emblems of national or party virtues and of exuberant bourgeois aspirations that might include luxuries like women's seclusion in the home and multiple wives, which display distinction in certain conservative Islamic contexts.[5]

The consolidation of nationalism historically has meant a rediscovery of women as symbols to be displayed in the shop window of the new nation. In the nationalist pantheon, women represent family, propriety, and sexual vulnerability. They are carriers of Muslim and national values and bearers of sons to repopulate the nation. In her study of women's participation in Egypt's anticolonial struggle, Baron notes that while nationalist discourses and symbols do knit women into the nation to some extent, "real women were cut out of access to the state at the critical moment when the nationalists seized power. . . . In short, the nationalist movement may have eventually ended the British occupation, but it did not make women full citizens of the state."[6]

In addition to sharing a highly gendered understanding of the nation, Muslim and secular nationalists in Turkey also espouse authoritarianism and the centrality of Muslim identity. They share a belief in the efficacy of social engineering, which results in fierce attention to educational molding and a barrage of interdictions, ranging from restrictions on religious clothing and alcohol; laws against insulting Ataturk, the army, and Turkishness; to a ban on YouTube. There is little tolerance of heterodoxy, criticism, or pushback. Democracy is widely understood as a mandate for the winning party to impose its values. Here again the patriarchal family serves as an explicit model for the relationship between Father State and his citizen children.

Other seemingly inalienable markers of membership in the Turkish nation, like the sacrality of blood and the embattled unity of the nation within its 1923 borders, appear more fungible as Muslim nationalists move away from a racialist toward a more culturally defined Turkish identity, and move the nation's focus slowly from fear of dissolution by enemy outsiders to promotion of outside opportunities. Despite Muslim nationalist emphasis on globalization and accommodation of minorities, however, polls show that much of the population still holds to the premise that Turkey's non-Muslims are the "enemy within," working as agents of "the enemy without"—the European Union, the United States, and Israel—to undermine Turkish territorial and national integrity.[7]

Muslim nationalists must be understood as rooted in powerful collectivist norms and an expansive historical understanding of national boundaries that make them more resistant to the perception of threat to national boundaries and identity. This rootedness in collective norms, however, contradicts their support for individual rights. Consequently, Muslim nationalist discourse is characterized by pragmatic switching between liberal and conservative positions,[8] for instance, supporting EU-mandated reforms and a new liberal constitution while simultaneously promoting in-group solidarity, obedience, and conformity, and undermining tolerance for difference. The AKP has displayed an à la carte approach to rights, an authoritarian intolerance, and a tendency to prosecute and repress critics. In 2011 Turkey led the world in number of jailed journalists, more than in China and Iran.[9] Dozens of journalists and writers have been jailed under Article 301 for "insulting the Turkish nation," for "supporting a terrorist cause" by writing about the Kurdish situation, and for being critical of the Gülen movement or religion in general.[10] Some of these prosecutions can be seen as attempts by various parties to consolidate power, but they also reflect a tradition mentioned previously that Muslim nationalists share with Kemalists—militarism, authoritarianism, an understanding of democracy as a mandate to impose the norms of one's own group, and a reliance on social engineering.

Just as Kemalist elites have lost the ability to wed young people to the Kemalist project, Islamists have lost control over Islam to the market, to media, and to choice-based experimentation. Islamism has ceded popularity to solidarity groups such as the Gülen movement that are not rule-based but service oriented, charismatic rather than scriptural. The individual has taken on new importance, not as a singular or even collective agent of change, but as a self-conscious member of solidarity groups that have been chosen rather than inherited. Personal choice is of particular importance for women whose development of subjectivity, that is, a consciousness of self as a social subject, continues to be more constrained than for their brothers. For many women within familial settings that strictly define their social roles and identities, choice remains a partial and sometimes illicit pursuit—a secret job, a leather jacket, a better hospital. However, some women, particularly young urban women, have taken control of defining their personhood, sometimes against family or community pressure. Their destination may be different from those of their peers and elders—for instance, civic or religious activism—or it may be the same—marriage and the solidarity of family—but they will have chosen their own path there, motivated by a search for justice, a desire for meaning or for upward mobility, or simply just by a desire to choose.

In the Third Turkish Republic, I suggest, the image of a coherent cultural tradition that makes up Turkish national identity has given way to a bewildering variety of choices of values, practices, and modes of affiliation. These choices have been expanded by the global media, a market in products and lifestyles through which one can express one's identity, NGOs, and the availability of alternative lifestyles and solidarity groups like the Gülen movement. Turkishness is being redefined in a variety of ways, and national identity, beyond certain core shared characteristics, has become a matter of choice. The choice is not only between Muslim or secular nationalism but, indeed, whether the individual chooses to build his or her subjectivity around nationalism at all.

This process may at times be muted by media-amplified crescendos of aggressive nationalism after PKK attacks on Turkish security services and civilians. Indeed, such attacks and aggressive responses by the state and ordinary people key directly into the "enemy within/enemy without" threat paradigm and masculinist, militarist definitions of national subjectivity ("We are all soldiers"). This response pulls the nation together in a familiar paroxysm of nationalist self-definition against a common enemy.

In the long run, however, this sort of exclusionary nationalism may be displaced in importance by other sources of solidarity and identity, the most powerful of which is a Muslim identity. Muslim nationalism is intrinsically Turkish, but its outlines, boundaries, rituals, and embodied representations are in flux. Current social tensions, I would argue, are in response to Kemalist fears that the social and political transformations of the Third Republic will result in the loss of a coherent, authentic national self, that is, an end to the Turkish nation as a pure, unalloyed representative of Turkishness.

A Turkish Model?

Turkey cannot be characterized as a Muslim or as a secular democracy without upending all the preconceptions the terms *Muslim* and *secular* entail in that context. This recognition allows us to reconsider the question of whether an Islam-rooted conservative party like the AKP is turning Turkey away from the West to the East, as some Western pundits have claimed. The AKP has been in power for more than a decade and in this time has reshaped Turkey's economic and political practices, not least its foreign policy. Under Foreign Minister Davutoğlu, Turkey has reached out to neighboring countries in the Middle East, primarily to open trade relations, but also in a bid to become a regional power broker and negotiator. Turkey also has expanded its diplomatic presence in Africa and South America. It has strengthened economic and political ties with Russia, Armenia, Greece, and Europe generally, as well as in the Middle East and Central Asia.

The AKP, in other words, has a postimperial vision based on its Ottoman past that is guiding its attempt to become a global power, not just an Eastern power. For Muslim nationalists, the emblematic founding moment for the Turkish nation is a moment of conquest (of the Byzantines in 1453), and their image of the future is of regional Turkish-led economic and political unions, not an Islamic *umma* in which Turkey will take equal place beside other Muslim nations. Indeed, Turks of every political persuasion with almost one voice proclaim Turkish Islam different from and superior to other forms of Islam, particularly that practiced in the Arab world.

This postimperial guiding vision also sets Turkey apart from other Middle Eastern nations that have spent the twentieth century throwing off the mantle of European conquest, only to be enveloped in authoritarian systems that rely on religion and repression to rule. Turkey has been proposed as a model for post–Tahrir Square Egypt and other countries in the region that, having been touched by the breeze of the Arab Spring, wish to develop electoral systems that integrate Islam with democracy. There are some similarities between Turkey and other countries in the region, particularly in the powerful role played by solidarity groups, in the patriarchal family as metonym for the state, and in cultural views of women's role in society and nation. What differentiates Turkey is its national self-confidence, regardless of whether that is based on racial pride or imperial heritage. Since long before Ziya Gökalp, Western lifestyles and institutions have been considered desirable and available for adoption. They are seen to be aspects of international civilization that do not in any way endanger Ottoman imperial tradition or compete with Turkish national identity, since the latter is based on a unique Turkish Muslim culture. In parts of the world that experienced Western conquest, by contrast, Western institutions are greeted with suspicion as postcolonial impositions hostile to native traditions. Furthermore, Turkey is the only country in the region engaged in EU accession procedures that have deeply transformed its laws and institutions. This process has accelerated a move from a communally embedded understanding of rights to one based on individual rights, although this change is incomplete, and contradictory traditions uneasily coexist.

Other unique aspects of the Turkish experience that have driven its success as a vibrant, if fractious, democracy are Ataturk's charisma, which allowed the relatively unchallenged imposition of enormous social and political changes early in the century (some of which had roots in the late Ottoman period); the role of the army as guarantor of democracy—it ensured free elections following every coup; and a continual process of inclusion of different parts of the population in national politics and economic development. Despite pressures against "mixing," this process has largely succeeded with the eventual integration of peasants and the pious sector but is still incomplete with regard to Kurds, Alevis, and non-Muslims.

In July 2011 the post-Mubarak Egyptian governing council, dominated by the military, came out in favor of a "Turkish model" of governance, but it was clear that they had in mind the authoritarian Kemalist model of military tutelage, not the "Muslim democracy" desired by the Arab street.[11] When Prime Minister Erdoğan visited Cairo in September, he was given a rapturous reception at the airport by the Muslim Brotherhood, which often cited the AKP as a model. The Brotherhood's opinion of Erdoğan was soon clouded by his speeches, in which he insisted that Turkey was not an Islamic democracy, but a secular one. In one of his speeches, Erdoğan pointed out that Arabic newspapers had translated his use of "secularism" wrongly as "atheism." Secularism, he explained, meant respecting all religions equally. He told the Egyptians not to fear building a secular state, and to make his point, he visited the elderly Coptic Patriarch of Alexandria. A dismayed Brotherhood spokesman hit back at Turkey's Islamic credentials, using women's sexual vulnerability as a metaphor for the Turkish nation's lack of honor: "In Turkey, when a man finds a woman in bed with another man, he can't punish her by law because it is permitted there. It means that Turkey . . . violates Islamic Shariah law."[12]

A few days later, Erdoğan repeated his message in Tunis, where he also received a heady reception. "A secular state has an equal distance to all religious groups," he told the press, "including Muslim, Christian, Jewish and atheist people.[13] . . . [T]his is not a secularism in the Anglo-Saxon or Western sense; a person is not secular, the state is secular. A Muslim can govern a secular state in a successful way. In Turkey, 99 percent of the population is Muslim, and it did not pose any problem. You can do the same here."[14] In this statement, Erdoğan was referring to the principles of Muslimhood, a model developed by the AKP and modernist theologians in Ankara that replaced Islamism. The Muslimhood model posits that Islam is a personal attribute that may be carried into the public arena, for instance, in the form of personal ethics, but does not define what a person does there.

On October 23, 2011, Tunisians held the first free election of the Arab Spring and gave the moderate Islamist Ennahda Party 40 percent of the vote. Ennahda explicitly models itself on the AKP and has stated its commitment to democracy and women's rights. Tunisia is known for having a comparatively secular outlook and progressive legislation on women's rights, unlike many other Arab states that to a greater or lesser extent incorporate shari'a in their legal institutions. Post–Arab Spring, the Muslim Brotherhood in Egypt and Islamists in Libya and elsewhere have insisted that their new governments and social and legal systems be based on Islam. Having faced down bullets and torture to remove their dictators, it is fair to say that most Arab Spring activists were motivated not by Islam, which played a minor role in the revolutions, but by a search for justice and freedom from oppressive governments. Young, modern Muslims seeking justice and material well-being would be more likely to find their mirror image in Turkey's Muslimhood model, not in a politically amorphous "Turkish model."

The desire on the part of these countries to duplicate Turkey's political and economic successes—to become vibrant "Muslim" democracies like Turkey—has led to the assumption that there is a "Turkish model." But a Turkish model, if such can be said to exist, is unique in ways that argue against its replication in countries whose commonality with Turkey might be said to be Islam and a desire for democracy, but that historically and in terms of culture, institutions, and driving motivators, are quite different. Even Islam and secularism in Turkey defy characterization, with the elaboration of a personalized Muslimhood in a secular state only one aspect of deep-rooted changes that have transformed Turkey. Such transformations affect not just the superficial mechanisms of governance but the core identity of what it means to be Muslim—or Turkish. This may indeed be a process underway among the Tahrir Square youth, but as power is consolidated in the new regime, the window for participation—and thus the possibilities for transformation—might well close for youth, as it has in the past for women.

DENATIONALIZATION

This is not to say that the processes outlined in this book are unique to Turkey. As we have seen, a similar complex of meanings links nationalism, masculinity, and women's honor elsewhere in the world, with particularly strong parallels in Israel. These similarities are not coincidental and suggest a further convergence in the roles played by religion, ethnicity, and national identity in both countries.

Indeed, in a study reminiscent of the Turkish case, Uri Ram examines the development of "religious nationalism" in Israel. He asks how religion and nationalism came to be so closely meshed that they were able to push aside modern secular Zionist nationalism. Israeli political culture, he argues, moved from a combination of strong nationalism/weak religionism in its early Zionist days to strong nationalism/strong religionism today.[15] The strong nationalism/weak religionism ideal type is strongly reminiscent of Kemalism, as Ram himself points out. Secular national culture acts as a "civic religion," and religious institutions are separated from or, in the Turkish case, subordinated to the state. Turkey arguably (though some might disagree) has not moved as far along the path toward strong nationalism/strong religionism as Israel, which is politically dominated by religious parties like the Israeli-Jewish Block of Faithful, making secularism increasingly unviable.[16] Nevertheless, the resulting "indissoluble mesh of 'religious nationalism'" (Ram invokes Irish Catholicism) has certain important parallels to the Turkish case.

Israel, Ram argues, is becoming increasingly nonsecular, because only Jewish nationality is officially recognized, not Israeli nationality, giving religious groups sway over defining the nation. Why is this the case? Jewish nationality means that belonging is determined by family of birth, while Israeli nationality is a potentially universal category open to all—Jews, Arabs, and other citizens. "In order to avert such a potential 'mix' and to secure the boundaries and membership of a 'pure' Jewish nationality, the state leans on Jewish religion(ism)." Judaism is thus deployed as a shield against civic nationalism. Since they cannot be nationals, non-Jews perforce are members of the devalued category of citizens. Religion used as a national standard thus disguises what is really political exclusion on the basis of ethnic racism. Jewish nationalism is intensely focused on monitoring the boundaries between Jews and Arabs and their demographic ratio—many believe that the high Arab birthrate threatens the very existence of a Jewish nation. Jewish nationalists use religion as a criterion of exclusion and to specify "the 'essence' of the 'core nation' of the state of Israel and to tell it apart from others."

In this way, religion (understood as lineage-based ethnicity) dominates over the state and sets the boundaries of the "nation." As a result, even Jews who are secular may observe religious codes and participate in some religious ceremonies, "not because they 'believe' in God, but because they 'belong' to the nation." That is, secular Jews must balance secular individual choices with the nonsecular demands of their national community.

A precondition for the secularization of Israel, Ram writes, is its denationalization, a transmutation from ethnic to civic nationalism, that is, from a Jewish state to a state of its citizens. In other words," he concludes, "as long as the state of Israel remains Jewish, it will remain nonsecular."[17] In the Turkish case, the blood-based definition of national identity originates in Kemalism's strong nationalism/weak religionism, which also masks race with religion (only Muslims are Turks), and thereby excludes its non-Muslim citizens from belonging to the Turkish nation. Turks and Israelis share a fear of disappearing as a nation, in the one case a nation of Muslim Turks and in the other, of Jews.

It is unclear how far Muslim nationalists have moved beyond blood and belonging toward a more civic nationalism that is inclusive of non-Muslims and Kurds (as well as women)—not through the unequal model of millet, not just as citizens, but as Turkish nationals. It would be instructive, indeed, if Turkey's strong nationalism/strong religionism, unlike in the case of Israel, would lead toward a more pluralist, civic state. Such a possibility points to the importance of local, contextual factors, such as the recent change in the public definition of Islam from being an indicator of Turkish blood to being an attribute of the individual, Muslimhood as a personalized value system. That is, the meaning of some of the basic elements that make up Ram's model for Israel—ethnic lineage, culture, secularism, and religion—are historically malleable. It is fair to conclude, then, that for Turkey, as for countries of the Arab Spring, religion is not incompatible with civic nationalism, but also that secularism is not the only route there. Personalized Islam or Muslimhood can be a model for incorporating pious individuals and principles into the public sphere without excluding non-Muslims. The conditions under which Islam has become personalized can be said to include rural to urban migration, neoliberal globalization and the commercialization of identity, and a young demographic. There are likely other factors at work in the Turkish case, like Ottoman modeling, that may or may not translate to countries in the region. Bayat writes about the "quiet encroachment of the ordinary" in Iran and Egypt, the subtle actions taken by individuals within a collective society that resocialize government and religious movements and thereby create new identities and opportunities for change.[18] The Turkish case constitutes an ongoing experiment in Casanova's *aggiornamentos*, small adjustments to tradition that lead to change.[19] However, contrary to Casanova's expectation that such accommodations in Muslim societies would cause democratic discourse to be framed in an Islamic idiom, it seems, rather, that nontraditional influences—ranging from literature to the market—elicit values not directly linked to religion—like social justice—that may lead individuals to personal piety and to democratic participation outside an Islamic idiom.

Despite these promising changes, at present Turkey's secular and Muslim nationalists remain in thrall to a hostile and competitive communalism that, as in Israel, excludes some parts of the population from national membership for reasons deeply embedded in the nation's culture and history. This exclusion is fueled by a much-elaborated fear of the enemy outside and within, and a fear of disappearing as a nation. Perhaps, as Soli Özel suggested, Turks can be released from mutual suspicion and obsessive boundary maintenance only if the institutions of the state provide an objective framework that can be relied upon to be fair and impartial and to protect the individual citizen's interest, regardless of his or her identity. Such an institutional framework would allow the individual to step outside the protective boundaries of the group and encourage civic nationalism. Otherwise, as Özel put it, "you are carried off by wolves."

THE UNBEARABLE LIGHTNESS OF TRUTH

Society is a disordered system, not a coherent model or a puzzle that has a solution if only we fit the pieces together properly. In these chapters I have tried to ask how Turkish social, cultural, and political reality is constructed in practice by individuals who bring their own concerns and characteristics to the business of being Turkish, being modern, being democratic. The process of acting out Turkishness generates some degree of order and shape, but also contradictions. We can examine discourse as an expression of shared practices, of models of and for reality. These practices, however, are always interactional and contextualized; that is, they involve both the individual and community. Without the link to practice, culture and society are abstractions, and nationalism—like Turkishness, Muslimhood, and modernity—becomes an empty category, a puzzle piece on a one-dimensional board.

The hope is that we can observe enough connections so that we can model practices that make up traditions of knowledge—what people believe they know about being Turkish, how they have come to know it, and how different people inhabit Turkishness—that is, how people act out that knowledge under different circumstances. Individuals bring to their pragmatic interpretation their age, sex, social class, education, and the accidents of living that have made them sensitive to life concerns.

People rely on the availability of shared, coherent traditions of knowledge to orient themselves as Turks, as modern, as Muslim, as Kemalist; they build communities around these traditions. They rely on historical traditions, streams of knowledge about what happened in the past, to justify the "cultural stock" of the present.[20] But these are just words, labels that gain meaning only when they are acted out. And in the process of being performed, root identifying traditions—like the knowledge, concepts, and values that make them up—are continually modified by experience, manipulated to meet subjective commitments and concerns, and disordered by contradictory interpretations imposed by one's gender, religious, racial, and social class positions. In his discussion of multiple modernities, Casanova suggests that "common modern traits or principles attain multiple forms and diverse institutionalizations in various historical contexts. . . . These modern traits are not developed necessarily in contradistinction to or even at the expense of tradition, but rather through the transformation and the pragmatic adjustment of tradition."[21] I would add that aggiornamentos act not on "tradition" per se but on traditions of knowledge that bear within them the inevitability of change as they are acted out strategically in different contexts, and as urbanization, globalization, literacy, commercialization, and other revolutions transform that context.

"Truth" is relative, plural. People know different things about being Turkish, and what is known is contingent and disputed. This debate has led to a fevered search for certainty, control, and purity, for a golden age of communal solidarity, provincial modes of propriety, and cosmopolitan civility. The disordering of categories has also allowed experimentation and unexpected convergences, especially among the young. Such experimentation, however, takes place within the still-considerable constraints of community, whether that is based on blood, soil, religion, or like-minded affiliation. Traditions of knowledge about being Turkish and being Muslim share powerful ideas about solidarity and gender that when acted out, shape the "truth" and limit the possibilities of these identities. As Özel put it:

> The peculiarity of Turkey is imagining a society that doesn't exist, shaping it in your own image and believing you've done so. You fool yourself into thinking Turkey is something it isn't. After World War II everyplace else changed except here. Kemalism had an incredible ability to reproduce itself. . . . The Welfare Party was a Kemalist party in green, not red. AKP is as well. It's not questioning certain dogmas: The sanctity of sovereignty, borders, inbredness.

One might add women's place in the national family as another shared dogma. Secular and Muslim nationalisms, in other words, despite the animosity they have generated, may share more ideas about being Turkish than issues that divide them. In this last section, I use a conversation with a liberal friend, Hasan, to illustrate the plurality and relativity of the "truth" of Turkishness.

We Have No Serial Killers

Hasan is a liberal from a conservative family background. Now in his early forties, he has worked in Istanbul's Covered Bazaar all his adult life. We meet on a summer evening with two of his friends at a special restaurant on the second floor of a non-descript building that specializes in grilled goat's throat. Özgür is a hairdresser; his girlfriend, Müjdan, works in the service sector. They are in their thirties, dressed in jeans, shirts, and sporty sweaters, the *légère* look favored by the middle class. In what terms do they describe themselves? Who are they?

> HASAN: "Turkishness (*Türklük*). We have solidarity. We're not like other countries. We're a community. We have no serial killers. We leave everything to the last minute. We believe in last-minute miracles. We're practical; we find a solution. We're pragmatic, but not programmed. We love people. We have shamanistic roots. We're Muslims, but don't resemble Arab Muslims because we became Muslims much later. We believe in soul and sorcery (*ruh* and *büyü*). We believe in people, trust one another, but there's a contradiction because we trust no one. There's always gossip. Turks have been humiliated by outsiders. We bind tightly together against foreigners."

> ÖZGÜR: "We have many relatives, big families. We show respect. It's a natural hierarchy —genetic—even in the most modern families. We show respect to elders. . . . Forty percent of our budget goes to the military. To some, this might sound high, but our geography doesn't resemble Holland's. We have a special geography, mountains; we can grow every kind of plant. We have energy sources and are a transit way. Therefore, we're very valuable and many countries want to rule us. To protect against that is expensive. We have lots of outside threats."

There is a park opposite the restaurant, which is located in a conservative area. Hasan points out the window at the working-class women in the park with their children. The women are dressed in long coats, their heads enveloped in scarves. "This isn't Turkish culture, those covered women," Hasan insists. "It's Arab culture. We're shamanic."

The liberalism displayed by Hasan and Özgür is a perfect storm of hybridity and mixing of sometimes contradictory ideas: the Kemalist threat paradigm, Republican history thesis, Central Asian shamanistic folk Islam versus Arab Islam, nationalist suspicion of outsiders, Turkish exceptionalism, the "genetic" patriarchal family, and the golden ideal of community solidarity ("We have no serial killers," that is, people who kill for impersonal reasons). Both Hasan and Özgür identify with conservative norms of family and obedience. They value trust, but trust only people in their group. At the same time, they appreciate the mixed nature of Turkishness, its boundlessness. "Turkishness means Ataturk, the state, the flag," Hasan sums up, then adds, "Everyone is mixed. We were an empire and we're still a small part of that empire. Religion and nonreligion, all ethnicities." And Müjdan? She joins the conversation but has nothing to say about nationalism or the nation, thereby illustrating, perhaps accidentally, the estrangement of women from the masculinist nation.

Like the 1998 study that represented the identities of Turkish youth as columns of simultaneously existing, sometimes conflicting, layers of ideological identities, Hasan and his friend exhibit deeply held convictions about their place in the world that combine conservative traditions and firmly patrolled national and social boundaries with postimperial expansiveness and ethnic mixing. The Turkish nation is understood to be both an open and a closed community. It might shock Hasan and Özgür to know that they share many of these views with Muslim nationalists.

ON JUNE 24, 2013, as the van sped from Ataturk Airport into the entrails of the city along new bypass roads carved through congested neighborhoods under AKP's infrastructural overhaul, I peered out the window, as I always did, to see what had changed since my last visit. Even though I had been to Turkey only a few weeks before, change had reached such a fever pitch that in the meantime anything could have happened. And something had happened. It began in Taksim, the Istanbul square that, since the beginning of the Turkish Republic, has served as the symbolic epicenter of both state patriotism and antigovernment protest. In the center of the vast plaza is the 1928 Monument of the Republic, commemorating its founding. One side of the square is dominated by the modernist rectangle of the Ataturk Cultural Center, an icon of Kemalist Republicanism and secular modernity. Built in the 1960s, this was where modern (*çağdaş*) citizens gathered to appreciate symphony, ballet, opera, and Turkish folk and classical music.[1] The upscale Marmara Hotel towers over the square. On the horizon is an enormous church, a reminder of the non-Muslim population of this district, now lost to history. Today the square is the central stop on the new Metro, another improvement under the AKP, and the gateway to Turkey's nightlife. Taksim Square also has long been the destination for all manner of parades, marches, and demonstrations and a sometimes bloody arena of confrontation between rival groups.[2] Gezi Park is a raised green area just opposite the Marmara Hotel, easy to miss and, until recently, not much used except by old men sitting on park benches and women pushing babies in strollers under the sycamore trees.

However, in response to the Erdoğan government's announcement that Gezi Park would be razed and turned into an Ottoman-themed mall, in mid-May several dozen young activists began staging a peaceful sit-in to save the park, one of the last green spaces in central Istanbul. Its location in Taksim gave it a larger, symbolic importance. On May 28, the protest was violently put down by the police, but instead of fading away, the dissent expanded into a spontaneous, countrywide, mass series of protests. The more the police attacked the protesters, the more people came out into the streets—tens of thousands of them in cities across the country, prompted to act by the increasing brutality of the police who shot tear gas canisters and rubber bullets directly into the crowd, causing severe injuries and deaths.[3] Water cannon trucks sprayed protesters with a liquid mixed with a caustic substance that burned the skin. As of mid-September, more than eight thousand people have been injured, six protesters have been killed, and one policeman died while in pursuit. Hundreds of people have been arrested and initially arraigned under draconian terrorism statutes. Police arrested lawyers and medical personnel who helped the protesters, and they attacked journalists. Newspapers that covered the protests were subjected to government censure. As of this writing, after a summer hiatus, the protests are continuing. On September 10, a sixth young protester died in unclear circumstances in the southern province of Hatay at a demonstration in part over the death of another protester.[4] The police have ordered an enormous new stockpile of tear gas canisters and armored riot-control vehicles.[5] And although the sycamores in Gezi Park are safe for the moment, the cutting down of trees and massive redevelopment projects in Istanbul and across the country are advancing without letup.

The Gezi protesters were a diverse group, mostly young, middle-class, liberal, and secular, many of them women, but as the protests spread, participants also included older people, taxi drivers, small business owners, conservatives, nationalists, leftists, Kemalists, Alevis, Kurds, LGBT, some pious young people who described themselves as anticapitalist Muslims, and a few who admitted to having voted for the AKP. Various organizations took part in the Gezi protests, but none defined it. Leftists and unionists put up their banners, LGBT their rainbow flag; Kemalists held signs saying they were Mustafa Kemal's soldiers; others skateboarded through the chaos wearing gas masks or read books to the police behind their Plexiglass riot shields. In some cases, these were individuals and groups whose interests had collided in the past. Even the young machos of rival soccer clubs, notorious for their violent clashes, worked together to protect the protesters.

In a country with a long history of violent clashes between protesters and police, May 28 was not the first instance of police brutality, but Turkey had come to a tipping point. In the Gezi clashes, a new generation of citizens, whose expectations have been shaped by twenty-first-century global concerns, social justice issues, and neoliberal expectations, confronted the remnants of twentieth-century structures of power based on autocratic, strongman rule that rests on the legitimacy of a ballot box majority and on patriarchal authority over the national "family." Just as the economic opening that began in the mid-1980s was a pivotal moment for the development of Turkish society and politics, the Gezi uprising is another, one that originates from the transformations that the economic changes brought about.

The anticapitalist Muslims, for instance, argue that in the AKP's neoliberal paradise, those who call themselves pious have in actuality forgotten their faith and instead are moving toward Islam as an upwardly mobile lifestyle choice. To protest the over-the-top fancy *iftar*, or fast-breaking celebrations, put on by AKP in Taksim

Square during Ramadan in July 2013, anticapitalist Muslims organized "ground iftars" that consisted of a line of newspapers and cloths placed on the ground along Istiklal Boulevard to which everyone was invited and everyone brought food. Compelling images emerged of a wide variety of Gezi characters sitting on the street, partaking of a communal iftar. As I explained in chapter 7, choices about "how" to be Muslim, along with deep engagement with meaning and social justice, are at the heart of the new generation's piety, especially for young women. In this, they are influenced by books, media, globalization, the market, and new opportunities, thus shaping new "truths" about what it means to be Muslim and Turkish.

The Gezi protests marked the first time in Turkey that a mass popular movement had appeared that was not linked to any particular political party, group, or ideology. In fact, the protesters in Gezi Park explicitly rejected these things. One woman held up a sign that said:

We are taking ownership of (*sahip çıkarız*)
religion without AKP
Ataturk (*Ata*) without CHP
the nation (*vatan*) without MHP
the Kurd without BDP
We are the people (*halk*)

This protest movement shattered once and for all the Western (and Turkish) cliché that Turks are divided between those who advocate secularism, Westernization, modernization, and nationalism on the one side, and Islamists who oppose Westernization and modernization and wish to impose Islamic values on the other. Both Kemalism and Islamism have, in the end, become desacralized and pushed from their plinths. As I have tried to show in the previous chapters, while categories of secular and Islamic continue to exist as identity markers ("Who is with me, and who is against me?"), they have long ceased to apply to reality on the ground, especially among Turkey's youth, who make up half of the population. Much like the studies that described Turkish youth as having simultaneous, sometimes contradictory multiple identities (p. 175), one of the lessons of Gezi is that it is becoming harder and harder to draw any firm lines. While many Kemalists still despise the headscarf, it is not uncommon to hear secularists say something like, "So what if someone covers her head, as long as they don't tell *me* what to do." During the research for this book I met a variety of pious covered women, some educated feminists, others whose families belonged to the most conservative religious traditions in Turkey; among them were the most liberal and open-minded women I had spoken to, as well as some of the most conservative, but their politics could not be predicted by the extent and form of their piety (chapter 6). Given the opportunity, pious women are primed to enter the political field. One sequence of photographs from the nighttime Istanbul protests posted on Facebook shows a veiled woman holding a large Turkish flag against her body, approaching and then arguing with a group of policemen.

Given the powerful draw of traditional family structure (in its classic form with an authoritarian patriarch and tightly choreographed male-female interaction), men's interest in maintaining the status quo differs from that of women. While men benefit from the patriarchal family system, a liberal loosening of restrictive norms tends to expand women's possibilities. Will the window of opportunity that the Gezi movement has afforded women protesters close again as power is reconsolidated in whatever shape the movement next assumes, as has been the fate of women in other uprisings discussed in chapter 8? Or can we expect a further transformation of Turkish national and social dogma, such as the cluster of ideas that links family to nation and women's sexual honor to national integrity, as women and men continue to choose their lifestyles and identities, practice hybridity, and experiment with new roles and forms of community despite government attempts to restrict them? As described in chapter 7, this process is well under way, but has been given national prominence through the protests.

Erdoğan's Masculine Impenetrability

In chapter 6, I discussed how the Turkish national image is founded upon militant masculinity and fears about penetration by outsiders, incursions that affect national honor much as the penetration of the female body affects family "honor." National and state discourse, I suggested, are mirror images of widely accepted relations within the conservative, patriarchal, authoritarian family. Nation, state, and family thus continually reinforce one another. Korkman and Aciksoz analyzed the role of masculinity and gender in Prime Minister Erdoğan's response to the Gezi uprising.

> With an aggressive, uncompromising, and domineering 'personality,' he aspires to act as every citizen's father, brother, and husband. (Indeed, one of the inventive feminist graffiti of the Gezi Park 'divorces' Erdoğan through *talaq*: 'Talaq Tayyip, talaq!') So far, this patriarchal authoritarian masculinity has been seen as one source of the charismatic popularity that has propelled Erdoğan's successful political career.[6]

Precisely because Erdoğan plays the role of the father, brother, and husband, the language of the protestors targets Erdoğan's masculinity through swearwords that question his penis size, heterosexuality, and impenetrability. . . . This masculine language of the resistance threatens to feminize Erdoğan through swear words derived from penis- and penetration-centered sexual acts. . . . In other words, the resistance is speaking the language of power.

In a counterpoint to some protesters' transgressive use of the language of penetration, a theme used by Prime Minister Erdoğan in his speeches and that was repeated in pro-government newspapers was that protesters had attacked covered women in the street. This image arouses the fear of penetration, loss of honor, and undermining of the traditional family around which the patriarchal father spins his web of protective authority. For decades, the state and the government fashioned themselves as all-powerful father figures that demanded complete obedience from their citizen children and, in return, protected them. An account of attacks on covered women is a morality tale of what will happen if you lose your father figure and submit yourself to the chaos of the global, liberal mob, a community without boundaries and without honor. Women will be the first victims if the patriarchal father (viz. Prime Minister Erdoğan) is no longer watching their backs.

THE PERSONAL IS POLITICAL

Initially, much of the Turkish media simply did not report the Gezi protests at all. Between May and September, fifty-nine journalists were fired, mostly for covering the protests from any other than the government line. Many others resigned in protest at not being allowed to do their jobs. While CNN International reported about protests so massive that cities were shrouded in tear gas, on June 1 CNN Türk played a documentary on penguins that has come to stand for the wholesale sellout of the media to corporate and government interests. People relied on social media, Facebook and Twitter, for on-the-spot news. YouTube carried footage, for instance, of police breaking into a court of law and forcibly removing lawyers and judges who had demonstrated in support of Gezi. One of the most moving images was of thousands of people—some news sites estimated up to forty thousand—crossing the Bosphorus Bridge on foot from the Asian side on June 1 after the government had ordered ferry service canceled to stop the protesters from reaching Taksim. Or you could zoom in and watch a live video feed by one man walking in the crowd from Kadiköy to Taksim.

One consequence of this new form of guerilla reportage was the personalization of activism and of the "news." This opened the door to a wide variety of creativity and humor, much of it ephemeral, but captured in a permanent record by ubiquitous individual smartphones and iPads. Turkey's youth is connected, as never before, to global discourses about environmentalism, social justice, the Occupy movement, and much else, giving them multiple references for their own desires and a grasp of what should be expected in a democratic society. They are able, for the first time, to distance themselves from the ideological indoctrination of institutions like the classroom that had shaped previous generations and that I described in chapter 3.

Indeed, a magazine cover that was never published has become one of the most famous images of the Gezi protests. The cover of *NTV Tarih*, a popular history magazine, shows an iconic Gezi scene that had been captured in a photo—police spraying pepper gas directly into the face of a surprised young woman in a red dress, an innocent passerby—but rendered as an Ottoman miniature drawing. The use of widely recognizable Ottoman imagery was especially forceful in that it co-opted the AKP's identification with the Ottoman past and its ubiquitous use of Ottoman themes. The magazine had prepared an article, "#History Written While Living," that chronicled the first nineteen days of the Gezi protests hour by hour as a form of historical documentation. The issue was never distributed. Instead, under government pressure, the owner, a large media group, closed the entire magazine down. But the cover was widely distributed on social media and itself became the basis for creative refashioning.[7]

The speed and flexibility with which "news" was processed led to rapid multiple reinterpretations and allowed the immediate co-optation of imagery and discourse by the protesters. When the prime minister used the term *çapulcu*, or looters, to refer to the protesters, they began to use the term as a self-referential logo. Hereafter, *çapulcu* (anglicized as chapuller) meant a person who fights for his or her rights; the term was widely reproduced visually and verbally, and picked up by the international media and used by sympathetic protesters abroad. A chalkboard in a cafe downhill from Taksim, where people gathered to discuss the protests, listed their new cocktails: the *Çapulcu,* the *Ayyaş* (drunkard), the *Biber Gazı* (pepper gas), and the *TOMA* (water cannon truck). Most involved a heady shot of tequila.

Individuals embodied protest in the name of the nation whether by standing before the police, imbibing provocatively named drinks, or wearing a Guy Fawkes mask[8] (quite a change from the image on p. 76), and their stance was then multiplied through the crowd. For instance, at a time when running and even walking through Taksim Square carried the risk of arrest, Erdem Gündüz stopped, faced the giant flags draped from the Ataturk Cultural Center along the side of the park, and stood still. It was hours before someone noticed that this was a form of protest, but then the image of the "standing man" (*duran adam*) spread through social media. People "stood still" in Ankara and Izmir, causing the frustrated police to arrest people for "insisting on standing." Such embodiment of national identity is familiar to Turks (p. 183). Every November 10 at 9:05 a.m., Turks across the country observe two minutes of silence to commemorate Ataturk's death in 1938. Wherever they are, they stop, get out of their cars, and stand still, literally embodying respect for the man and for the nation and communally reinscribing their national identity onto their bodies and into their lives.

The Gezi experience is an ongoing experiment in Casanova's notion of *aggiornamentos*, small adjustments to tradition that lead to change. It also illustrates my exception to Casanova's expectation that in Muslim societies emerging democratic discourse will be framed within a Muslim idiom. Instead, I argued that in today's Turkey (p. 192), nontraditional influences—from literature to the market—elicit values not directly linked to religion (or any of the other dominant ideologies like Kemalism), but that may lead people to personal piety and democratic participation. In the case of Gezi, social media, globalization, environmental and social justice discourses, and a variety of other influences converged not to overthrow tradition, but to rewrite it.

Crossing Lines

The protest was not about Islam versus secularism; the issues crossed those lines. Gezi Park has become emblematic of a much larger malaise and discontent with the increasing autocracy and authoritarianism of the ruling party, and its disregard for the wishes of the population on many issues. Grandiose urban development schemes are despoiling the environment and erasing entire historic neighborhoods, often ethnically mixed, replacing them with middle-class housing for the Muslim bourgeoisie. Government schemes include building the world's largest mosque, a third Bosphorus bridge, a third airport, and a canal between the Black Sea and the Sea of Marmara that will bisect the European half of Istanbul. These and other projects have provoked accusations of corruption, that the networks around AKP are reaping profit from private development of public land. Laws protecting public land, historical sites, and the environment and that require expert and citizen consultation have been weakened.

What the protesters had in common was a visceral reaction against Prime Minister Erdoğan's increasingly heavy-handed authoritarianism and social engineering that attempted to shape people's private lives and the environment in which they lived to fit a neoliberal, conservative, restrictive, and, in many ways, misogynist national model. As Edhem Eldhem put it in a *New York Times* opinion piece, "It is disturbing that Mr. Erdoğan, after years of successfully fighting the legacy of military control, has now chosen to revive precisely the same methods and strategies that characterized his predecessors' rule. . . . [H]e is seeking to do with the help of the police what previous governments did with the help of the army."[9] In other words, the AKP had become Kemalist.

The AKP bases its demand for obedience on its legitimacy won at the ballot box, what it calls the "national will." This constitutes a majoritarian understanding of democracy that gives the ballot box the same magical power as a military tank to manufacture rule with no checks on power. A majoritarian understanding of democracy is shared by many Turks who believe that democracy means that whichever party gets the most votes has won the right to impose its values on society. This has been the case whether the government in power banned the headscarf or banned alcohol. The result has been a weak formulation of citizenship and its attendant rights (pp. 178–179). "Democracy" then becomes a defensive gesture wielded by groups victimized by the "national will."[10] Defensive democracy and majoritarian legitimacy are both deformations of democracy that disguise the absence of tolerance and rights. Democracy requires more than legitimacy; it must also safeguard the basic rights of individuals and minorities.

As described in chapter 1, in the years immediately after AKP's 2002 election, there was an upsurge of optimism as the party appeared to combine a respect for conservatism with a liberal agenda and a healthy business orientation. This attracted a variety of supporters from across the spectrum and allowed the party to win a larger and larger percentage of the vote in every subsequent election.

The AKP toppled the military from its role as enforcer of Kemalist rule and made it a servant to the elected government, improving Turkey's democratic credentials. The Ergenekon trial, in which hundreds of officers were charged with aiding plots to topple the elected government, has ended with many former military leaders in jail for life.[11] Out of danger, however, the AKP has snapped back to deploying the formula that worked so well under previous regimes—playing on divisions in society (inside and outside enemies), top-down social engineering, and an appeal to enduring conservative values like the authority of the paterfamilias and protecting the honor of women and the family. Prime Minister Erdoğan responded to the Gezi protests in the guise of the authoritarian father punishing disobedient citizen children and protecting the national family against outsiders, a familiar and comforting role to many who fear a return to instability.

Yet, just as pious Turks once were incensed by restrictions imposed by previous secular governments on Islamic expression and wearing of headscarves in certain public places, participants in the Gezi protests were enraged by government intrusions into their private lives—what they should wear, what they should drink (restrictions on alcohol), what they should do with their bodies (for instance, the government urging that women should have three children and stay at home, and attempts to restrict abortions and Caesarian sections), and where they should live (unrelated men and women should not share a dormitory or apartment)—and the increasing arrogance of AKP supporters in demanding that only their norms be represented in society (confronting men and women kissing in public or strolling in a park together). Although on October 31, 2013, the rules were changed to allow pious female MPs to wear headscarves in the Grand National Assembly for the first time, other issues affecting women as a whole have not received the same attention. Despite an increase in violence against women, for instance, the government has shut down women's shelters and shown little interest in dealing with the problem. Many of these are issues that concern both pious and secular citizens, especially women.

Another issue that crosses pious/secular lines is anger at the AKP government for its policies on neighboring Syria, particularly for supporting a radical Islamist militia known as Jabhat al Nusra, or the Nusra Front, which has pledged allegiance to al-Qaeda, and is fighting against the Syrian regime of Bashar al-Assad. AKP has made it clear that it wants the Assad regime to fall, although public opinion in Turkey is strongly against any Turkish intervention. Consequently, al Nusra and other radical jihadis have been allowed to enter Turkey and cross into Syria to fight. Syria's brutal conflict has become a proxy war between Shiite Iran, which is supporting the Assad regime, and Sunni opponents, like al Nusra, that are funded by Saudi Arabia and Qatar. The jihadi presence in Turkey and the vast numbers of Syrian refugees from the conflict have begun to polarize Turkey as well, turning Sunni Turks against their fellow Alevi citizens, although Alevis differ from Syria's Alawites and stand outside the Syrian conflict. Even Turkish Sunnis on the border are afraid of the armed, bearded strangers in their midst. This is an issue that divides the ranks of the AKP as well as the population.

Furthermore, Prime Minister Erdoğan is attempting to change the constitution to make Turkey's parliamentary system into one that gives the president much greater powers and that would, in essence, remove the checks and balances on that power. It is clear that he himself would like to occupy that position when he reaches the end of his last term as prime minister. AKP's primary partner in reformulating the presidential system was the Kurdish party in parliament. Just before the Gezi protests began, Prime Minister Erdoğan had guided the AKP to a peace deal with the PKK that would potentially end decades of bloodshed and enmity between the Turkish state and the Kurds. This was in everyone's interest as Turkey wished to develop the area on the Turkish side of the Iraqi border, and the PKK would be free to stand with Syrian and Iraqi Kurds in a rare opportunity provided by the breakdown of the Syrian state to develop a formal regional Kurdish presence.

Indeed, Kurds initially stayed away from the Gezi protests so as not to undermine the peace deal. But Erdoğan's heated rhetoric and uncompromising stand in response to the Gezi protests soon also encompassed the Kurds, leading to a loss of faith that the government would hold up its end of the bargain, which included, among other things, an end to the indiscriminate use of the antiterror law to imprison Kurds (and that was now being used to arrest Gezi protesters). Kurds promptly joined the snowballing Gezi ranks, leading to the possibility that the prime minister's aggressive response to the Kurds might make them unwilling partners in procuring for him a more powerful presidency.

AKP has a long history of contradictory discourses supporting universalist principles of human rights while at the same time curtailing freedom of speech and opposing lifestyles that do not conform to a conservative worldview (p. 17), rooting its right to impose those norms in the "public will." The Gezi response shows the natural limit of such contradictions. The Gezi generation views social and political life as open to innovation and resents the imposition of limitations based on norms that are not their own. Nevertheless, almost half the voters will likely continue to support AKP because they desire the stability and prospects for upward mobility that the party has afforded them, and they see no other political steward into whose hands they might place their fates.

PIETY AND PROFIT

The desire for upward mobility is a powerful force both for moderation (stability is good for business) and for repression (law and order is more stable than unknown liberal openings). The AKP has played on this desire for stability by pointing over and over to its own good stewardship of the economy and the many infrastructural improvements like roads and mass transport. But a 2013 Gallup poll noted that more than one in three Turks (35 percent) rated their lives as "suffering," nearly double the 18 percent found in 2012. Most of the increasing poverty was in large cities, as people, including both supporters and detractors of the government, find it increasingly hard to make ends meet. Inflation in July reached 8.9 percent,[12] and the country is running a serious trade deficit.

Now that AKP's regional foreign policy, described in chapter 2, has largely failed and the government has received a black eye internationally for its brutality against the protesters, its 2014 election eggs are all in the increasingly unsteady economic basket. Erdoğan has tried to shift blame for economic damage to the protesters and outside enemies. For example, he blamed the protesters for destroying public property ("Who is going to pay for that?") and for chasing away tourists and shoppers and thus driving small businesses into the red. The identity of the "enemy without" changed several times, but AKP finally settled on a mysterious international cabal of Jewish financiers who plotted with the Gezi "looters" to undermine Turkey's international creditworthiness.

While his country was roiling in the initial wave of Gezi protests and their brutal repression, Prime Minister Erdoğan left the country for a few days of trade meetings in Morocco. When he arrived back at Ataturk Airport at 3 am on June 6, he was met by thousands of supporters. The prime minister was unrepentant and combative, contradicting more conciliatory statements made by officials of his own party while he was gone that offered dialogue with the protesters. He insisted that the destruction of Gezi Park would continue and that a mall would be built on that site. He reiterated his plan to tear down the Ataturk Cultural Center. He made a halfhearted apology for the extreme use of tear gas against protesters, but insisted that all countries use tear gas. He blamed the violence and destruction on the outlawed Revolutionary People's Liberation Party/Front (DHKP/C), a fringe far left group. He dismissed out of hand the protesters' demands that they had passed on to Deputy Prime Minister Bülent Arınç on June 6.

He contrasted the *çapulcu* in Gezi Park and their supporters, who banged pots and pans from their windows every night at 9 pm, with his own supporters, who instead had their eyes on piety and profit, on continuing the stability that safeguarded their upward mobility. "You won't be like those with pots and pans in their hands on the street, but [you are] youth with computers in your hands."

The crowd's response, however, makes clear another disturbing sentiment that animates the AKP's base and that echoes Turkey's Kemalist past. The crowd chanted, "Let us go, let us crush Taksim," and "Minority, do not mistake us, do not test our patience." (*Azınlık şaşırma, sabrımızı taşırma.*) Some of the protesters have been attacked by bands of stick-wielding men, at times chanting religious phrases or military march lyrics. Videos of these incidents posted on YouTube make the abstract concept of militant masculinity real.[13] After decades of Kemalist education, Edhem Eldhem points out, elements of the Turkish public react instinctively to a powerful brew of national pride, xenophobia, paranoia, and Islam as cultural elements that define them. "The average Turk isn't born a democrat."[14]

While young nationalists differ from their elders in terms of political predictability, polls show that young people also exhibit high levels of intolerance and "othering" and have conservative views on family relations and the relationship between men and women (p. 109). The Gezi generation, however, is bucking the trend toward intolerance and lack of trust and an aversion to mixing with anyone different described in chapter 5, a tradition of knowledge about "being Turkish" that had shaped most of Republican history. As I discussed on page 113, "mixing" can become nonthreatening only if it is denationalized, and, indeed, it seems that the Gezi protesters have taken that next step away from ethnic and religio-racial nationalism toward a civic nationalism in which citizenship is attributed to individuals, regardless of group membership. The Gezi phenomenon can be seen as a form of cosmopolitanism that is detached from restrictive forms of identity and parochial allegiances to nation, state, and ethnos. As nationalism is acted out in brand-new contexts during the protests, national discourse about what and who is a Turk has been transformed. New knowledge can fundamentally change what individuals think they know, initiating a cascade of variation in systems of thinking and practice, resulting in a phenomenon like Gezi.

WHAT HAS GEZI WROUGHT?

Turkey's government was freely elected, and no one, not even the protesters, disputed that. There was no desire to overturn the system or even kick out the elected AKP. There was dissatisfaction that Prime Minister Erdoğan was not acting democratically, and people would have liked to see his party remove him as prime minister (although realistically no one believed this would happen, even though he has to some extent become a liability to his party). A June poll put AKP support at 44 percent (down 6 percent since the protests began), still enough to win local elections in March 2014.[15]

Prime Minister Erdoğan, however, seemed to view the Gezi protests as attempts to unseat his government and to see himself in the same situation as President Muhammad Morsi of Egypt, a leader who also was elected by a majority and then challenged by crowds of protesters who eventually lent legitimacy to a military coup that removed him from power on July 3, 2013. In some ways, the situations of Erdoğan and Morsi were similar in that both understood their power and authority to derive from a majority at the ballot box, but had not internalized democratic principles of representing the national whole. The difference was that Turkish protesters had faith in the electoral system and agitated to be heard within the existing system, while Egyptian protesters believed that a majority by ballot box could be pushed aside by an equivalent majority behind an army.

As the last few months have shown so clearly, the AKP sees "the public will" as a mandate to make unilateral decisions without input by citizens, experts, or sometimes even parliament. Like Morsi, Erdoğan seems unable to move out of the twentieth-century definition of statesman as single-handed ruler of his people to statesman as skillful manager of diverse interests and lifestyles. The AKP and many of its followers are uncomfortable with the organized chaos that is social media and unable to envision a society composed of freely interacting individuals. Rather, they are used to looking behind a group of people for their leader or ideological visionary.

The most important outcome of Gezi is that a sizable new constituency has emerged, as yet with no name, no platform, no leader. It is the first time in Turkish history that such masses of people—many with contradictory or competing interests—have come together without any ideological or party organization. They cross class boundaries and bridge left/right, conservative/liberal, pious/secular. The protests are an urban movement, but since almost 80 percent of Turkey is now urban, with Istanbul's inhabitants alone making up 20 percent of the country's population, the protests are arguably a national phenomenon. Despite government claims that there is an international cabal steering them, the protesters' aim is to air a wide variety of complaints, but central is their demand that an elected government must also protect the rights of the people who did *not* vote for them, the rights of minorities, the rights of people whose ideas or lifestyle the electoral winners might not agree with.

However, the many people—particularly women and youth—who came out into the streets over Gezi have little say in Turkey's formal political life. After an election, the voices of those on the "wrong" side of the ballot box are discounted. The streets were the only venue where they could make themselves heard. To change the institutions that reproduce this flawed system, they will need to find a way to get into the system, perhaps as a new party. That, however, is difficult given Turkey's restrictive election rules that forbid raising funds for a new party and a 10 percent vote threshold for getting into parliament (after which the state funds the party).[16]

Nevertheless, the protests have reframed debates in Turkey and abroad away from Islamism/Kemalism as an explanatory framework and instead put the focus on shared rights and tolerance of difference. They have revealed mass discontent with the paternalism that characterized relations between society and the army and state throughout the twentieth century. As Graham Fuller noted, the Gezi uprising indicated "greater public awareness and knowledge, heightened participation, the emergence of new political forces out of traditional rural Anatolian classes, and expanded economic awareness and participation. The Turkish public simply expects more today—on economic, social, environmental and political levels."[17]

Are We Romanticizing Gezi?

In mid-July, when I returned to Turkey, I spoke with a number of small business owners, taxi drivers, housewives, and others in Istanbul. I heard a great deal of support for AKP and the prime minister and a lack of sympathy for Gezi protesters, phrased in much the same language as Erdoğan used when he said protesters were destroyers of property who caused financial damage to people and who were likely steered by outside interests. They said that the protesters threw Molotov cocktails and tore up paving stones, and therefore the police should be cracking down on them. There was sometimes a reluctant acknowledgment that there may have been excessive force used (with this statement usually coming from women, rarely from men), but the overall assessment was that the protesters deserved it for causing trouble. I suggested in one case that the people causing damage were only a small number compared to the other peaceful protesters on the street. The response: If you have fifty eggs and you find that several are rotten, what are you supposed to do with the rest? You smash them too.

In the village, Gezi might have been happening on another planet. People were not very interested, having made up their minds that this was a bunch of hooligans and that the government had the situation under control. They talked about an escaped cow, the nighttime fog that blighted the vegetables, whose granddaughter is going to school where, headache cures, food (it was Ramadan, and when people are fasting they like to talk about food). People praised AKP for the sleek highways and metro-buses that made the trip from Istanbul to the village a snap, rather than a difficult drive of many hours. But I saw little sign of AKP's promised prosperity in their lives beyond that. They are still living in an economy of pennies. A neighbor buys morning milk from another who has a cow. A family returning to the city buys two watermelons from a relative. A woman sells Amway to her network of other women. Another woman buys embroidered blouses from a relative and sells them at a stand in the city at a slight profit. But the AKP municipality, they made a point to tell me, had provided the stand. For these citizens, Prime Minister Erdoğan's promise of piety and profit still resonates. The Gezi phenomenon remains a cautionary tale, the end of which is not clear.

What Next?

How do you make democracy the weapon and discourse of power, rather than the defensive tool of the weak? How can the example of Gezi lead to a Turkey that is comfortable with a diverse and changing identity, a country based on civic nationalism where mixing is not a source of dishonor, and where the rule of law is institutionalized and the judiciary is independent enough to protect citizens' private lives and the rights of minorities? Where, as Soli Özel would put it, people can dare to be individuals (p. 105).

Some in the Gezi constituency fear a loss of innocence if they join the system by entering formal politics, by starting a party or joining an existing one. In a kind of political anarchism, they make it a point not to have political structures derived from their activism. In stark contrast to the hostile communalism being whipped up by Prime Minister Erdoğan, the Gezi protesters reject all parties and all categorizations. Instead, to show respect for diversity and to foster urban civility, they have set up local forums where residents of neighborhoods can come forward and share their views.

The Gezi youth are the product of the enormous changes in Turkish society after 1980. They are global, playful, consumerist. Turkishness is a personal attribute, just as AKP suggested that Muslimhood is a personal attribute. They represent themselves, not an ideological position, a political party, or a scheming foreign power. But as I discussed in chapter 8, the rules of power in twenty-first-century Turkey are still twentieth-century rules, and much of the country is in thrall to the familiar symbiosis of traditional family values and the state. Erdoğan even invoked the Kemalist threat paradigm—that the protests were led by shadowy outsiders (chapter 3). And many responded as they always have, by calling for the autocratic father to protect the family from penetration by outsiders, by the "marginals," by those seeking to undermine the Turkish national family's honor. The Gezi protests have heralded important steps in Turkey's transformation away from twentieth-century values and incomplete political structures toward civic nationalism and a more tolerant democratic order, but the traditional family retains a powerful hold on the national imagination and, through that, on a political system dominated by older males.

Nevertheless, between my last visit to Turkey and the next on June 24, the definition of the nation, what it means to be Turkish, and what represents that identity had already changed in the space of only a few weeks. From the window of the airport van, I saw a number of homes with Turkish flags hanging from the windows. Wait a moment, I said to myself, I thought this was a conservative neighborhood. Homes flying the flag outside of holidays tended to be Kemalist or nationalist. For Kemalists, the flag has always been a powerful statement that often went along with a picture of Ataturk displayed in the window facing out. So what did these flags mean? I realized that it was no longer possible to tell.

During the protests, both sides used the flag to mark their identity as authentic Turks. In mid-June, for instance, protesters had occupied the Ataturk Cultural Center in Taksim Square and draped it with Gezi posters and assorted leftist banners. The police chased the protesters away, pulled down their banners, and then replaced them with a giant portrait of Ataturk on a cloth hung from the top of the building and flanked by two enormous Turkish flags. I was surprised, since the flag had until then been used to signal discontent with the AKP and countered by AKP loyalists with Islamic or Ottoman symbolism (chapter 1). Social media reported that the police had decorated some of the TOMA, or armed water cannon trucks, with Turkish flags. Someone described how a protester ripped the flag from one of the TOMA and, clutching it to his chest, shouted at the driver, "You don't deserve this!"

Traditions of knowledge about what it means to be Turkish—and the symbols through which they are expressed—bear within them the inevitability of change as they are acted out strategically in different and sometimes novel contexts, and as urbanization, globalization, social media, and other revolutions transform that context. The disordering of categories has encouraged experimentation and allowed unexpected convergences, especially among the heterogeneous young. For others, change has been unsettling and evoked in them instead a desire for certainty and control, for communal solidarity and familiar modes of propriety. Turkey's *aggiorna-*

mentos, like the Gezi protests, are small earthquakes that shift the ground just enough to destabilize dogmas and make it difficult for inbred institutions to reproduce themselves fully.

Notes

1. The Kurdistan Workers' Party (*Partiya Karkerên Kurdistan, PKK*) has been fighting an armed struggle against the Turkish state since 1984 over autonomy of the Kurdish region and greater cultural and political rights for Kurds in Turkey.

2. "13 oğrenci kanlarıyla bayrak yaptı, Paşa'yı duydulandırdı [sic]," *Ihlas Haber Ajansi,* January 11, 2008. Unless otherwise specified, all translations are by the author.

3. *bianet,* January 13, 2008.

4. *Today's Zaman,* January 14, 2008. Oran is referring to the killings of Trabzon's parish priest, Father Andrea Santoro, in February 2006; the murder of three Christians accused of being missionaries in Malatya in April 2007; and other incidents. See, for instance, Grossbongardt (2006).

5. *bianet,* January 13, 2008.

6. Gündüç (2008).

7. Knaus (2009).

8. On September 14, 2010, the European Court of Human Rights issued a judgment that the Turkish state had failed to protect Dink's life by not acting on information police had about the planned murder, and that the guilty verdict had infringed his freedom of expression and made him a target for nationalist extremists. ECHR press release on the Dink case: http://cmiskp.echr.coe.int/tkp197/view.asp?action=html&documentId=873693&portal =hbkm&source=externalbydocnumber&table=F69A27FD8FB86142BF01C1166 DEA398649.

9. Samast was put up to the crime by a local man active in nationalist circles. The investigation revealed that the regional military police commander had known of the murder plan in advance but had told his subordinates (who later testified against him) to say and do nothing. In January 2012, the court sentenced Samast and his associate to lengthy prison terms but did not pursue evidence of collusion. It is widely believed that the assassination of Dink was part of a wider plot to destabilize Turkish society in preparation for a coup. A separate case, against alleged military and civilian plotters in a shadowy state-linked group called Ergenekon, is still in the courts.

10. Spickard (2004, 2). I debated using the term *ethnic* to describe the link between Turkish identity (for which the term *soy* is commonly used) and Islam but chose religio-racial as a better descriptor of the meaning of *soy*, with its emphasis on blood ties, lineage, and descent.

11. Here I am referring to mainstream Muslims, such as followers of the preacher Fethullah Gülen, AKP supporters, self-consciously Muslim businessmen, and young people experimenting with modern Muslim lifestyles. Fringe groups, like the *Alperen Ocakları* ultranation-

alist youth group, combine Muslim and racial identities and serve as shock troops for nationalist demonstrations. Although highly visible in the media, they do not represent the mainstream.

12. Cagaptay (2006).

13. Turkstat (2011). The median age of Turkey's population is 29.

14. Kandiyoti (1992, 256); Atak and Çok (2008).

15. Casanova (2011); see also Hurd (2011).

16. Quoted from Seligman's formal response to Casanova's September 15, 2010, lecture at Boston University, "The Secular, Secularizations, and Secularisms." Ahmet Kuru (2009) dissects these national practices, contrasting France and Turkey's "assertive secularism, which aims to establish a secular public sphere and confine religion to the private domain, with the "passive secularism" of the United States, which allows public visibility of religion. See also Hurd's (2008) comparison of secularism and its political effects in Turkey, Iran, the United States, and the European Union.

17. See, for instance, Ahmet Yükleyen's discussion (2011) of the ways in which various Islamic organizations in Germany and Netherlands have been transformed by their competition for European Muslim members in the "religious markets" within the different national policy and legal environments of Netherlands and Germany.

18. As it is used here, *cosmopolitanism* refers to a worldview that envisions a single "universal civilization" that renders religion invisible or reduces it to just another form of cultural group identity. (Casanova 2011, 253–254).

19. Citizens in Turkey are easily and frequently accused of high treason for a variety of reasons ranging from arguing for a democratization packet to tackle the Kurdish question (interpreted as succumbing to terrorist demands) to supporting the Annan plan to reunite Cyprus. The Turkish Law on Treason is so broad as to lend itself to different interpretations. Acts of treason include, among other things, "damaging the unity of the state" and "acting against national interests." Society's polarization is regularly expressed in mutual accusations of treason. (Yavuz 2009b)

20. Quoted in Zürcher (2010, 62).

21. Özyürek (2004, 381). For an artist's take on the ubiquity of Ataturk's image, see Mandel and Zakari (2010).

22. Toprak (2008).

23. A 2008 Pew Global Attitudes Survey found very unfavorable Turkish opinions on almost every major country asked about in the survey, and on Hamas, Hezbollah, and Osama Bin Laden. The German Marshall Fund Transatlantic Trends Survey showed similar results, as well as a decline in support for Western institutions like NATO and less interest in joining the European Union. The number of Turkish isolationists (who believe that Turkey should act alone) dropped from 48 percent in 2008 to 34 percent but still outnumbered those supporting increased alliances with other countries and groups. http://www.gmfus.org/trends/2010/about.html.

24. White (2005).

25. Navaro-Yashin (2002).

26. Turam (2007); Yavuz and Esposito (2003).

27. Personal communication, November 3, 2007.

28. White (2005).

29. Demir and Gam (2010); Demirbaş (2009).

30. Işıl Eğrikavuk, "'Holy Birth Week' causing controversy in Turkish schools," *Hürriyet Daily News*, April 22, 2011.

31. Yılmaz (2004). Türeli (2010) describes Miniaturk, Turkey's first theme park of models representing "Turkey in miniature," as an alternative to Ataturk's mausoleum in Ankara, which until then had been the epicenter of national symbolism. She suggests that visitors to the park satisfy "a yearning for alternative models in which to examine the nation." See also Hart (1999) and Özyürek (2007).

32. Bosphorus University and the Open Society Institute (2007).

33. Ali Bayramoğlu's 2006 study of pious and secular views on democratization makes clear that these are not opposing homogenous camps but, rather, exhibit similarities, particularly shared attitudes about authority, patriarchy, and community. Within each camp, there are individuals who resist change and others who creatively adapt to and embrace social transformation.

34. "Davutoğlu suggests new paradigm in Turkish–Egyptian relations, *Today's Zaman*, March 7, 2010.

35. The Roma, another officially unacknowledged minority, have been deracinated as "slum dwellers" and moved from their traditional neighborhoods by the government's urban renewal and gentrification policies. They have also been occasional targets of mob violence. See, for example, the attack on Roma residents in Manisa in January 2010, http://bianet.org/english/minorities/125087-finally-it-is-a-crime-to-humiliate-roma (accessed November 5, 2011).

36. Kasaba (2009).

37. I owe this insight to Murat Somer.

38. Watts (2010); Barkey and Fuller (1998).

39. Somer and Liaras (2010, 162).

40. Shankland (2007).

41. Yavuz (2005a, 68).

42. Some Alevi fear that recognition would give the state more control over their activities. Erdemir (2004).

43. A first step toward a new constitution was taken in September 2010 when a popular referendum approved a number of amendments to the existing constitution. The changes improve women's and children's rights, and rights of the disabled and elderly; protect the right to privacy; empower civilian courts to try military personnel; and increase the number of justices on the Constitutional Court, allowing parliament to appoint some of them. The latter two changes herald an era when the military and the high courts can no longer easily act against elected parties and governments. Secular nationalists fear that these changes will remove the last safeguards against Islamism and that Turkey will come under the sway of an authoritarian AKP that will impose conservative, religious lifestyles and eliminate its enemies without opposition.

44. A survey by Çarkoğlu and Toprak (2007) shows that a third of the population are

highly intolerant toward others who are different (Kurdish, Jewish, Armenian, Greek, atheist, gay) and a full 98 percent are intolerant to some extent (pp. 49–51). AKP and MHP voters were less tolerant than CHP voters on some of these issues (p. 55), but on the issue of veiling, 51 percent of people who considered themselves secularist and 43 percent of those with higher education said that it would disturb them if they received service from a civil servant who was covered (p. 79). More recent surveys show similar results.

45. Sancar and Atılgan (2009).

46. White (1994).

47. White (2002).

48. A survey by Çarkoğlu and Toprak (2007, 56, 86) shows that the majority of the population value democracy and civil liberties but show little sensitivity toward others' rights. Democracy is understood as a system that represents the views of the majority rather than protecting the rights of minorities.

49. Barth (1993).

50. Kentel, Ahıska, and Genç make a similar observation (2007, 3): "Although a 'shared history' is often mentioned in constructing [Turkish] nationalist discourse, individuals build up different 'histories' mainly through their personal experiences and by 'communicating' through the existing historiography."

51. *Türkiye'de Ortak Kimlik Olarak Ötekilik* (Ankara: Eğitim Bir-Sen, August 2010, 41). I have rounded off all survey numbers.

52. Yılmaz (2010). (I have summarized the last two categories as ethnic and regional.) These results are somewhat similar to those obtained in a study by Çarkoğlu and Toprak (2000) ten years earlier, in which 34 percent chose citizen; 35 percent, Muslim; 20 percent, Turk; 4 percent, Muslim Turk; and 1 percent each, Kurd and Alevi. One major difference is a consequence of the greater differentiation among "Muslim" identities in the 2010 study. Thus, while 35 percent identified themselves as "Muslim" in 2000, only 18 percent chose "devout Muslim obeying Islamic precepts" in 2010. The category Turk (based on ancestry or blood) increased by 9 percent. Comparing surveys with such different terminology is an impossible task, but it is noteworthy that the extreme Islamic right appears to have decreased in numbers, while Turkish blood–based nationalism has increased over this decade.

53. Yılmaz (2007, 38).

54. Konrad Adenauer (1999).

CHAPTER 2
ISLAM AND THE NATION

1. Tucker (1978, 595).

2. Eissenstat (2004, 245). Europeans, however, had long used the term interchangeably with Ottoman.

3. Kasaba (2009).

4. Meeker (2002) describes how the semiautonomous relationship between Black Sea coast elite families and the Ottoman center was reproduced in the Republican era within new

national structures (such as tea cooperatives). Even the hierarchy of local families remained the same.

5. Eissenstat (2004, 248).
6. Zürcher (1997).
7. Magnarella and Türkdoğan (1976).
8. Lewis (2002); Aytürk (2004).
9. Tanyeri-Erdemir (2006).
10. Cited in Tanyeri-Erdemir , p. 382.
11. Ibid.
12. Ibid.
13. Bozdoğan (2002).
14. Zürcher (1997, 136).
15. Ibid.
16. Cagaptay (2006).
17. Recently, scholars have begun to challenge this thesis by pointing to continuities in personnel, political and economic structures, and culture between the Ottoman and Republican periods. See, for instance, Meeker (2002).
18. Duben and Behar (1991).
19. Kuru (2009).
20. Ahmad (2009).
21. Baer (2009).
22. Cagaptay (2006).
23. Eissenstat (2004, 251). Early Republican magazines often featured blond and blue-eyed individuals. See, for instance, Libal's (2000) account of the nationalization of the image and care of infants.
24. Enacar (2009, 112).
25. Spickard (2004, 2).
26. Eissenstat (2004, 247).
27. Özbudun, cited in Cagaptay (2006, 106).
28. Eissenstat (2004, 251).
29. Ibid., 246.
30. Cagaptay (2006, 97).
31. Eissenstat (2004, 250; see also Guttstadt (2006).
32. Eissenstat (2004, 252).
33. Cagaptay (2006, 139).
34. Bali (2006).
35. Cagaptay (2006, 62).
36. Kasaba (2009) discusses the remarkable cultural variation and religious heterodoxy that characterized the Ottoman hinterland.
37. White (2010a).
38. Zürcher (1997, 244–245).
39. Eighty-three percent of Turks define themselves as religious (Çarkoğlu and Kalaycıoğlu 2010).

40. Zürcher 276–277.

41. I tell the story of an attack with a sledgehammer that I witnessed in White (2002, 39–40).

42. Zürcher, 277.

43. In 1977 a British friend, an apolitical English teacher living in Ankara, was attacked on the street by a group of ultranationalists and beaten up. Eventually, my friend related, his attackers seemed to grasp that he was English. They stopped hitting him, dusted him off, and indicated his mustache. Later, someone explained to him that he was sporting a "leftist" mustache.

44. See de Bellaigue's account of the history of an eastern Turkish town in which he untangles overlapping layers of politics, history, shifting ethnic and religious identities, family feuds, and personal animosities (2010).

45. Marcus (2007).

46. Zürcher, 277

47. Ibid., 292.

48. Özal had links to the Nakşibendi Sufi order, but he lived a secular lifestyle, and the Motherland Party platform was not based on Islam.

49. When I returned to Turkey in 1983, I was startled by some of the changes that had occurred in the five years I had been absent. An entire generation—the politicized youth of the 1970s—had been silenced. Close friends refused to speak about politics, even in private. Many encouraged their children to be apolitical, not to join organizations, to focus instead on education, jobs, marriage, and upward mobility. The population appeared to have been struck by amnesia about the previous two decades and even the vicious crackdown following the coup. Some of this amnesia can be explained by fear and emotional exhaustion. Hundreds of leftists, some of my friends among them, were tortured in jail and their lives irrevocably altered by death, disease, mental illness, and the inability to resume their careers or to build stable family lives.

50. White (1994).

51. *Turkey's Tigers: Integrating Islam and Corporate Culture* (2006), Films for the Humanities and Sciences.

52. ESI (2007).

53. Saktanber (2002).

54. Navaro-Yashin (2002).

55. Turam (2007); Yavuz and Esposito (2003).

56. Toprak (2009).

57. Çarkoğlu and Toprak (2000, 45).

58. Ibid., 43, 27.

59. Gülalp (2004).

60. Erbakan's earlier National Salvation Party had drawn its main support from towns in the underdeveloped eastern and central Anatolian provinces and did not do well in the cities.

61. In 2010 the AKP mayor of Ankara proposed a smiling Angora cat as a city logo, presumably to circumvent the court's decision, but the court did not allow the substitution of cat for Hittite sun.

62. Kentel (1995); see also Çarkoğlu and Toprak (2000).

63. Öncü (1995, 60–62).

64. White (2002).

65. Güvenç (2009).

66. Çarkoğlu and Toprak (2000).

67. This may be changing as Islamic activists and the media bring "modern" Islamic practices and encourage conformity. See, for example, Hart (2009).

68. White (2005).

69. Interview with the author, Istanbul, 1995.

70. Yılmaz (2007, 39–40).

71. Led by a figurehead, since Erbakan was banned from political office.

72. Kuru (2006, 8).

73. For a comparison of Turkey's laicism and secularism as these are expressed in other societies, see Kuru (2009).

74. Yumul (2010).

75. Reformist modernist theologians affiliated with Ankara University's School of Theology developed a Turkish brand of Islamic philosophy that influenced the AKP government (White 2005).

76. Interview with the author, Ankara, November 30, 2002.

77. "Northern Iraq's first Turkish university opens," *Today's Zaman*, August 29, 2010. See also the statement by Harun Akyol on Fethullah Gülen's website, "An Alternative Approach to Preventing Ethnic Conflict: The Role of the Gülen's Schools in Strengthening the Delicate Relations Between Turkey and the Iraqi Kurds with Particular Reference to the 'Kirkuk Crisis,'" December 2, 2008, http://en.fgulen.com/conference-papers/gulen-conference-in -washington-dc/3126-an-alternative-approach-to-preventing-ethnic-conflict.html.

78. Davutoğlu (2001).

79. Davutoğlu's address to Kokkalis Foundation Forum, Harvard University, September 28, 2010.

80. "Davutoğlu suggests new paradigm in Turkish–Egyptian relations," *Today's Zaman*, August 29, 2010.

81. "Yeni Osmanlılar sözü iyi niyetli değil," *Sabah*, December 4, 2009.

82. Personal communication from Ayşe Önal, November 2009.

83. Finkel (2008).

84. Steinvorth (2008).

CHAPTER 3
THE REPUBLIC OF FEAR

1. Beller-Hann and Hann (2001).

2. For a critical review of the evidence in the case, see Jenkins (2009).

3. There are many Turkish anthropologists working outside the nationalist paradigm, some of whom are cited here, but the institutional setting, the charged social atmosphere, and

age-based hierarchies of academic power make nationalism a default framework that scholars have told me they must sidestep or appease to do their work.

4. The fact that Dalan understood Obama's "racial" lineage in terms of his religion is in line with Turkish beliefs that to be of the Turkish 'race' means to be Muslim. It is also somewhat ironic in that some right-wing Americans have since maintained that Obama is Muslim through his father.

5. Guler (2003).

6. Bila (2007).

7. Aydinli (2009) suggests that the generals' relative acquiescence to the AKP government's recent actions, including the Ergenekon trial, means that the progressive minority position in the Turkish military, that seeks global engagement and integration with the EU, might be on the ascendance. Cook, however, writes (2007, 132) that "ultimately Turkish military commanders chose to consent to certain aspects of the EU reform program in the belief that they could control the process," a miscalculation.

8. Since our conversation was not explicitly on the record, I will not identify the officers further.

9. See Birand's (1991) account of life within the Turkish military, and Cizre (2008) on military–government relations. As of May 2012, family members may no longer be excluded from military social establishments for wearing religious clothing, nor will officers be punished if their wives wear headscarves.

10. The term *luminous* plays on *aydın* (light) and its New Turkish meaning of "intellectual." The idea is that Ataturk provided the light by which the nation could see a path forward, led by its enlightened intellectuals and leaders. Light is also a central metaphor in the Gülen Movement, but using the term *nur*, which has the additional traditional meaning of the "light of saintliness." And, finally, the AKP logo is a lightbulb—a symbol of modernity and technological progress, as well as intimations of light in the sense of nur. Critics have compared the shape of the filament inside the lightbulb to a Quran stand.

11. "Sanık paşaların eşleri de mitingdeydi," *Radikal*, May 17, 2009.

12. Özakman (2005).

13. Abdullah Gül, an economist, worked at the Islamic Development Bank in Saudi Arabia between 1983 and 1991.

14. These terms have been in use since the nineteenth century to distinguish between the "old" *a la Turka* Ottoman and "new" *a la Franga* Westernized lifestyles, including habits of bodily comportment (for instance, sitting on the floor at a low table to eat versus sitting on a chair at table). Europeans were referred to as Franks. The term *a la Turka* today is often used to disparage behavior that is seen to be rural or lower class, not sufficiently modern or Westernized.

15. Interview with the author, December 17, 2008.

16. German Marshall Fund (2009).

17. The term was first used in 1923 in a debate in Turkish parliament about repatriating Turkish troops from Yemen. The speaker used *Türkiye'li* for Turkish, meaning literally "of" or "from" Turkey. This precipitated a discussion about what that meant. If it meant "an officer residing within our borders," then that might prevent those of "Turkish blood" who had been

raised outside the new borders, but who had "maintained their Turkish identity," from being repatriated (Eissenstat 2004, 249).

18. Prime Minister Erdoğan has suggested that Turkish *üst kimlik* (upper identity, like the German *Leitkultur*) is *Türkiyeli* and its lower identity is Muslim, but in the *Eğitim-Sen* study of national identity, only 2.3 percent of respondents chose Türkiyeli as their primary cultural identity.

19. Survey questionnaires that list such categories as the only potential answers force all respondents, both men and women, to choose a label, even if they would not do so in daily practice. In my open-ended discussions with women, they were less likely than men to present themselves by reference to these categories.

20. Şirin (2009).

21. Akyol (2006).

22. Bozkurt (2009).

23. Yavuz (2009).

24. White (2005).

25. Kaplan (2006, 191).

26. Despite their emphasis on good-quality secular education in Gülen-sponsored schools, the Gülen Movement is a major supporter of creationism. Another proponent is the cult leader Adnan Oktar, who has spent a fortune on publishing and disseminating works promoting creationism, including an enormous, high-quality coffee-table book that was mailed to nearly every scholar in the United States. I interviewed Oktar at his home in 2008. He is not affiliated with the Gülen movement but, rather, claims to have a following of wealthy young Turks who have given him this money. The easy availability of such books, free of cost, with color photographs mimicking science texts, has led to their entering the chronically underfunded Turkish school system.

27. Çayır (2004).

28. Ibid., 103.

29. Bora (2004).

30. Cited in Kaplan (2006, 61).

31. Ibid.

32. Altınay (2004a).

33. Altınay (2004b).

34. Ibid., 86.

35. Altınay (2004a).

36. Bora (2004, 62–65).

37. Ibid., 67–68.

38. Çayır (2004, 98).

39. Altınay (2004a, 68).

40. Cited in Bora (2004, 62–65).

41. Bora (2004, 69).

42. Altınay (2004b, 88–89).

43. "Bayburt'ta 93. yıl zulmü," *Radikal*, February 22, 2011; "From the Bosphorus: Straight—'Pity' is the only word," *Hürriyet Daily News*, February 23, 2011.

44. Çayır (2004, 103).

45. Altınay (2004b, 82–83, 68).

46. Ceyhan (2009).

47. Jones (2009).

48. "Evinde Kürtçe ders veren 10 yaşındaki kıza soruşturma açıldı," *Radikal*, August 26, 2009.

49. Sinclair-Webb (2006).

CHAPTER 4

THE MISSIONARY AND THE HEADSCARF

1. Özyürek (2009).

2. "TSK: Misyonerler, Alevileri ve Kürtleri hedef aldı," *Zaman,* December 31, 2004. The original report is no longer available on the Armed Forces website.

3. Cited in Özyürek (2009, 100). Ecevit, who lived a secular lifestyle, claimed Islamic identity as an expression of her nationalism. She said she wanted to live a "healthy Islam . . . cleaned up from superstition and religious exploitation" and railed equally at Islamic veiling and at Christian conversion.

4. "Suspicious villagers reject EU funding," *Today's Zaman*, October 7, 2007.

5. Yıldırım (1999).

6. Özalpdemir (2005).

7. Özyürek (2009, 92).

8. Pew (2008).

9. Özyürek (2009, 101).

10. Vick (2006).

11. Özyürek (2009, 101).

12. *Cumhuriyet* 1: http://www.youtube.com/watch?v=CBSs9YYzH88 (accessed November 8, 2009).

13. "Europe keeps eye on Assyrian monastery ownership," *Hürriyet*, December 16, 2008.

14. Özkırımlı and Sofos (2008, 169); see also Dinçşahin and Goodwin (2011).

15. Özkırımlı and Sofos (2008, 166, 171).

16. Garih, who was Jewish, was stabbed to death in 2001 beside the tomb of a Sufi sheikh that he admired and visited regularly. Although the assailant was arrested and claimed robbery as a motive, it is asserted by people close to the family that Garih was murdered as part of an extortion attempt linked to shady figures in Turkey's "deep state," some of whom are under indictment in the Ergenekon trial.

17. Laws become effective when published in the *Resmi Gazete, (Official Gazette)*.

18. Jenkins (2004).

19. Oran (2007).

20. *Hürriyet*, December 15, 2008.

21. Hudson (2009).

22. Ceylan and Irzık (2004).

23. "Bahçeli'den üstü kapalı tehdit: Anadolu yeniden fethedilir," *Radikal*, August 29, 2009.

24. Çarkoğlu (2009, 456).

25. Göle (1996, 2011) has written extensively about the relation between veiling and modernity.

26. Scott (2007, 10). See Kuru (2009) for a comparison of the roles of religion and the state in France and Turkey.

27. *Cumhuriyet* 2: http://www.youtube.com/watch?v=WwTzascPpCQ&NR=1 (accessed November 8, 2009).

28. *Cumhuriyet* 3: http://www.youtube.com/watch?v=wfbygWnBTqo (accessed November 8, 2009).

29. While this would imply a no vote, the same independent producer also made a film promoting a yes vote, so the political intent behind the videos is unclear. Nevertheless, both videos use elements of a common recognizable discourse to make powerful statements, http://vimeo.com/14527052 (accessed September 9, 2010).

30. Personal communication, November 12, 2009.

31. "President Gül files lawsuit against CHP's Arıtman," *Today's Zaman*, December 23, 2008.

32. "'Let the deputy PM perform circumcisions on PKK members,' says BDP head," *Hürriyet Daily News*, August 31, 2010.

33. Village guards are hired and armed by the state to guard villages against PKK incursions. Akyol interview, 2008.

34. Although de Bellaigue, in his account of an eastern Turkish town (2011), mentions that local Armenians joined the PKK.

35. Baer (2009, 64). Moving to Turkey saved the Dönme from the Holocaust. Almost all of Salonica's Jews were killed under the Nazis, who would also have considered Dönme to be Jews.

36. Baer, 172.

37. Bulun (2010).

38. Poyraz (2007).

39. Özyürek (2009, 9).

40. Quoted in Özcan (2009).

41. Lewis (2002).

42. Cited in Özyürek (2009,106).

43. Ceyhan and Irzık (2004,78). The gendered aspect of this definition of citizenship should also be noted. "Dying for the homeland" refers to the male soldier and provides no obvious role for a female citizen.

44. Nagel (1998, 256); Najmabadi (1997, 445).

45. Özyürek (2004).

46. Çinar (2001).

47. Hart (2009).

48. Neyzi (2001, 421). Özyürek suggests (2009, 109–110) that the murders in Malatya, in which the three Christians were tied up and killed like sacrificial animals, were meant to ritually cleanse Malatya of its Armenian roots. Since the assassination of Hrant Dink, a Malatya native, several months earlier, Malatyans had been taunted by outsiders (for instance, rival

soccer teams) who called them Armenians and implied they could not be true nationalist Turks. The Malatyans in turn taunted the opposing team by calling them PKK (Kurdish guerillas), leading to a violent fight between fans. Malatyan nationalists responded with a You-Tube video replete with ultranationalist and religious slogans that was viewed 10,553 times in eight months. Christians responded with a video of massacres of Armenians in Malatya with Christian music, viewed 14,409 times. Özyürek concludes that within this context the killers "sacrificed" the three converts "with the hope that their mixed past would be forgotten and forgiven."

49. Scott (2007, 1).

50. Ibid., 15, 61.

51. Çinar (2001).

52. I would like to thank Cemal Kafadar for this insight.

53. Davutoğlu's address to Kokkalis Foundation Forum, Harvard University, September 28, 2010.

54. Barçın Yinanç, "Turkey courts Chinese tourists with Iskender and ice cream at Shanghai Expo 2010." *Hürriyet Daily News*, September 17, 2010.

55. Çarkoğlu (2003).

56. Küçükural (2005, 78, 70, 117).

57. Yılmaz (2007).

58. Çarkoğlu and Kalaycıoğlu (2010).

59. Pew Transatlantic Trends (2007).

60. Şirin (2009).

61. Based on content analysis of secular and Islamic newspapers, Somer (2011, 511) suggests that Turkish Islamists' thinking democratized considerably during the 1990s, although their approach to pluralism and liberal values remains a work in progress. He makes the observation that "religious actors' adoption of more democracy may paradoxically make some secular actors less democratic."

62. Bayramoğlu (2009, 144–145).

63. Çınar (2001).

Chapter 5
No Mixing

1. The list included six Sufis and other religious leaders, one Alevi poet, an Armenian musician and a rock musician of Armenian-Azeri descent, two Kurdish poets, two leftist writers, a nationalist academic who wrote Turkey's national anthem, and one woman, Sabahat Akkiraz, a Turkish folk musician. "Erdoğan lists controversial people central to Turkey's culture," *Hürriyet Daily News*, October 9, 2009.

2. "MHP'li Vural: Türk milleti mozaik degil mermer," *Radikal* October 5, 2009.

3. Ibid.

4. Kentel et al. (2007).

5. Personal communication, March 26, 2008.

6. Lindholm (2008).

7. Neyzi (2001, 425, 423).

8. Atak and Çok (2008).

9. UNDP Development Report: State of Youth Survey, Turkey (2008).

10. Young women's labor force participation rate in 2009 was only 28 percent, but even so, it was higher than women's overall participation rate of 24 percent (compared with men's 72 percent). Ercan (2010); World Bank and TSPM (2009).

11. Neyzi (2001, 426).

12. Kandiyoti (1992, 256).

13. Neyzi, 425.

14. Respondents in the OECD *Education at a Glance 2010* study were asked to place themselves on a scale from 0 to 10, where 0 means "You can't be too careful," and 10 means "Most people can be trusted." Sweden showed a one-point decline in trust at higher educational levels but at much higher levels of trust overall.

15. Pew (2007).

16. Baer (2010, 143,147).

17. Eissenstat (2004), cited in Baer (2010, 143).

18. Baer (2010, 147). The Greek minority of Istanbul and several other small populations were allowed to remain.

19. Eissenstat (2004, 248).

20. Baer (2010, 144, 239).

21. Ibid., 142.

22. Akdamar was spared further destruction because for at least a decade it was an off-limits military camp. Prior to that it had reportedly been used as a discotheque.

23. Chaliand (1993, 58). One bomber was piloted by Sabiha Gökçen, Ataturk's adopted daughter and Turkey's first female military officer and pilot.

24. Pew (2008, 2009, 2010). In line with Turkey's defensive posture, 36 percent of respondents also had unfavorable views of Saudi Arabia and Pakistan; 24 percent, of Iran and China; and 27 percent, of India. Indeed, few Turks held favorable views of any of the countries asked about in the poll. Only 6 percent had a favorable view of Hamas, and 3 percent of Hezbollah in Lebanon. The United States received its lowest favorability rating in every Pew Global Attitudes survey conducted between 2006 and 2009, when it had risen to 17 percent. Positive views of the European Union plummeted from 58 percent in 2004 to 22 percent in 2009, although they rose somewhat to 28 percent in 2010. Nevertheless, 54 percent still wish to join the European Union (down from 68 percent in 2005). Turks tend to believe the negative feelings are mutual; 68 percent think their country is generally disliked, the highest percentage among the 22 countries surveyed, matched only by the United States—60 percent of Americans think the United States is generally disliked abroad.

25. Toprak (2009); Çarkoğlu and Toprak (2000, 2006); see also "Farklılıklar zenginliğimiz değil korkumuz olmuş," *Radikal*, September 30, 2009; "4 kişiden 3'ü 'içki içen komşu' istemiyor," *Milliyet*, May 31, 2009.

26. Toprak et al. (2009, 6).

27. Toprak et al. (2009).

28. Küçükural (2005).

29. Cited in Karaveli (2009, 2).

30. "'Kurdish' firetruck 'divides' Black Sea town." *Hürriyet Daily News*, March 4, 2010.

31. Greek nationalists backed by the Greek military junta had attempted to stage a coup in Cyprus, with the aim of annexing the island. Turkey sent in troops, dividing the island into Greek and Turkish sectors, a situation that remains unresolved today. In 2004, the Greek sector joined the European Union, disregarding a referendum that indicated a strong desire on the part of Turkish Cypriots to reunite. At present, the Turkish sector has diplomatic recognition only from Turkey.

32. Mills (2010).

33. Üstel and Kaymaz (2009, 5–53) interviewed forty well-educated secular professionals and found that they divided society into "us and them" and felt threatened by those with different values. They did not like to be around women wearing headscarves, did not like the AKP or Kurds, and did not support broader rights for non-Muslim minorities. They admitted to having non-Muslim and other minority-group friends, but said they avoided talking about these issues with them for fear of creating tension. Nevertheless, they expressed a "nostalgic unity" with Turkey's non-Muslim minorities that was bound up with nostalgia for the modern (*çağdaş*) city, with Kurds being the most distant from that civilized ideal.

34. Şirin (2009).

35. Barth (1993).

36. Starr argues (2009, 5–53) that the possibility of cosmopolitanism and its "sense of an expanded world" is intimately linked to empire, to "the cultural fusion made possible by military conquest," making it short-lived in the nationalist present. In her study of Egypt, Starr describes how contemporary filmmakers and writers negotiate the recollection and representation of Egypt's "cosmopolitan era" in order to undermine the romantic myth of coexistence.

37. Barth (1993).

38. "Lawyer and writer Fethiye Çetin: 'My identity has never been purely Turkish,'" May 20, 2006, http://www.journalistinturkey.com/stories/human-rights/fresh-air_22/.

39. Altınay and Türkyılmaz (2011, 4).

40. Interestingly, I saw few covered heads among the demonstrators. Islamist men would be unmarked, but if there are no covered women—always placed in the forefront of public political statements—there is unlikely to be any sizable contingent of pious men.

41. "Dikkat! Melezler geliyor!" *Taraf*, November 20, 2008.

42. "NGO files complaint against minister," *Hürriyet Daily News*. February 29, 2012, http://www.hurriyetdailynews.com/ngo-files-complaint-against-minister.aspx?pageID=238&nID=14874&NewsCatID=339 (accessed February 29, 2012).

43. Öncü (2002, 185).

44. Stokes (1993); Özgür (2006).

45. Aracı (2010).

46. Öncü (2002, 185).

47. Öncü (1999,105).

48. Ibid., 112. Nationalist fears of hybridity expressed as stereotypes of migrant men's

sexual rapaciousness and their dangerous penetration into urban, civilized space afflict other populations as well. Like *maganda*s, Arabs in France are hybrid creatures perceived to be a threat to the social order and polluting the city. The French, Scott writes (2007, 52), see Arab men as obscene, lascivious, excessively and unacceptably sexual, far from the tradition and religion in their place of origin that might have restrained their impulsivity. Even if they changed their clothing, assimilation was not possible.

49. Interview with the author, December 17, 2008.

50. For an account of urban migration and the development of illegal housing from the beginning of the Republic to the present, see White (2010b).

51. A similar debate erupted over whether pissoirs were un-Islamic. In August 2009 the governor of Ordu Province asked the official religious authorities whether the pissoir was allowed in Islam. The *müftü* responded that urinals were against the Islamic religion and, furthermore, were unhealthy, since they were unhygienic and because urinating while standing up caused prostate cancer. As a result, urinals in mosques throughout the province were moved. A few weeks later the governor was recalled and the pissoirs reinstalled. "Pisuvarlar özgürlüğüne kavuştu," *Radikal*, September 16, 2009.

52. "Hair today, prime minister tomorrow," *Monocle*, August 24, 2010, http://www.monocle.com/monocolumn/2010/08/24/hair-today-prime-minister-tomorrow/.

53. Knudsen (2006, 2008) analyzes the Black Sea coast fishing industry to explain the cultural link between urban restaurant fish consumption, alcohol consumption, and Kemalism.

54. Berrin Karakaş, "Evleri ayırdık!" *Radikal*, November 28, 2010.

55. Turkstat (2011). In 2008 the World Economic Forum ranked Turkey 123rd among 130 countries on measures of gender empowerment. Turkey's low ranking on this and other measures of gender status is due primarily to women's extremely low and still-declining labor participation rate (down from 34 percent in 1988) and the low numbers of women in public life. (World Bank 2009)

56. Nine percent of the Grand National Assembly is female; only 27 of 3,000 mayors are women.

57. Ayata (2002).

58. Navaro-Yashin (2002).

59. *Sabah*, November 24, 2002.

60. *Milliyet*, November 14, 2002.

61. *Zaman*, October 28, 2002.

62. Seufert (2002).

63. Meeker (1991, 37). Çarkoğlu and Kalaycıoğlu also found in their 2009 national survey that about half the Turkish population is for some kind of social change, but for 34 percent of those desiring change, it would ideally take the form of going back to a past age "to reconstruct the old social order of the passing traditional, agricultural society in Turkey" (p. 113).

64. Toprak (1981, 101).

65. Meeker (1994, 31).

66. White (2002).

67. Erdoğan laid claim to the unity of Turkey's diversity—Turkey as a mosaic, not marble

—by listing the names of those who have suffered from PKK terrorism and from torture in Turkish jails, and by listing eastern cities of which "we are children" and those who are "our true [*öz*, biological] siblings": Turk, Kurd, Laz, Circassian, Bosnian, Georgian, Romani, and Arab. He followed this up by naming the Ottoman victories these "siblings" had participated in together and emphasizing that they pray together and in the same direction and are walking toward the same future. "Erdoğan Dıyarbakır'da konuştu: Sizi çok seviyoruz be...," *Radikal* September 3, 2010.

68. Somer and Liaras (2010); Üstel and Kaymaz (2009, 5–53).

69. http://www.tarlabasiistanbul.com/.

70. Potuoğlu-Cook (2006).

71. Susanne Fowler, "Art walk turns into street fight in Istanbul," *New York Times*, November 10, 2010, http://www.tarlabasiistanbul.com/2010/10/under-construction-a-stroll-through-tophane/.

72. Foucault (1975).

73. Delaney (2004).

74. Hall (1996).

75. "Turkey alcohol curbs raise secular fears," *BBC*, January 12, 2010, http://www.bbc.co.uk/news/world-europe-12174905. The following are some of the regulations passed over the past two years: alcohol is banned from food and sports advertising and from events for young people; sales are limited to licensed shops and restaurants; alcoholic beverages and cigarettes may not be sold outside their original packaging or be presented as promotional prizes; zoning has become more restrictive; the number of available liquor licenses has been reduced; and taxes have been raised. Harassment of liquor store owners has been reported in the news.

76. Ahmad (2003).

77. "Turks barred from receiving sperm or egg donations abroad," *Hürriyet Daily News*, March 15, 2010.

78. Demirel's story received heavy media coverage. "5 aylık olan Sevda Demirel çocuğunu aldırması için tehdit edildiğini dile getirdi," *En Son Haber*, August 21, 2010, http://www.ensonhaber.com/sevda-demirel-tehdi-ediliyor.html.

79. Translation from the Turkish by Yigal Schleifer, http://istanbulcalling.blogspot.com/2010/10/sowing-seeds-of-paranoia.html.

CHAPTER 6
SEX AND THE NATION

1. Interview with the author, November 24, 2008.

2. I use a pseudonym to safeguard her privacy. For the same reason, I do not identify individuals I spoke with unless my interlocutors are professionals or public persons, and the conversation is officially "on the record"; or if the person has given me permission to use her name, and the content of our conversation is such that no harm could result from publishing it.

3. This reminded me of a comment made in the 1990s by a young Islamist man from a squatter area. When I asked him why he had switched his vote from Erbakan, the Islamist party leader, to right-of-center Tansu Çiller, he replied, "She's very manly (*erkekçe*)."

4. Tekeli (2010, 122) notes that women's share in property ownership is 8 percent.

5. See Önal's 2008 interviews with men jailed for having carried out "honor killings" to get a sense of the intense social pressure that "requires" purification of the family's honor and pushes men to kill the women closest to them— their sisters, wives, mothers. The pressure may come from women in the family and community as well as from men, as the loss of namus affects the entire family.

6. The term *ibne* is from the Arabic, where it also has the learned meaning "daughter." (*Redhouse Sözlüğü* 1990)

7. "CHP'den Erdoğan'a mayın sorusu," *Vatan*, May 25, 2009. For more about the mine clearing law, see Akgonenc (2009).

8. *Hürriyet Daily News*, March 6, 2009.

9. Çarkoğlu and Kalaycıoğlu (2009a 133). It was widely believed that this treatment was U.S. retaliation for the March 1, 2003, vote by the Turkish parliament that denied the United States the right to use Turkish soil to stage the invasion of Iraq.

10. "Yargı'nın Dağlıca kararı: Asker silah bırakıp teslim olmaz," *Radikal*, January 20, 2010.

11. Ayşe Karabat, "Sexist journalist condemned by women's rights groups," *Today's Zaman*, December 6, 2008.

12. This makes an interesting comparison with women's views that they are naturally more "open" than men, something they value positively.

13. Amnesty International (2006).

14. "İlköğretim öğrencisine gebelik testi," *Radikal*, April 27, 2011.

15. Parla (2001).

16. Ibid.

17. The impetus was the election of Şafak Pavey as CHP Istanbul representative. Pavey wears a prosthetic leg. She herself has said she is not bothered by wearing skirts. The proposal to change the regulations failed when a rider was added to allow headscarves. An exasperated Pavey has called the intense media focus on her leg a form of harassment.

18. Parla (2001); Berktay (1995).

19. Kaplan, for instance, described this in textbooks in a southern Turkish village. The books used in the curriculum would have been issued by the state and would presumably have been the same at all schools (2006, 186).

20. This explains the widespread belief that any children who suckled at the same semen-originating breast are related and may not marry. See Kaplan (2006, 212fn32).

21. Ibid., 185.

22. White (1994).

23. Emine Özcan, "Prosecutor denies transsexual singer right of free speech," *bianet*, February 11, 2009.

24. Altınay (2004b, 84).

25. Delaney (1991). Women from elite families, like former Prime Minister Tansu Çiller,

are exceptions in that they carry on family identity, especially in the absence of sons. In a class-based hierarchy like Turkey, status trumps gender. When they married, Çiller's husband was the one to change his name.

26. Interview with the author, December 17, 2008.

27. Baron makes the important observation that the convention of presenting political abstractions in female form dates to antiquity. Imperial centers and their colonies often were rendered as a woman, although the practice was neither universal nor consistent (2005, 7).

28. Berkovitch (1997).

29. Sasson-Levy (2002).

30. Baron (2005, 5).

31. Baron (2005, 1–3).

32. Nagel (1998, 254).

33. Scott (2007, 54–55).

34. Baron (2005, 219).

35. Nagel (1998, 261), citing Young (1993, 26).

CHAPTER 7
CHOICE AND COMMUNITY

1. Çarkoğlu and Kalaycıoğlu (2009a, 119).

2. Deeb (2006).

3. Turam (2007, 14–15).

4. Mahmood (2005).

5. For an example, see White (2002, 216–218).

6. Çayır (2006).

7. White (1994).

8. Mandaville (2011, 24, 26, 23). Patton describes AKP's attempt to combine neoliberalism with an Islam-flavored communitarianism as "responsible individualism, self-help, market-based inclusion, and the ethics of community combined with the dynamics of the free market" (2009, 448).

9. Census figures show that 65 percent of Turkey's population lives in urban areas.

10. Çarkoğlu and Kalaycıoğlu (2009a,119).

11. Hyden defines the economy of affection as "a network of support, communications and interaction among structurally defined groups connected by blood, kin, community or other affiliations, for example, religion" (1983, 8).

12. Özyürek (2004).

13. Konrad Adenauer Foundation (1999); Seufert (2002).

14. Şirin (2009); Jan Felix Engelhardt, "Interview with Selçuk Şirin," http://en.qantara.de/webcom/show_article.php/_c-476/_nr-1215/i.html (accessed April 9, 2011).

15. Çarkoğlu and Kalaycıoğlu (2009a, 79, 142).

16. Ibid., 92, 78, 79.

17. The Konrad Adenauer study (1999) showed a distinct social class divide in attitudes

toward relations between unmarried men and women and premarital sex, and the willingness to discuss one's relationship or marriage with outsiders, with lower-class respondents showing much lower tolerance for these than middle- and upper-class respondents. Seufert (2002).

18. This situation was extensively documented by Human Rights Watch (2011) in their report "'He Loves You, He Beats You': Family Violence in Turkey and Access to Protection."

19. Turkstat (2011); World Bank and Turkish Prime Ministry (2009).

20. "Erdoğan'ın 'İstikrar sürsün' hükümeti," *Radikal*, July 7, 2011.

21. A play on feminist writer Duygu Asena's pathbreaking 1987 novel about women's oppression, loveless marriage, and their agency and desire, *The Woman Has No Name* (*Kadının Adı Yok*).

22. Kandiyoti (1992, 256).

23. Nagel (2010).

24. Parla (2001).

25. Saigol (2008); Najmabadi (1997, 445).

26. Yıldırım (1999).

27. Najmabadi (1997, 446).

28. Interview with the author, December 2, 2008.

29. Aydın (2005, 8).

CHAPTER 8
CONCLUSION

1. A 2010 study by Küçükcan reported that 74 percent of Turks have a negative attitude toward Armenians and 72 percent toward Jews, although the numbers are somewhat lower for younger people. Thirty-nine percent have negative feelings toward Arabs, 35 percent toward Europeans, and 65 percent toward Americans.

2. Polls cited in the text break down the percentages of the population holding these views in various ways. Perhaps more important is the insight that there is a continuum: some parts of the population exhibit entrenched Kemalist and Islamist views and a suspicion of change, while a more mobile flank welcomes choice and change, whether it is in the direction of more liberal cosmopolitanism or a golden age of Islamic conservatism.

3. "Hürrem hatırası," Milliyet.com.tr, April 20, 2011; "Osmanlı hatırası!" *Radikal*, July 9, 2011.

4. Deeb (2006); Clark and Schwedler (2003).

5. It is relevant to point out that during the crisis years of World War II, American women were celebrated for entering the labor force in great numbers, but in the postwar American Dream of the 1950s and 1960s, women ideally were housewives who had the luxury of not working. They were able to devote themselves entirely to family life in suburbs that, during the day, were largely female spaces. The declining rate of female labor force participation in Turkey coincided with a movement from agricultural labor to city living, upward mobility, and a concomitant desire to gain attributes of distinction within that context.

6. Baron (2005, 219–220).

7. Altınay (2004b); Ceylan and Irzık (2004).

8. Islam recognizes no difference among Muslims other than in degree of piety. This egalitarian model of Islamic personhood is often used by pious Turkish Muslims to explain their individual-rights discourse (White 2001). In other words, while switching between liberal and conservative discourses may well be a pragmatic response to the national political context, it does not mean that individual-rights discourse is wielded cynically. Contradictions between individualist and collectivist discourses about rights are often obscured by the Turkish public's general lack of clarity about both humanistic philosophy and Muslim theology, allowing a practical and inexact approximation of meaning.

9. International Press Institute, http://www.freemedia.at/site-services/singleview-master/5419/ (accessed April 29, 2011).

10. For instance, in April 2011, security services carried out intensive unannounced searches of the homes and offices of a number of writers, journalists, and other citizens looking for copies of an unpublished book manuscript, *Imamın Ordusu* (*The Imam's Army*) by Ahmet Şık, that asserts that the Fethullah Gülen movement has infiltrated Turkey's security forces. The authorities jailed the writer and wished to find and destroy all copies of the manuscript. It has since been widely circulated on the Web under a different title, *Dokunan Yanar* (*Whoever Touches It Will Burn*), even though it is illegal to download or own a copy of the manuscript. Gareth Jenkins (2011) has written an interesting analysis of the spate of arrests in this case as well as the Ergenekon case (to which prosecutors are trying to tie Şık) in the context of a possible power struggle between AKP and the Gülen movement, which until recently had operated in tandem but whose goals, Jenkins argues, have now begun to diverge.

11. Kirkpatrick (2011).

12. "Erdoğan presents Turkey as model for Arabs," *Today's Zaman*, September 14, 2011.

13. His inclusion of atheists caused some consternation in Turkey.

14. "Erdoğan offers 'Arab Spring' neo-laicism," *Hürriyet Daily News*, September 15, 2011.

15. Ram's emphasis is not on the symbolic or phenomenological content of religion but on its social, organizational, and political aspects (2008).

16. The campaign by ultraorthodox extremists in Jerusalem to deface billboards that featured women's faces is uncomfortably reminiscent of Islamist and later AKP mayors' removing statues depicting women from town squares across Turkey Greenwood (2011).

17. Ram (2008, 58, 61, 62, 71); see also Tepe (2008) for a detailed comparison of religious politics in Israel and Turkey.

18. Bayat (2010).

19. Casanova (2011).

20. Barth (1993, 173).

21. Casanova (2011, 263).

AFTERWORD TO THE NEW PAPERBACK EDITION

1. The building has been closed for renovation since 2008.

2. Deniz Göktürk, Levent Soysal, and Ipek Türeli, eds. 2010. *Orienting Istanbul: Cultural Capital of Europe?* London: Routledge.

3. According to media reports, the police used 130,000 canisters of tear gas during the first twenty days of the demonstrations. *Amnesty International*, September 12, 2013. http://www.amnesty.org/en/for-media/press-releases/turkey-fresh-protests-spark-fears-over-pending-tear-gas-shipments-2013–09–1.

4. The police say that Ahmet Atakan fell from a building. Eyewitnesses say that he was also struck by a tear gas canister fired by police.

5. *Amnesty International*, September 12, 2013.

6. Zeynep Kurtulus Korkman and Salih Can Aciksoz, "Erdogan's Masculinity and the Language of the Gezi Resistance," *Jadaliyya*, June 22, 2013. http://www.jadaliyya.com/pages/index/12367/erdogan%E2%80%99s-masculinity-and-the-language-of-the-gezi.

7. http://www.gazeteciler.com/gundem/ntv-tarihi-bu-kapak-yuzunden-kapandi-67999h.html.

8. The Guy Fawkes mask has become internationally known as a symbol of the hacktivist group Anonymous and has been taken up by protest groups such as Occupy. It was ubiquitous during the Gezi protests and sold by vendors alongside gas masks.

9. "Turkey's False Nostalgia," *New York Times*, June 16, 2013. http://www.nytimes.com/2013/06/17/opinion/turkeys-false-nostalgia.html?_r=0.

10. Interview with Edhem Eldhem, "A Turkish Spring?" L.I.S.A. Das Wissenschaftsportal der Gerda Henkel Stiftung, July 29, 2013. http://www.lisa.gerda-henkel-stiftung.de/content.php?nav_id=4493.

11. Among the 270 people arrested in the case, most were military officers, but there were also lawyers, academics, and journalists. On August 5, 2013, the court announced verdicts in the case. Fourteen defendants, including former chief of staff Ilker Başbuğ, who led the military between 2008 and 2010, received life sentences, and others received lengthy sentences of up to forty-seven years. Twenty-one were acquitted.

12. http://www.gallup.com/poll/164075/suffering-increases-turkey.aspx.

13. For instance, this video of an attack on protesters in Kocamustafapaşa: https://www.facebook.com/IlericiKadinlarDernegi/posts/481519751931535. Accessed December 3, 2013.

14. "A Turkish Spring?"

15. "Bugün seçim olsa partilerin oy oranları kaç olurdu?" *T24*, June 30, 2013.

16. CEOs of several companies told me that the ban on funding parties was no obstacle and that companies give large donations to political parties all the time. The parties don't count them as such and "put them in a different drawer." In other words, while anyone can register a new party, they cannot grow it unless they can recruit special interests to support them. On November 12, 2013, the AKP introduced a package of reforms in parliament, among them a possible lowering of the election threshold and broadening of treasury support for political parties.

17. Graham E. Fuller, "Turkey's Growing Pains," *New York Times*, June 13, 2013.

References

Abu Lughod, Lila. 1990. "The Romance of Resistance: Tracing Transformations of Power through Bedouin Women." *American Ethnologist* 17 (1): 41–55.

Ahmad, Feroz. 2008. "The Special Relationship: The Committee of Union and Progress and the Ottoman Jewish Political Elite, 1908–1918." In *From Empire to Republic: Essays on the Late Ottoman Empire and Modern Turkey*, 2:149–173.

Ahmad, Norhayati Haji. 2003. "Assisted Reproduction—Islamic Views on the Science of Procreation." *Eubios Journal of Asian and International Bioethics* 13:59–60.

Akgonenc, Oya. 2009. "Clearing Up an Explosive National Issue: Demining the Turkey–Syria Border." *Eurasia Critic*, July 2009.

Akgun, Birol. 2002. "Twins or Enemies: Comparing Nationalist and Islamist Traditions in Turkish Politics." *Middle East Review of International Affairs* 6 (March): 7–35.

Akyol, Mustafa. 2006. "How Turks See the Pope—Part I." *Turkish Daily News*, November 24.

Altınay, Ayşe Gül. 2004a. *The Myth of the Military Nation: Militarism, Gender, and Education in Turkey*. New York: Palgrave.

———. 2004b. "Human Rights or Militarist Ideals? Teaching National Security in High Schools." In *Human Rights Issues in Textbooks: The Turkish Case*, ed. Deniz Tarba Ceylan, Gürol Irzık, and Ismet Akça, 76–90. Istanbul: Tarih Vakfı Yayınları.

Altınay, Ayşe Gül, and Yektan Türkyılmaz. 2011. "Unravelling Layers of Gendered Silencing: Converted Armenian Survivors of the 1915 Catastrophe." In *Untold Histories of the Middle East: Recovering Voices from the 19th and 20th Centuries*, ed. Amy Singer, C. Neumann, and S. A. Somel, 25–53. London: Routledge.

Amnesty International. 2006. "Caring for Human Rights: Challenges and Opportunities for Nurses and Midwives." June. http://www.amnesty.org/en/library/info/ACT75/003/2006/en (accessed February 21, 2011).

Aracı, Emre. 2010. "The Turkish Music Reform: From Late Ottoman Times to the Early Republic." In *Turkey's Engagement with Modernity*, ed. Celia Kerslake, K. Öktem, and P. Robins, 336–345. New York: Palgrave Macmillan.

Atak, Hasan, and Figen Çok. 2008. "The Turkish Version of Inventory of the Dimensions of Emerging Adulthood (The IDEA)." *International Journal of Human and Social Sciences* 2 (3): 148–154.

Ayata, Sencer. 2002. "The New Middle Class and the Joys of Suburbia." In *Fragments of Culture*, ed. Deniz Kandiyoti and A. Saktanber, 25–42. London: I.B. Tauris.

Aydın, Suavi. 2005. *"Amacımız Devletin Bekası": Demokratikleşme Sürecinde Devlet ve Yurttaşlar*. Istanbul: TESEV.

Aydınli, Ersel. 2009. "A Paradigmatic Shift for the Turkish Generals and an End to the Coup Era in Turkey." *Middle East Journal* 63 (Autumn): 581–596.

Aytürk, Ilker. 2004. "Turkish Linguistics against the West: Origins of Linguistic Nationalism in Atatürk's Turkey." *Middle Eastern Studies* 40 (6): 1–25.

Baer, Marc David. 2009. *The Dönme: Jewish Converts, Muslim Revolutionaries, and Secular Turks.* Palo Alto, CA: Stanford University Press.

Bali, Rıfat. 2006. "The Politics of Turkification during the Single Party Period." In *Turkey Beyond Nationalism: Towards Post-Nationalist Identities*, ed. Hans-Lukas Kieser, 43–49. London: I. B. Tauris.

Barkey, Henri J., and Graham E. Fuller. 1998. *Turkey's Kurdish Question.* New York: Rowman and Littlefield.

Baron, Beth. 2005. *Egypt as a Woman: Nationalism, Gender, and Politics.* Berkeley: University of California Press.

Barth, Fredrik. 1993. *Balinese Worlds.* Chicago: University of Chicago Press.

Bayat, Asef. 2010. *Life as Politics: How Ordinary People Change the Middle East.* Palo Alto, CA: Stanford University Press.

Bayraktar, Özlem. 2007. *The National Outlook and Its Youth in the 1970s.* Master's thesis, Bosphorus University.

Bayramoğlu, Ali. 2009. *"Modernity Does Not Tolerate Superstition": The Religious and Seculars in the Democratization Process.* Istanbul: TESEV.

Beller-Hann, Ildiko, and Chris Hann. 2001. *Turkish Region: Culture and Civilization on the East Black Sea Coast.* Oxford: James Currey.

Berktay, Fatmagül. 1995. "Has Anything Changed in the Outlook of the Turkish Left on Women?" In *Women in Turkish Society: A Reader*, ed. Şirin Tekeli. London: Zed Books.

Berkovitch, Nitza. 1997. "Motherhood as a National Mission: The Construction of Womanhood in the Legal Discourse in Israel." *Women's Studies International Forum* 20 (5–6): 605–619.

Bila, Fikret. 2007. *Komutanlar Cephesi.* Istanbul: Detay Yayınları.

Birand, Mehmet Ali. 1991. *Shirts of Steel: An Anatomy of the Turkish Armed Forces.* London: I.B. Tauris.

Bora, Tanıl. 2008. *Türkiye'nin Linç Rejimi.* Istanbul: Birikim Yayınları.

———. 2004. "Nationalism in Turkish Textbooks." In *Human Rights Issues in Textbooks: The Turkish Case*, ed. Deniz Tarba Ceylan and Güral Irzık, 49–75. Istanbul: The History Foundation of Turkey.

———. 2003. "Nationalist Discourses in Turkey." *South Atlantic Quarterly* 102 (2/3): 433–451.

Bosphorus University and Open Society Institute. 2007. "Defining the Middle Class in Turkey."

Bozdoğan, Sibel. 2002. *Modernism and Nation Building: Turkish Architectural Culture in the Early Republic.* Seattle: University of Washington Press.

Bozkurt, Abdullah. 2009. "BBP leader calls for active engagement in diplomacy, advocates democratic freedom." *Today's Zaman*, June 9.

Bulun, Mehmet Ali. 2010. "Turkish church defaced with Islamist graffiti." *Hürriyet Daily News*, July 14.

Cagaptay, Soner. 2006. *Islam, Secularism, and Nationalism in Modern Turkey: Who Is A Turk?* London: Routledge.

Çarkoğlu, Ali. 2009. "Women's Choices of Head Cover in Turkey: An Empirical Assessment." *Comparative Studies of South Asia, Africa and the Middle East* 29 (3): 450–467.

——. 2003. "Who Wants Full Membership? Characteristics of Turkish Public Support for EU Membership." *Turkish Studies* 4 (1): 171–194.

Çarkoğlu, Ali, and Ersin Kalaycıoğlu. 2010. *Social Inequality in Turkey, 2009.* International Social Survey Program.

——. 2009a. *The Rising Tide of Conservatism in Turkey.* New York: Palgrave Macmillan.

——. 2009b. "Türkiye'de Dindarlık: Uluslararası Bir Karşilaştırma." Istanbul: Sabancı University, TÜBITAK.

Çarkoğlu, Ali, and B. Toprak. 2007. *Religion, Society and Politics in a Changing Turkey.* Istanbul: Türkiye Ekonomik ve Sosyal Etüdler Vakfı.

——. 2000. *Türkiye'de Din, Toplum ve Siyaset.* Istanbul: Türkiye Ekonomik ve Sosyal Etüdler Vakfı.

Casanova, José. 2011. "Cosmopolitanism, the Clash of Civilizations and Multiple Modernities. *Current Sociology* 59 (2): 252–267.

——. 2010. "A Secular Age: Dawn or Twilight?" In *Varieties of Secularism in a Secular Age,* ed. Michael Warner, Jonathan VanAntwerpen, and Craig Calhoun, 282–299. Cambridge, MA: Harvard University Press.

Çayır, Kenan. 2006. "Islamic Novels: A Path to New Muslim Subjectivities." In *Islam in Public: Turkey, Iran, and Europe,* ed. Nilüfer Göle and L. Ammann. Istanbul: Bilgi University Publications.

——. 2004. "Consciousness of Human Rights and Democracy in Textbooks." In *Human Rights Issues in Textbooks: The Turkish Case,* ed. Deniz Tarba Ceylan, Gürol Irzık, and Ismet Akça, 100–101. Istanbul: The History Foudation of Turkey.

Çetin, Fethiye. 2008. *My Grandmother: A Memoir.* Brooklyn, NY: Verso.

Ceyhan, Müge Ayan. 2009. "Emergence of Individualism, Entrepreneurialism and Creativity in Turkey's State-Run Educational System: Anthropological Contributions to Educational Sciences." *Procedia Social and Behavioral Sciences* 1:101–104.

Ceylan, Deniz Tarba, and Güral Irzık. 2004. *Human Rights Issues in Textbooks: The Turkish Case.* Istanbul: The History Foundation of Turkey.

Chaliand, Gérard. 1993. *A People Without a Country: The Kurds and Kurdistan.* London: Zed Press.

Çinar, Alev. 2001. "National History as a Contested Site: The Conquest of Istanbul and Islamist Negotiations of the Nation." *Comparative Studies in Society and History* 43 (2): 364–391.

Cizre, Ümit. 2008. "Ideology, Context and Interest: The Turkish Military." In *Cambridge History of Modern Turkey,* ed. Resat Kasaba, 4: 301–332. Cambridge: Cambridge University Press.

Clark, Janine Astrid, and Jillian Schwedler. 2003. "Who Opened the Window? Women's Activism in Islamist Parties." *Comparative Politics* 35 (3): 293–312.

Cook, Steven A. 2007. *Ruling But Not Governing: The Military and Political Development in Egypt, Algeria, and Turkey*. Baltimore: The Johns Hopkins University Press.

Davutoğlu, Ahmet. 2001. *Stratejik Derinlik: Türkiye'nin Uluslararası Konumu*. Istanbul: Küre Yayınları.

de Ballaigue, Christopher. 2011. *Rebel Land: Unraveling the Riddle of History in a Turkish Town*. New York: Penguin.

Deeb, Lara. 2006. *An Enchanted Modern: Gender and Public Piety in Shi'i Lebanon*. Princeton, NJ: Princeton University Press.

Delaney, Carol. 1994. "Untangling the Meanings of Hair in Turkish Society." *Anthropological Quarterly* 67 (4): 159–172.

———. 1991. *The Seed and the Soil: Gender and Cosmology in Turkish Village Society*. Berkeley: University of California Press.

Demir, Gül, and Nikki Gam. 2010. "Istanbul's Panorama 1453 History Museum brings history to the present." *Hürriyet Daily News*, August 6.

Demirbaş, Betül Akkaya. 2009. "Istanbul's panoramic museum enchants visitors with visual feast." *Today's Zaman*, February 15.

Devinim. 2009. http://www.devinim.tv/.

Dinçşahin, Şakir, and Stephen R. Goodwin. 2011. "Towards an Encompassing Perspective on Nationalisms: The Case of Jews in Turkey During the Second World War, 1939–1945." *Nations and Nationalism* 17 (4): 843–862.

Eğitim Bir-Sen. 2010. "Türkiye'de Ortak Bir Kimlik Olarak Ötekilik." Ankara, July.

Eissenstat, Howard. 2004. "Metaphors of Race and Discourse of Nation: Racial Theory and State Nationalism in the First Decades of the Turkish Republic." In *Race and Nation: Ethnic Systems in the Modern World*, ed. Paul Spickard, 239–256. London: Routledge.

Enacar, Ekin. 2009. "*Education, Nationalism and Gender in the Young Turk Era (1908–1918): Constructing the "Mother Citizens" of the Ottoman Empire*." Master's thesis. Saarbrücken, Germany: VDM Verlag, Bilkent University. http://www.thesis.bilkent.edu.tr/0003432.pdf.

Ercan, Hakan. 2010. "EEO Review: Youth Employment Measures, 2010, Turkey." Birmingham, UK: European Employment Observatory.

Erdemir, Aykan. 2004. "Incorporating Alevis: The Transformation of Governance and Faith-Based Collective Action in Turkey." PhD diss. Harvard University.

ESI (European Stability Initiative). 2007. "Sex and Power in Turkey: Feminism, Islam and the Maturing of Turkish Democracy." Berlin/Istanbul, June 2.

Eurofound (European Foundation for the Improvement of Living and Working Conditions). 2009. *Second European Quality of Life Survey*. Dublin.

Findley, Carter Vaughn. 2010. *Turkey, Islam, Nationalism, and Modernity: A History, 1789–2007*. New Haven, CT: Yale University Press.

Finkel, Andrew. 2008. "The morning after." *Today's Zaman*, July 31.

Foucault, Michel. 1975. *Discipline and Punish: the Birth of the Prison*. New York: Random House.

German Marshall Fund. 2010, 2009, 2007. *Transatlantic Trends Survey*. http://www.gmfus.org/trends/2010/about.html.

Golder, W. Evan. 2005. "Missionaries in Turkey Build On Trust, Character and Empathy." *United Church News*, June–July.

Gökalp, Ziya. 1959. *Turkish Nationalism and Western Civilization: Selected Essays of Ziya Gökalp.* Trans. and ed. Niyazi Berkes. New York: Columbia University Press.

Göktürk, Deniz, Levent Soysal, and Ipek Türeli, eds. 2010. *Orienting Istanbul: Cultural Capital of Europe?* London: Routledge.

Göle, Nilüfer. 2011. *Islam in Europe: The Lure of Fundamentalism and the Allure of Cosmopolitanism.* Princeton, NJ: Markus Wiener.

———. 1996. *The Forbidden Modern: Veiling and Civilization.* Ann Arbor: University of Michigan Press.

Greenwood, Phoebe. 2011. "Jerusalem mayor battles ultra-orthodox groups over women-free billboards." *Guardian*, November 15.

Grossbongardt, Annette (2006) "Fear prevails after a priest's murder." *Spiegel Online*, April 12.

Gülalp, Haldun. 2004. "Whatever Happened to Secularism? The Multiple Islams of Turkey." *South Atlantic Quarterly* 102 (2/3): 381–395.

Guler, Habib. 2003. http://www.turks.us/article.php?story=20030519100545582, May 19.

Gündüc, Gökce. 2008. "Büyükanit Spreads Militarism Among Children." http://bianet.org/english/education/104134-buyukanit-spreads-militarism-among-children, January 13.

Guttstadt, Corinna Görgü. 2006. "Depriving Non-Muslims of Citizenship as Part of the Turkification Policy in the Early Years of the Turkish Republic: The Case of Turkish Jews and Its Consequences during the Holocaust." In *Turkey Beyond Nationalism*, ed. Hans-Lukas Kieser, 50–56. London: I.B. Tauris.

Güvenç, Murat. 2009. *Türkiye Seçim Atlası 1950–2009.* Istanbul: Bilgi University Yayınları.

Hall, Stuart. 1996. "Introduction: Who Needs Identity?" In *Questions of Cultural Identity*, ed. Stuart Hall and Paul duGay, 1–17. London: Sage.

Hart, Kimberly. 2009. "The Orthodoxization of Ritual Practice in Western Anatolia." *American Ethnologist* 36 (4): 735–49.

———. 1999. "Images and Aftermaths: The Use and Contextualization of Atatürk Imagery in Political Debates in Turkey." *Political and Legal Anthropology* 22 (1): 66–84.

Hudson, Alexandra. 2009. "Turkish Jews fearful of anti-Semitism after Gaza." Reuters, January 26.

Human Rights Watch. 2011. "He Loves You, He Beats You": Family Violence in Turkey and Access to Protection." http://www.hrw.org/node/98418 (accessed May 5, 2011).

Hyden, Goran. 1983. *No Shortcuts to Progress: African Development Management in Perspective.* Berkeley: University of California Press.

Hurd, Elizabeth Shakman. 2011. "A Suspension of (Dis)Belief: The Secular-Religious Binary and the Study of International Relations." In *Rethinking Secularism*, ed. Craig Calhoun, M. Juergensmeyer, and J. VanAntwerpen. New York: Oxford University Press.

———. 2008. *The Politics of Secularism in International Relations.* Princeton, NJ: Princeton University Press.

Jenkins, Gareth. 2011. "The Fading Masquerade: Ergenekon and the Politics of Justice in Turkey." *Turkey Analyst* 4 (7): 4.

———. 2009. "Between Fact and Fantasy: Turkey's Ergenekon Investigation." Washington,

DC: Central Asia–Caucasus Institute & Silk Road Studies Program, Johns Hopkins University.

———. 2004. "Non-Muslim Minorities in Turkey: Progress and Challenges." *Turkish Policy Quarterly* 3:1. http://www.turkishpolicy.com/category/84/2004–1.

Jones, Dorian L. 2009. "Turkey: A Revolution Long in the Making." Open Society Institute, February 17.

Kalaycıoğlu, Ersin, and B. Toprak. 2004. *İş Yaşami, Üst Yönetim ve Siyasette Kadın*. Istanbul: TESEV.

Kandiyoti, Deniz. 1992. "Women, Islam, and the State: A Comparative Approach." In *Comparing Muslim Societies: Knowledge and the State in a World Civilization*, ed. Juan Cole, 237–260. Ann Arbor: University of Michigan Press.

Kaplan, Sam. 2006. *The Pedagogical State: Education and the Politics of National Culture in Post-1980 Turkey*. Palo Alto, CA: Stanford University Press.

Karaveli, Halil M. 2009. "Turkish Society Increasingly Marked by Intolerance Toward 'The Other.'" *Turkey Analyst*. January 30. http://www.silkroadstudies.org/new/inside/turkey/2009/090130B.html.

Kasaba, Reşat. 2009. *A Moveable Empire: Ottoman Nomads, Migrants, and Refugees*. Seattle: University of Washington Press.

Kentel, Ferhat. 1995. "Carrefour des identities socials et culturelles en Turquie: Les cas de Parti de la Prospérité." *Cahiers d'études sur la Méditéranée orientale et le monde turco-iranien* (*CEMOTI*) 19 (January–June): 211–227.

Kentel, Ferhat, M. Ahıska, and Fırat Genç. 2007. *"Milletin Bölünmez Bütünlüğü": Demokratikleşme Sürecinde Parçalayan Milliyetçilik(ler)*. Istanbul: TESEV.

Kirkpatrick, David. D. 2011. "Egyptian military aims to cement muscular role in government." *New York Times*, July 16.

Knaus, Gerald. 2009. "The virtue of boldness—Meeting Perihan Magden." *Rumeli Observer*, April 24.

Knudsen, Ståle. 2008. *Fishers and Scientists in Modern Turkey. The Management of Natural Resources, Knowledge and Identity on the Eastern Black Sea Coast*. Oxford: Berghahn Books.

———. 2006. "Between Life Giver and Leisure. Identity Negotiation through Seafood in Turkey." *International Journal of Middle East Studies* 38 (3).

Konrad Adenauer Foundation. 1999. "Turkish Youth 98: The Silent Majority Highlighted," Ankara and Istanbul. http://www.pecya.com/pdfviewer/?w=MTQ0OTFeMV4gXi0y&query=turkish%20youth.

Küçükcan, Talip. 2010. *Arab Image in Turkey*. Istanbul: SETA Foundation for Political, Economic and Social Research.

Küçükural, Önder. 2005. *Dynamics of Youth Euroscepticism*. Master's thesis. Ankara: Middle East Technical University.

Kuru, Ahmet T. 2009. *Secularism and State Policies toward Religion: The United States, France, and Turkey*. New York: Cambridge University Press.

———. 2006. "Reinterpretation of Secularism in Turkey: The Case of the Justice and Development Party." In *The Emergence of a New Turkey: Democracy and the AK Party*, ed. M. Hakan Yavuz. Salt Lake City: University of Utah Press.

Lewis, Geoffrey. 2002. *The Turkish Language Reform: A Catastrophic Success*. Oxford University Press.

Libal, Kathryn. 2000. "The Children's Protection Society: Nationalizing Child Welfare in Early Republican Turkey." *New Perspectives on Turkey* 23:53–78.

Lindholm, Charles. 2008. *Culture and Authenticity*. Malden, MA: Blackwell.

Magnarella, Paul J., and Orhan Türkdoğan. 1976. "The Development of Turkish Social Anthropology." *Current Anthropology* 17:273–274.

Mahmood, Saba. 2005. *Politics of Piety*. Princeton, NJ: Princeton University Press.

Mandaville, Peter. 2011. "Transnational Muslim Solidarities and Everyday Life." *Nations and Nationalism* 17 (1): 17–24.

Mandel, Mike, and C. Zakari. 2010. *The State of Ata*. Eighteen Publications.

Marcus, Eliza. 2007. *Blood and Belief: The PKK and the Kurdish Fight for Independence*. New York: NYU Press.

Meeker, Michael. 2002. *A Nation of Empire: The Ottoman Legacy of Turkish Modernity*. Berkeley: University of California Press.

———. 1991. "The New Muslim Intellectuals in the Republic of Turkey." In *Islam in Modern Turkey: Religion, Politics, and Literature in a Secular State*, ed. Richard Tapper, 189–219. London: I.B. Tauris.

Mills, Amy. 2010. *Streets of Memory: Landscape, Tolerance, and National Identity in Istanbul*. Athens: University of Georgia Press.

Nagel, Joane. 1998. "Masculinity and Nationalism: Gender and Sexuality in the Making of Nations." *Ethnic and Racial Studies* 21 (2): 242–269.

Najmabadi, Afsaneh. 1997. "The Erotic Vatan [Homeland] as Beloved and Mother: To Love, to Possess, and to Protect," *Comparative Studies in Society and History* 39 (3).

Navaro-Yashin, Yael. 2002. "The Market for Identities: Secularism, Islamism, Commodities." In *Fragments of Culture*, ed. Deniz Kandiyoti and A. Saktanber, 221–253. London: I.B. Tauris.

Neyzi, Leyla. 2001. "Object or Subject? The Paradox of 'Youth' in Turkey," *International Journal of Middle East Studies* 33:411–432.

OECD. 2010. *Education at a Glance: OECD Indicators*. Paris: Organisation for Economic Cooperation and Development.

Önal, Ayşe. 2008. *Honour Killing: Stories of Men Who Killed*. London: Saqi Books.

Öncü, Ayşe. 2002. "Global Consumerism, Sexuality as Public Spectacle, and the Cultural Remapping of Istanbul in the 1990s." In *Fragments of Culture: The Everyday of Modern Turkey*, ed. Deniz Kandiyoti and A. Saktanber, 171–190. London: I.B. Tauris.

———. 1999. "Istanbulites and Others: The Cultural Cosmology of Being Middle Class in the Era of Globalism." In *Istanbul: Between the Global and the Local*, ed. Çağlar Keyder, 95–120. Lanham, MD: Rowman and Littlefield.

———. 1995. "Packaging Islam: Cultural Politics on the Landscape of Turkish Commercial Television." *Public Culture* 8 (1): 51–71.

Oran, Baskın (2007) "Minority Concept and Rights in Turkey: The Lausanne Peace Treaty and Current Issues." In *Human Rights in Turkey*, ed. Zehra F. Kabasakal Arat, 35–52. Philadelphia: University of Pennsylvania Press.

Özakman, Turgut. 2005. *Şu Çılgın Türkler*. Istanbul: Bilgi Yayınevi.

Özalpdemir, Ramazan. 2005. "Misyonerlik." *Diyanet Aylık Dergisi*, June.

Özcan, Emine. 2009. "'Irkım Türk, Dinim Islam'dan Ötesi Devinim.tv de." *bianet*, September 22.

Özel, Soli, and Şuhnaz Yılmaz. 2009. "Rebuilding a Partnership: Turkish-American Relations for a New Era: A Turkish Perspective". Istanbul: TUSIAD.

Özgür, Iren. 2006. "Arabesk Music in Turkey in the 1990s and Changes in National Demography, Politics, and Identity." *Turkish Studies* 7 (2): 175–190.

Özkırımlı, Umut, and Spyros A. Sofos. 2008. *Tormented by History: Nationalism in Greece and Turkey*. New York: Columbia University Press.

Özyürek, Esra. 2009. "Convert Alert: German Muslims and Turkish Christians as Threats to Security in the New Europe." *Comparative Studies in Society and History* 51 (1): 91–116.

———. 2007. "Public Memory as Political Battleground: Islamist Subversions of Republican Nostalgia." In *The Politics of Public Memory in Turkey*, ed. E. Özyürek, 114–137. Syracuse, NY: Syracuse University Press.

———. 2004. "Miniaturizing Atatürk: Privatization of State Imagery and Ideology in Turkey." *American Ethnologist* 31 (3): 374–391.

Parla, Ayşe. 2001. "The 'Honor' of the State: Virginity Examinations in Turkey." *Feminist Studies* 27 (1): 65–88.

Patton, Marcie J. 2009. "The Synergy between Neoliberalism and Communitarianism: 'Erdoğan's Third Way.'" *Comparative Studies of South Asia, Africa and the Middle East* 29 (3): 438–449.

Pew Research Center. 2010. "Turks Downbeat About Their Institutions." Pew Research Center Publications, September 7.

———. 2007, 2008, 2009. Global Attitudes Survey.

Potuoğlu-Cook, Öykü. 2006. "Beyond the Glitter: Belly Dance and Neoliberal Gentrification in Istanbul." *Cultural Anthropology* 21 (4): 633–660.

Poyraz, Ergün. 2007. *Musa'nın Çocukları Tayyip ve Emine*. Istanbul: Togan Yayıncılık.

Ram, Uri. 2008. "Why Secularism Fails? Secular Nationalism and Religious Revivalism in Israel." *International Journal of Politics, Culture and Society* 21:57–73.

Saigol, Rubina. 2008. "Militarization, Nation and Gender: Women's Bodies as Arenas of Violent Conflict." In *Deconstructing Sexuality in the Middle East: Challenges and Discourses*, ed. P. Ilkkaracan, 165–175. Hampshire, England: Ashgate.

Saktanber, Ayşe. 2002. "'We Pray Like You Have Fun': Islamic Youth in Turkey Between Intellectualism and Popular Culture." In *Fragments of Culture: The Everyday of Modern Turkey*, ed. Deniz Kandiyoti and Ayşe Saktanber, 254–276. London: I.B. Tauris.

Sancar, Mithat, and Eylem Ümit Atılgan. 2009. *"Adalet Biraz Es Geçiliyor . . .": Demokratikleşme Sürecinde Hâkimler ve Savcılar.* Istanbul: TESEV.

Sasson-Levy, Orna. 2002. "Constructing Identities at the Margins: Masculinities and Citizenship in the Israeli Army." *Sociological Quarterly* 43 (3): 357–383.

Scott, Joan Wallach. 2007. *The Politics of the Veil.* Princeton, NJ: Princeton University Press.

Seufert, Günter. 2002. "Religion und Nationalismus unter der türkischen Jugend." *Schweizerische Gesellschaft Mittlerer Osten und Islamische Kulturen Bulletin* 4 (14): 4–11.

Shankland, David. 2007. *The Alevis in Turkey: The Emergence of a Secular Islamic Tradition.* London: Routledge.

Sinclair-Webb, Emma. 2006. "Our Bülent Is Now a Commando: Military Service and Manhood in Turkey." In *Imagined Masculinities: Male Identity and Culture in the Modern Middle East,* ed. Mai Ghoussoub and E. Sinclair-Webb, 65–102. London: Saqi Books.

Şirin, Selçuk. 2009. "Genç Kimlikler Araştırması Sonuç Raporu." New York University and Bahçeşehir University.

Somer, Murat. 2011. "Does It Take Democrats to Democratize? Lessons from Islamic and Secular Elite Values in Turkey." *Comparative Political Studies* 44 (5): 511–545.

Somer, Murat, and Evangelos G. Liaras. 2010. "Turkey's New Kurdish Opening: Religious Versus Secular Values." *Middle East Policy* 17 (2): 152–165.

Spickard, Paul, ed. 2004. "Race and Nation, Identity and Power: Thinking Comparatively About Ethnic Systems." In *Race and Nation: Ethnic Systems in the Modern World,* 1–29. London: Routledge.

Starr, Deborah A. 2009. *Remembering Cosmopolitan Egypt.* London: Routledge.

Steinvorth, Daniel. 2008. "Turkey's faltering reform drive: Erdogan striking nationalist tones." *Der Spiegel,* December 9, 2009.

Stokes, Martin. 1993. *The Arabesk Debate: Music and Musicians in Modern Turkey.* New York: Oxford University Press.

Tanyeri-Erdemir, Tuğba. 2006. "Archaeology as a Source of National Pride in the Early Years of the Turkish Republic." *Journal of Field Archaeology* 31 (4): 381–393.

Tekeli, Şirin (2010) "The Turkish Women's Movement: A Brief History of Success." *Quaderns de la Mediterrània* 14:119–123

Tepe, Sultan. 2008. *Beyond Sacred and Secular: Politics of Religion in Israel and Turkey.* Stanford: Stanford University Press.

Toprak, Binnaz. 2009. *Türkiye'de Farklı Olmak.* Istanbul: Metis Yayınları.

Toprak, Binnaz, et al. 2009. "Being Different in Turkey—Alienation on the Axis of Religion and Conservatism." Istanbul: Open Society Institute and Bosphorus University.

Tucker, Robert, ed. 1978. *The Marx-Engels Reader.* New York: W. W. Norton.

Turam, Berna. 2007. *Between Islam and the State.* Palo Alto, CA: Stanford University Press.

Türeli, Ipek. 2010. "Modelling Citizenship in Turkey's Miniature Park." In *Orienting Istanbul: Cultural Capital of Europe?* ed. Deniz Göktürk, L. Soysal, and I. Türeli, 104–200. London: Routledge.

Turkstat. 2011. "Household Labour Force Survey Results, July 2011." Ankara: Republic of Turkey Turkish Statistical Institute.

———. Ankara: 2011. *Statistical Indicators 1923-2010*.

UNDP Development Report. *State of Youth Survey*. 2008. Ankara: United Nations Development Programme.

Üstel, Füsün, and Birol Kaymaz. 2009. *Seçkinler ve Sosyal Mesafe*. Istanbul: Bilgi University.

Vick, Charles. 2006. "In Turkey, a deep suspicion of missionaries." *Washington Post*, April 9.

Watts, Nicole F. 2010. *Activists in Office: Kurdish Politics and Protest in Turkey*. Seattle: University of Washington Press.

White, Jenny. 2010a. "Fear and Loathing in the Turkish National Imagination." *New Perspectives on Turkey* 42:225–246.

———. 2010b. "Tin Town to Fanatics: Turkey's Rural to Urban Migration from 1923 to the Present." In *Turkey's Engagement with Modernity*, ed. Celia Kerslake, Kerem Öktem, and Philip Robins, 425–442. London: Palgrave.

———. 2008. "Islam and Politics in Contemporary Turkey." In *Cambridge History of Modern Turkey*, ed. Resat Kasaba, 4:357–387. Cambridge: Cambridge University Press.

———. 2007. "The Ebbing Power of Turkey's Secularist Elite." *Current History*, December.

———. 2005. "The End of Islamism? Turkey's Muslimhood Model." In *Modern Muslim Politics*, ed. Robert Hefner, 87–111. Princeton, NJ: Princeton University Press.

———. 2003. "State Feminism and the Turkish Republican Woman." *National Women's Studies Association Journal* 15 (3): 145–159.

———. 2002. *Islamist Mobilization in Turkey: A Study in Vernacular Politics*. Seattle: University of Washington Press.

———. 2001. "The Islamist Movement in Turkey and Human Rights." *Human Rights Review* 3 (1): 17–26.

———. 1994. *Money Makes Us Relatives: Women's Labor in Urban Turkey*. Austin: University of Texas Press.

World Bank and Turkish State Prime Ministry (TSPM). 2009. "Female Labor Force Participation in Turkey: Trends, Determinants and Policy Framework." Washington, DC.

World Economic Forum. 2008. "Global Gender Gap Report." Geneva.

Yavuz, Ercan. 2009a. "Alperen Ocakları may become loose cannon after losing leader." *Today's Zaman*, April 5.

———. 2009b. "Reform drive sparks treason debate." *Today's Zaman*, August 18.

Yavuz, M. Hakan. 2005. *Islamic Political Identity in Turkey*. New York: Oxford University Press.

Yavuz, Hakan, and J. Esposito, eds. 2003. *Turkish Islam and the Secular State: The Gülen Movement*. Syracuse, NY: Syracuse University Press.

Yıldırım, Hasan. 1999. "Misyonerlik Dalgaları Islâm'ın Sağlam Duvarlarına Çarpıp Durmaktadır." *Diyanet Aylık Dergisi* 106 (October).

Yılmaz, Hakan. 2010. *"Biz"lik, "Öteki"lik ve Ayrımcılık: Kamuoyundaki Algılar ve Eğilimler*. Istanbul: Open Society Institute and Boğazici University, May.

———. 2007. *Türkiye'de Orta Sınıfı Tanımlamak*. Istanbul: Boğazici University and Open Society Institute.

Yılmaz, Önay. 2004. *"Çanakkale'ye 'ruhani' akın."* *Milliyet*, July 29.

Yinanç, Barçın. 2010. "Turkey courts Chinese tourists with Iskender and ice cream at Shanghai Expo 2010." *Hürriyet Daily News*, September 17.

Young, Crawford, ed. 1993. *The Rising Tide of Cultural Pluralism: The Nation-State at Bay*. Madison: University of Wisconsin Press.

Yükleyen, Ahmet. 2011. *Contextualizing Islam in Europe: Turkish Islamic Communities in Germany and the Netherlands*. Syracuse, NY: Syracuse University Press.

Yumul, Arus. 2010. "Fashioning the Turkish Body Politic." In *Turkey's Engagement with Modernity*, ed. Celia Kerslake, Kerem Öktem, and Philip Robins. Basingstoke, UK: Palgrave Macmillan, 349–369.

Zürcher, Erik J. 1997. *Turkey: A Modern History*. London: I.B. Tauris.

Zürcher, Erik-Jan. 2010. "The Importance of Being Secular: Islam in the Service of the National and Pre-National State." In *Turkey's Engagement with Modernity: Conflict and Change in the Twentieth Century*, ed. Celia Kerslake, Kerem Öktem, and Philip Robins, 55–68. Basingstoke, UK: Palgrave Macmillan.

Index

a la Franga (Westernized lifestyle), 63, 204n14
a la Turka ("old" Ottoman lifestyle), 63, 204n14
Abdulhamid II (sultan), 24–25
Achamenids, 26
Africa, 25, 26; North Africa, 12, 93; sub-Saharan Africa, 12
Ahmad, Feroz, 29
Akdamar Island, 108, 209n22
AK-DER (*Ayrımcılığa Karşı Kadın Hakları Derneği* [Association for Women's Rights Against Discrimination]), 171
AKP. *See* Justice and Development Party (*Adalet ve Kalkınma Partisi* [AKP])
Aktütün, 149
Akyol, Taha, 109
Akyol, Mustafa, 8, 67, 87, 91, 93; on citizenship, 178–179
al Banna, Hasan, 36
Alaton, Ishak, 84–85
Albanians, and Turkish citizenship, 29, 30–31
Alchemist, The (Coelho), 163, 164
alcohol, 17, 18, 48, 51, 118, 185; consumption of and Ataturk, 120–121; as a cultural marker, 132–133, 211n53; laws concerning, 212n75; ban on, 17, 133, 212n75
Alevi(s), 12, 34, 38, 49, 66, 80, 108, 114, 139, 189; Alevi Kurds, 14; assembly houses of (*cemevleri*), 14; massacre of Alevi Kurds (Dersim massacre), 14, 108; oppression of under the Ottomans, 14; religious communities of, 14; role of women in religious ritual, 14; secularism of, 14
Alevism, 71
Alp, Tekin, 26
Alparslan, 102
Alperen Ocakları (Alperen Hearths), 67, 68, 90, 197–198n11
Alperenler (followers of Alper), 54, 56
Altaylı, Fatih, 153
Altınay, Ayşe Gül, 72, 73, 75, 114, 159
Anatolia, 6, 25, 31, 36, 42, 57, 63, 83
Anatolian Tigers, 8, 36, 37
Ankara, 27, 31, 40, 104, 107; city logos of, 40, 202n61
Annan, Kofi, 136

Annan Plan (for the reunification of Cyprus), 198n19
anthropology: in Turkey 54–58, 204n3
anti-Semitism, 86
Arab Spring (2011), 5, 23, 51, 184, 188
arabesk, 117
Arabs, and Turkish citizenship, 29, 30
archaeology, and the rewriting of Turkish history, 26, 57
Arıtman, Canan, 151
Armenia, 12, 19, 188
Armenian diaspora, 2
Armenian genocide, 56, 112
Armenian Genocide Resolution, 51
Armenian massacre (1915), 49–50, 111
Armenians, 30, 59, 87, 91, 111–112, 132, 148; massacre of Azerbaijani citizens by Armenians (1992), 114; "secret history" of Armenian children ("leftovers of the sword") taken in by Turks, 112
Arnavutköy, 110–111
art, Turkish/Ottoman, 123
Article 301 (Penal Code), 2, 3, 163, 186
Asena, Duygu, 215n21
Assyrians, 87
Ataturk. *See* Kemal, Mustafa (Ataturk)
Ataturk Cultural Center, 40
Ataturk Thought Society, 62
Atatürkçü (Ataturk admirer, secularist), 64
authenticity, 28, 39, 72, 74, 84, 103–104, 106, 116–117, 123, 130–131, 133, 169, 187
authoritarianism, 3, 39, 185, 186
auto-Orientalism, 130
Avşar, Hülya, 112–113
Ayata, Sencer, 122, 123
Aybay Law Research Foundation, 85
Aydinli, Ersel, 59, 204n7
Aytuğ, Yüksel, 125
Ayvalık, 108
Azerbaijani citizens, massacre of by Armenians (1992), 114

Baer, Marc David, 29, 92, 106, 107
Bahçeli, Devlet, 87
Bali, Rıfat, 31–32

Balinese identity, 18
Balkan Wars, 30
Balkans, the, 25, 26, 56
Baron, Beth, 161–162, 185, 214n27
Barth, Fredrik, 18, 65; on traditions of knowledge (nationalism, Islam, democracy, modernity), 113; on change, 173
Bayat, Asef, 192
Baykal, Deniz, 118
Bayramoğlu, Ali, 99–100, 199n33
Beirut, 184
belly dancing, 130–131
Benli, Fatma, 171
Beyaz, Zekeriya, 94
Beyoğlu, 108
Bila, Fikret, 59
birth control, 175
Black Sea, 55, 211n53
Black Turks, 46–48, 49, 120, 132, 133
Bora, Kerim, 93
Bora, Tanıl 71, 72, 73, 74
boundaries/borders, 3, 11, 34, 65, 79, 94, 101, 102, 103, 106, 107, 117, 121, 128, 135, 178, 196; the border as honor (sınır namustur), 149–154; communal and group boundaries, 33, 39, 151, 193; and identity, 5, 6, 95; and Judaism, 191; metaphorical boundaries, 4; national boundaries, 19, 25, 50, 94, 151–152, 178, 186, 191; openness of boundaries, 19, 96, 100; Ottoman imperial boundaries, 19; and purity, 22, 100, 135, 191; racial boundaries, 179; sexual boundaries, 23, 183; women's boundaries, 153
Brazil, 11
breastfeeding, 157–158, 213n20
Bugün, 153
Büyükanıt, Yaşar, 1, 11
Byzantine civilization, 27, 96; conquest of by the Turks (1453), 9, 83, 135, 188

Cagaptay, Soner, 29, 30, 31, 32, 118, 120
Capital City Women's Platform, 142–143, 148, 171, 173
capitalism, 36, 39; capitalist relations, 174
Çarkoğlu, Ali, 99, 152, 166, 167, 173–174, 175, 199–200n44, 200n48
çarşaf, 140
Casanova, José, 194; and the concept of aggiornamento, 5–6, 192
Çatalhöyük, 96
Çayırbaşı, 109

Çayır, Kenan, 71; on "Islamist fiction," 170
Central Asia, 26, 27, 54, 55, 66, 67, 188; legacy of gender equality in, 116; pre-Islamic Central Asia, 66, 71
Central Intelligence Agency (CIA), 62, 63
Çerezcioğlu, Burçak, 163
Çetin, Fethiye, 112
Cevdet, Abdullah, 26
Ceyhan, Müge, 75, 77
Chaldeans, 87
Chechens, and Turkish citizenship, 29
China, 26, 68, 183, 186
Christianity, 31, 90; conversions to in Turkey, 80; spread of, 81
Christians, 12, 15, 31, 79, 90, 148; Christian Crusaders, 84; Christian monasteries, 15; and women's identity, 160; Greek Christians, 111; Orthodox Greek Christians (Rum), 107, 110, 148; population of Christians in Turkey, 81–82
Çiçek, Cemil, 85–86, 114
Çiller, Tansu, 213–214n25
Circassians, and Turkish citizenship, 29
citizenship: consciousness of, 174; gendered aspect of, 94, 156, 161, 184, 207n43; and martyrdom, 159–160; and nationalism, 73; residual citizenship, 177–184, weak, 94, 178. See also citizenship, Turkish
citizenship, Turkish, 8–9, 64, 94, 137, 141; decisions about awarding, 29. See also Turkish national identity (soy); Turkishness (Türklük); Türkiyeli
civic activism, 3, 90, 104
civilization (medeniyet), 27–28, 57, 115, 118; Arabian Islamic civilization, 27; contemporary civilization (çağdaş medeniyet), 48; incorporation of Western practices and lifestyles into Turkish modernity as "civilization," 27; international civilization, 48, 188; Ottoman civilization, 48–53
Coelho, Paulo, 163, 169
collective identity, 103–105; among women, 148; individual liberties and collective logic, 16–18, 90
colonialism, 51, 87, 95
commercialization, 100, 170, 192, 194
Committee of Union and Progress (İttihat ve Terakki Cemiyeti [CUP]), 24–25, 30; relationship with Jewish political elites, 29
communalism, 193
community, 3, 94, 135, 193–194; and change,

173–177; and choice, 172, 173; community membership, 6–7; community pressure 7, 69, 100, 123, 187; defined through "ethnicity," 31; homogenous middle-class communities (*siteler*), 121–122; idealized Muslim community, 176; individual choice and community loyalty, 165–166; Muslim national community, 3–4; and personhood, 97, 99–101; and protection, 106; and race, 30; and values, 7
conservatism, 126, 173–174, 181, 215n2; among high school students, 174–175; conservative view of women, 177; Islamic conservatism, 10; paradox of in Turkey, 175–176; types of in Turkey, 68–69
Constitutional Court, 33, 43, 45, 52, 63–64, 199n43
consumerism, 3, 60, 90, 104, 121–122, 171, 173
consumption, 103, 104, 122, 129, 211n53; patterns of consumption, 173
constitution, Turkish: 14, 15, 33, 35. 46, 51, 81, 85, 86, 89, 91, 100, 176, 186, 199n43
cosmopolitanism, 5, 129, 131, 198n18, 210n36, 215n3; cosmopolitan civility, 12, 128; definition of, 113; and Jews, 106; "lost cosmopolitanism" (nostalgia for Muslim-Christian togetherness), 111, 149, 210n33; Ottoman cosmopolitanism, 29; in present-day Turkey, 113–114
Council of Higher Education (YÖK), 134; regulations of, 120
coup, 7, 14, 19, 24, 33, 35, 36, 42, 165, 181–182, 189, 197n9, 202n49; and anti-minority violence, 95; coup plots, 56, 66, 75, 87; in Cyprus, 210n31; and gender, 146; "soft coup," 43; "slow-motion coup," 52; "cyber-memorandum," 78
creationism, 71, 205n26
creolization, 65
Çubukçu, Nimet, 147
culture, 115, 132; Arab culture, 66; civilizing cultures versus folk/minority cultures, 58–59; cultural religiosity (Turkish Islam), 91; "folk culture" (*halk kültürü*), 115; and masculinity, 160–161; Muslim culture, 48–53, 188; "national culture," 71; pre-Islamic Central Asian culture, 66, 71; purity of culture and Turkish food, 133, 150–151; purity of culture linked to purity of lineage, 133–134; Turkish cultural complexity, 58–59
Curzon, George, 107
"cyber-memorandum," 78

Cyprus, 12, 49, 51, 86, 96, 198n19; attempted coup in, 110, 210n31; "Cyprus is Turkish" campaign, 83

Dalan, Bedrettin, 36, 54–56; belief that Obama is a Jew, 58, 91, 204n4; claim that the Kurdish language contained only 600 words, 58
Davutoğlu, Ahmet, 12, 50, 96, 188; and neo-Ottomanism, 50; "zero-problem" approach to foreign relations , 50
Deeb, Lara, 167, 169
Değirmencioğlu, Serdar, 1
Demirel, Sevda, 134, 212n78
democracy, 15, 43, 51, 73, 113, 185, 189, 200n48, 208n61; authoritarian democracy, 39; Kemalist democracy, 3; "Muslim" democracies, 190; skepticism of, 11
"Democratic Opening," 52
Democrat Party, 32–33
Democratic Society Party (*Demokratik Toplum Partisi* [DTP]), 13
democratization, 5
denationalization, 190–193
Dersim massacre, 14, 108
desacralization, in the suburbs, 121–126; and homogenous middle-class communities (*siteler*), 121–122; and Islam as a form of personal expression, 123–124; and *sosyete* (high-society) individuals, 126
devletçi (supporter of a strong state), 64
Dink, Hrant, assassination of, 2–3, 56, 67, 78, 114, 197nn8–9
Directorate of Religious Affairs (*Diyanet İşleri Başkanlığı* [Diyanet]), 28, 40, 43, 80, 97, 178
divorce, 175
Doğan, Ali, 66, 68
Dönme (Sabbateans), 29, 91, 92, 107, 120, 207n35; as "hidden Jews," 107, 152; identity of, 107

Ecevit, Bülent, 81
Ecevit, Rahşan, 81, 206n3
education, 4, 17, 18, 24, 25, 41, 60, 65, 71–72, 77, 80, 105, 109, 142, 213n19; and creationism, 71, 205n26; educational reforms led by the EU, 75, 77; Gülenist contributions to, 37–38; Islamic education, 28; Kemalist Republican education, 6; and nationalism 71–77, 183; pledge of allegiance to Turkey recited in, 74–75; religious education, 43, 71; schools as arenas for expressing Turkishness, 75;

education (*cont.*)
  social outcomes of, 105; teaching concerning
  the Turkish flag, 74; textbooks referring to
  Ataturk's mother used in, 157, 213n19; xenophobic discourse in school "security courses,"
  72–73
Educators Labor Union (*Eğitim Bir-Sen*), 21
egg donation 134
Egypt, 184, 185, 188, 189, 190; "cosmopolitan
  era" of, 210n36
Egypt as a Woman (Baron), 161
Eighteenth Brumaire of Louis Bonaparte, The
  (Marx), 24
Eissenstat, Howard, 25, 30
elections, 7–8, 13, 43, 45, 51, 52, 63, 78, 118,
  127, 189; in Egypt, 185; first multi-party elections in Turkey (1950), 32–33; success of the
  AKP in the 2002, 2007, and 2009 elections,
  8, 46–47, 52; success of Islamist parties in
  elections throughout the 1980s and 1990s,
  40–42
Enacar, Ekin, 30
Ennahda Party (Tunisia), 51, 190
Erbakan, Necmettin, 39–40, 42, 43, 44, 45, 68,
  202n60
Erdoğan, Recep Tayyip, 41, 44–46, 47, 52, 62, 86,
  102, 108, 118; attacks on as a "crypto-Jew,"
  92; views on Turkish diversity, 128, 211–
  212n67; depiction of as a man from the *varoş*,
  120; visit to Cairo and Tunis, 189
Ergenekon, 62, 67, 197n10, 204n7; coup plots of,
  56–57; and the gray wolf origin myth, 56
Ersoy, Bülent, 158–159
Erzurum, 83
ethics, Islamic, 9
Etruscans, 26
Europe, 25, 31, 185; southern Europe, 25, 93
European Court of Human Rights, 2
European Economic Community (EEC), 81
European Union (EU), 2, 10, 11, 15, 62, 72, 99,
  103, 181, 186; accusations against by Turkey,
  80–81; and educational reforms in Turkey,
  75, 77; EU accession procedures and Turkey,
  188–189; and France, 95; lukewarm response
  of to Turkey's membership bid, 22
European Union Customs Union, 40

Fatih Book Fair, 124
Fatsa, 34
Felicity Party (*Saadet Partisi* [FP]), 45
Finkel, Andrew, 52

food, Turkish, 133, 150–151
Foucault, Michel, 132
France, 25, 28; cultural homogeneity in, 95; national unity in and the refusal to recognize
  difference, 95; roots of Kemalism in, 89;
  threat to national sovereignty of, 95

Gaarder, Jostein, 163
Gallipoli, 9–10
Garih, Üzeyir, 85, 206n16
Gaza, 86, 92
gazi (one who fights on behalf of Islam), 71
genocide, 112. *See also* Armenian genocide, Armenian massacres
gentrification, 118, 129–132, 199n35
globalization, 3, 10, 11, 47, 60, 61, 68, 80, 95,
  100, 170, 180, 181, 186, 192, 194; support of
  by conservative Turkish Muslims, 182; and
  Turkey, 129
Gökalp, Ziya, 26, 27, 32, 48, 57, 67, 69, 116, 156,
  188
Gökçen, Sabiha, 209n23
Göktürk, Gülay, 143
"Golden Age" of the Prophet Muhammad, 170
Gönül, Vecdi, 147–148
Grand National Assembly, 28, 151; debates in
  concerning what constituted a Turkish citizen, 29; measure passed by forbidding conversion of Christians and Jews to Islam, 107; reform of Article 301 of the Penal Code, 2;
  women members of, 156, 211n56. *See also*
  parliament, Turkish
Grand Unity Party (*Büyük Birlik Partisi*), 67–68
Gray Wolves 34, 35, 66
"Greater Middle East Initiative," 52
Greece, 12, 19, 26, 29, 73, 77, 110, 188; Muslim
  population in, 25
Greek Orthodox, 87; attacks on the Greek Orthodox population in Istanbul, 83–84. *See
  also* Rum
Greeks, 26, 30, 59, 73, 108, 132; Greek national-
  ists (*Yunanlı*), 111; migration of Greek Mus-
  lims to Turkey, 107; in Turkey, 83–84
Green Wolves, 65–68
Gül, Abdullah, 44–45, 46, 47, 52, 78, 91; in Saudi
  Arabia, 62
Gül, Hayrünnisa, 46
Gülen, Fethullah, 3, 8, 37, 62, 97, 197–198n11
Gülen Movement, 62, 68, 90, 97, 104, 124, 186,
  187, 216n10; Gülenist foundations, net-
  works, and schools, 37–38, 50; support of for

creationism, 205n26; women in, 167–168, 169, 172
Gülenists, 10, 37–38
Gündeş, Ebru, 159
Güvenç, Bozkurt, 57

Hagia Sophia, 57
Hall, Stuart, 132
Hasan, 195, 196
Havva, 163–167, 171; political choices of, 164–165
headscarves, 7, 15, 17, 18, 21, 52, 115, 143, 160, 167, 175, 181; as an emblem of fear, 47, 79, 80, 87–89; and the Islamic form of covering (*tesettür* or *turban*), 88–89, 130, 131, 141; *tesettür* and the desire to be "modern," 89; *tesettür* and the fashion industry, 123; the *yemeni* (light cotton headscarf), 116; and social class, 116; video advertisements depicting headscarves as a threat, 89, 207n29
Hezbollah, 167, 169, 184, 198n23, 209n24
Higher Education Council (YÖK), 88
Hikmet, Nâzim, 102
history, 26, "shared history" and individual "histories," 200n50. *See also* Turkish Historical Society (*Türk Tarih Kurumu*); Turkish History Thesis (*Türk Tarih Tezi*)
Hittites, 26, 27, 40, 202n61
Holy Birth Week, 9
homogeneity, 51, 92, 109; cultural homogeneity in France, 95; Muslim homogeneity, 29
homosexuality, 109, 150
honor (*namus*), 15, 61, 99, 149–154; different words for in Turkish, 150; and food, 151; men's and women's honor, 150; and national boundaries, 34, 101, 151–152; national honor and female purity, 141, 161–162, 178, 183–184; and a person's *namus*, 150; and women's sexuality, 153–154, 183–184
"honor" killing, 150–151, 175, 213n5
"hooding incident," the, 152–153
Huntington, Samuel, 136
Hürriyet, 86
hybrid (*melez*)/hybridity, 71, 92, 117, 171, 180, 183, 195; as a form of liberalism, 23; nationalist fears of, 210–211n48

idealism, 174
Imamın Ordusu (*The Imam's Army* [Şık]), 216n10
Independent Industrialists and Businessmen's Association (*Müstakil Sanayici ve İşadamları*

Derneği [MÜSİAD]), 36–37; members of as Islamic Calvinists, 36
India, 26
individualism, 3, 15, 94, 100, 105, 113, 156; individual liberties and collective logic, 16–18, 90; "responsible individualism," 214n8; and the state, 105
Indonesia, 5
Inönü, Ismet, 57
International Anthropology Conference, 55, 57
intolerance, 7, 109, 186, 199n44, 210n33, 215n1
Iran, 26, 51, 80, 89, 186
Iraq, 14, 60, 63; U.S. invasion of, 22, 51
Iraqi Kurdistan, 50
Islah Party, 184
Islam, 3–4, 10, 27, 32, 49, 67, 68, 89, 97, 107, 113, 190, 216n8; and "Arabic" script, 123; as cultural identity, 27, 32, 48, 67, 91, 188; as faith, 32, 71, 89, 97, 164; as a form of personal expression, 123–124, 182, 192; as an imperial religion, 49; Islam in politics, 40, 127, 182; Islamic activism, 173; and the "Islamic language of being," 127; Islamic law, 36, 43; Islamic "love" (*sevgi*) and service (*hizmet*), 174; Islamic philosophy, 203n75; "nation" of, 30; and personhood, 216n8; privatization of, 5; public Islam, 30; Sunni Islam, 71; Turkish Islam, 101, 116, 208n61; Turkish Islam as distinct from Arab-influenced Islam, 27, 66, 68–69, 195
Islamcı (adherent of politicized Islam), 64, 65
Islamic Action Front (IAF), 184
Islamism, 39, 123, 170, 173, 186–187, 199n43; death of Islamism, 43; "Islamist fiction," 170
Islamists (Islamist political parties; Islamist movement), 8, 38, 44, 49, 186, 190; and Kemalists, 38–39; Turkish Islamists and liberal values, 100, 208n61
Israel, 134; commando raid of on the MV *Mavi Marmara*, 92; and the invasion of Gaza, 86; and the invasion of Lebanon, 184; orthodox extremists in, 216n16; "religious nationalism" in, 191; secularization of, 192; women in the Israeli army, 161
Israeli-Jewish Block of Faithful, 191
Istanbul, 16, 27, 40, 92, 104, 107; Arnavutköy district of, 110–111, 149; attacks on the Greek Orthodox population in, 83–84; Beyoğlu district of, 131–132; Greek minority in, 209n18; Jewish community in, 109; Kuzguncuk, district of, 110–111; Sulukule dis-

Istanbul (*cont.*)
   trict of (Roma population), 129; Tarlabaşı
   district of (Kurdish population), 128, 129–
   130; Tophane district of, 131
Istanbul Metropolitan Municipality, 9
Istanbul Music Festival, 129
Italy, 26

Jalil, Mustafa Abdul, 185
Jansen, Hermann, 27
Jeunes Turcs (Young Turks), 12, 15, 31, 38, 83, 87,
   91, 107, 108, 132, 192; and cosmopolitanism,
   106; and the Holocaust, 207n35; and Jewish
   nationality, 191; Ottoman Jews, 91; "Speak
   Turkish" campaign of, 29; in Turkey, 84–85.
   See also Dönme (Sabbateans)
Jordan, 184
journalists, 56, 216n10; jailing of, 186
Journalists and Writers Foundation, 37
Judaism, 191
Just Economic Order (*Adil Düzen*), 39, 42
justice, 10, 34, 148, 164, 165, 170, 187, 190; economic justice, 42; social justice, 42, 167, 171,
   192; Turkish justice, 86
Justice and Development Party (*Adalet ve
   Kalkınma Partisi* [AKP]), 3, 8, 10, 11, 12, 19,
   43–46, 50, 51–52, 56, 59, 61, 68, 71, 86, 89,
   97, 99, 137, 186, 189–190, 199n43, 216n10;
   appeal to Kurds as fellow Muslims, 13; Armenian members of, 207n34; celebration of
   the conquest of Constantinople, 96; conservatism of, 46, 181, 187–188; consolidation of
   power by, 123; contradictory discourses of,
   17–18; and the "democratic opening" for the
   Kurds, 13; and the EU accession process, 14–
   15; Gülenist members of, 37–38; heterogeneity of, 175–176; hostility of toward gay, lesbian, and transgendered citizens, 15;
   international diplomatic presence of, 188; Kemalist nationalist backlash against, 51; legal
   accusations against, 52; and the legality of alcohol sales, 133, 212n75; Muslim orientation
   of, 65; pious supporters of, 9; and the protection of women and women's rights, 176–177;
   relationships with Near East and Balkan countries, 96; success of, 78, 127; success of in the
   2007 elections, 46–47; vision of, 188–189.
   See also "Kurdish Opening" Kağan, Bilge, 102

Kalaycıoğlu, Ersin, 152, 166, 167, 173–174, 175
Kandemir, Selahattin, 26

Kandiyoti, Deniz, 104, 177
Kaplan, Sam, 72
Karman, Tawakkul, 184
Kasaba, Reşat, 201n36
Kaya, Ahmet, 102
Kaymaz, Birol, 109, 111
Kemal, Mustafa (Ataturk), 3, 6, 9, 102, 185;
   charisma of, 189; definition of the Turkish
   nation, 28–29; idolization of, 73; images
   and portraits of, 6, 120–121, 131, 174,
   182; influence of Gökalp on, 27; laicist reforms of, 39; liberation of Anatolia and
   Thrace by, 25; the "luminous road" of, 62,
   204n10; militias of, 61–63; and national
   unification, 25; mother and wife of, 157,
   213n19
Kemalism, 3–4, 11, 21, 39, 126, 135, 173, 191,
   211n53; decline of Kemalism as a form of
   identity among young people, 166; emphasis
   on the masculine nature of national identity,
   3; and France, 89; militarism of, 3; Kemalism
   as religion, 182; vision of solidarity and community for Turkey, 3. *See also* Kemalists; secularism, Kemalist
Kemalists, 39, 43, 56, 62, 64, 116, 120, 166, 182;
   backlash of against the AKP, 51; Kemalist
   identity, 100; Kemalist ultranationalists, 53;
   and modernism, 48; and their definition of
   contemporary civilization (*çağdaş medeniyet*),
   48; use of the term "Muslim" by, 30; as
   "White Turks," 48
Kentel, Ferhat, 18, 63, 103, 118, 160, 178, 179
Keyder, Çağlar, 103
Khan, Oghuz, 56
Kırşehir, 1
knowledge, forms of, 18, 22, 58, 79, 113–114
Kocaeli earthquake, the, 134
Kurdish Democratic Society Party (*Demokratik
   Toplum Partisi* [DTP]), 99
"Kurdish Opening," 52, 53, 77, 112–113
Kurdistan, 50
Kurdistan Workers' Party (*Partiya Karkerên
   Kurdistan* [PKK]), 1, 34, 51, 54, 60, 63, 80,
   128, 148, 152, 153, 187; armed struggle of,
   197n1; attacks on Turkish soldiers, 13–14,
   187; PKK terrorists as Armenians, 91
Kurds, 12–13, 15, 56, 80, 112, 114, 146–147,
   148, 189, 210n33; as "easterners," 128; massa-
   cre of Alevi Kurds, 14, 108; Muslim Kurds,
   30; and Turkish citizenship, 29
Kuru, Ahmet, 198n16

Kuva-i Milliye, 62
Kuzguncuk, 111

laicism, 6, 33, 39, 40, 46, 90, 128; compared to
    secularism, 181, 203n73; laicist Islam, 32; la-
    icist law, 46
laïcité, 28
laiklik (state Islam), 28, 46
Language Institute (*Dil Kurumu*), 58
Law on Duties and Powers of the Police, 154
Laz, the: Laz language, 55; and Turkish citizen-
    ship, 29
Lazistan, 55
Lebanon, 184
Liaras, Evangelos G., 13
liberals, 17, 21, 64, 101; as supporters of cosmo-
    politanism and freedom of speech, 64, 65
liberalism, 106, 186, 195–196; as an ideological
    form of hybridity, 23; and mixing, 114
Libya, 185, 190
Lindholm, Charles, 103
Lollobrigida, Gina, 88
Lydians, 26

maganda, 117, 210n48
Mağden, Perihan, 1, 2
Mahmood, Saba, 169
Mahmut Efendi mosque, 140
Malatya, 90, 207–208n48
Malaysia, 80, 89
Mandeville, Peter, 214n8
manhood, and military service, 159–160
Maraş, attack on Alevis in (1978), 34
marketing, and the creation of middle-class and
    elite Islamic styles, 122
martyrs (*şehit*), 1, 71, 184; and citizenship, 159–
    160; funerals of, 160; and the rearticulation
    of motherhood (from "mother of sons" to
    "mother of martyrs") under Kemalist nation-
    alism, 156–157; secular Kemalist military use
    of the religious term "martyr" for its dead sol-
    diers, 160
Marx, Karl, 24, 53
masculinity, 120, 190; "microculture" of, 160–
    161; and military service, 160, 161; and the
    nation, 3, 23; nationalist masculinity, 162,
    183
Mavi Marmara, Israeli commando raid on, 92,
    110
Mavi Saçlı Kız (*The Girl with Blue Hair*
    [Çerezcioğlu]), 163, 169

Mawdudi, Abul Ala, 36
Mazlumder (Islamic Human Rights Organiza-
    tion), 146–147
Meeker, Michael, 127, 200–201n4
Mehmed II (sultan), 9
Menderes, Adnan, 33
Mevlevi (whirling dervishes), 124–125; Sufi
    whirling, 125
Middle East, 12, 25, 26, 67, 188
Midyat, 83
militarism, 1, 3, 73–74, 75, 94–95, 186; secular
    Kemalist military use of the religious term
    "martyr" for its dead soldiers, 160
military. *See* Turkish army/military
military service, 22, 24, 69, 77–78, 151, 157–
    159, 183; conscientious objector status, 159,
    179; and manhood, 159–160; military ser-
    vice as a debt to the nation (*vatan borcu*),
    158; "We are all soldiers" ["*Hepimiz
    askeriz*"], 3, 6, 23, 157, 187. *See also* Turkish
    army/military
Milli Görüş (National Vision), 38–43, 45, 46, 68
Milliyet, 1, 9, 125
Milliyetçi (rightist nationalist), 64, 66, 137
Miniaturk, 199n31
Ministry of Family and Social Politics (*Aile ve So-
    syal Politikalar Bakanlığı*), 177
Mirsan, Kazim, 57, 58
missionaries, fear of, 15, 22, 78–79, 86–87, 90,
    93, 178, 181; expressions of concern about
    missionaries in the army and the press, 80;
    Kurdish areas of Turkey as vulnerable to mis-
    sionaries, 81; rhetoric against missionaries as
    part of the anti-EU campaign, 80–81; sup-
    posed goals of missionaries, 80; as the third
    largest threat to Turkey, 80
"modern living" (*çağdaşı yaşamı*), 115
modernism, 94; global modernism, 5; Kemalist
    modernism, 48
modernity, 113, 122, 131, 154, 193; incorpora-
    tion of Western practices and lifestyles into
    Turkish modernity as "civilization" (*medeni-
    yet*), 27; and Islam, 182, 203n67; and mod-
    ernization as a form of physical shame, 118;
    multiple modernities, 194; secular moder-
    nity, 5
Mor Gabriel Syriac Monastery, 83
Mor Jacob Syriac Orthodox Church, 92
mother, position of in nation, 156-158, 161
Motherland Party (*Anavatan Partisi*), 7, 35, 66
Muslim Brotherhood, 51, 189, 190

Muslim identity (*kimlik*), 1, 2, 3, 8, 15, 38, 187; Kemalist expressions of, 124; as modern (*çağdaş*), 21; "most important" types of, 21; "traditional" Muslim, 21

Muslimhood, 97, 182, 192, 193; as ethical nostalgia, 126–128; as a means of self-expression, 126; as a model of government, 49, 51, 189–192

Muslimness, 139, 173

Muslims, 95, 112, 181, 182; and alcohol consumption, 17; Balkan Muslims, 30, 31; "consciously" believing Muslim (*şuurlu*), 6, 8, 19, 20; Greek Muslims, 107; Muslim bourgeoisie, 10, 104, 182; Muslim Kurds, 30, 31; Muslim networks, 3; Muslim politics, 173; Muslim publics, 8, 10; Muslim secularists, 43–46; non-Turkish Muslims, 30–31; Sunni Muslims, 14, 38, 53, 71; Turkic Uyghur Muslims, 68; Turkish Muslims, 31, 216n8. *See also* culture, Muslim; Dönme (Sabbateans); homogeneity, Muslim; Muslim identity; nationalism, Muslim

mustache, 34, 202n43; as a marker of social class, 118, 120

My Grandmother: A Memoir (Çetin), 112

Nagel, Joanne, 160–161, 162

Nahdat Misr (the awakening of Egypt), 161

Narlı, Nilüfer, 134

nation, and the body: 103, 158, 178, 183

national identity, as forms of knowledge, 11, 18, 172

national rituals, 96, 101, 135, 160, 181, 187, National Police Academy, 78

National Salvation Party (NSP), 127, 202n60

National Security Council, 33, 35, 43, 80, 182

National Sovereignty and Children's Day, 9

national subjectivity, 18, 22, 78, 183; militarist definitions of 3, 23, 187; subjectivity and female choice, 171–172, 173, 186–187

national unmixing, 106–110

nationalism, 2, 3, 4, 43, 49, 60, 160; civic nationalism, 113, 191–193; consolidation of, 185; and control, 178; and different forms of knowledge, 18, 22; exclusionary nationalism, 187; gendered aspect of, 23; Jewish nationalism, 191; Kemalist nationalism, 53, 71, 167, 179–180; language of, 63; and personal identity, 103; and race/racism, 2, 60, 197n10; racialized nationalism, 91–92; "religious nationalism," 191; "secular nationalism," 21,

100, 183, 199n43; shared assumptions of secular and Muslim nationalists, 183–184; as traditions of knowledge, 113. *See also* nationalism, Muslim; nationalism, Turkish

nationalism, Muslim, 9–11, 19, 22, 23, 38, 53, 87, 182–186, 187, 192, 193, 196; as a collectivist national identity, 97; and cultural Turkism, 19; mainstream, 68; unorthodox, 69; and women, 19

nationalism, Turkish: basis of as absolute loyalty to the state, 73; and the EU, 103; forms of, 137; and the individual as the nation, 103; and honor, 149; and militarism, 73–74; and religion, 94, 148; and the state, 73–74; in the Third Republic, 69; views of young people concerning, 103–104, 111–112. *See also* women, as alienated from Turkish nationalism and as lesser citizens; women, views of nationalism

Nationalist Action Party (*Milliyetçi Hareket Partisi* [MHP]), 34, 60, 63, 66–67, 87, 102, 137, 200n44; militants of, 63; racism in, 66

nations/national states, gendered understanding of, 184, 185; the nation as a masculine institution, 160–161, 184; the nation as a vulnerable female, 178, 189; and purity, 132–135; symbolic role of women in as "Mothers of the Nation," 161

Navaro-Yashin, Yael, 123

neo-liberal norms, 173

"neo-Ottomanism," 50; as source of distinction, 129

Nesin, Aziz, 102

New Turks, 121

New York Times, 129

Neyzi, Leyla, 104

Niagara Foundation, 37

Nizam-ı Alem Ocakları, 67

non-governmental organizations (NGOs), 64, 187

non-Muslims, 7, 25, 31, 32, 111, 210n33; as the "enemy within" Turkey, 186; integration of non-Muslim religious communities within the Ottoman Empire, 12–13, 96; as *mukim yabancılar* (resident aliens), 86; non-Muslim minority students in Turkey, 72, 73

nostalgia, 94, 96, 110, 126, 127, 129, 149, 174, 182, 210n33

North Atlantic Treaty Organization (NATO), 40, 60, 61; declining Turkish support for, 99

Nursî, Sait, 26

Obama, Barack, 58, 91, 114, 204n4
Öcalan, Abdullah, 34
Oghuz, the, 55–56
Oğur, Yıld[ıray, 114
Oktar, Adnan, 205n26
Önal, Ayşe, 90, 150–151
Öncü, Ayşe, 117
Oran, Baskın, 1
Organisation for Economic Cooperation and Development (OCED), 105, 177, 209n14
Örmek, Medya, 77
Other, the: alienation from the "other," 109; identification and demonization of, 100; "otherization" (ötekileştirması), 115; social "othering," 21; violence and the identity of the "other," 95
Ottoman civilization, 48–53
Ottoman Empire, 19, 25, 26, 28, 30, 31, 50, 51, 96, 129, 189; consensus concerning non-Muslims in, 25; diversity in the Ottoman hinterland, 201n36; millet system of, 12–13, 96
Ottomania, 183
Ottomanism, 38; as model, 11–15
Ottomans, 9; conquest of Christian Byzantium by, 9, 83, 135, 188; devşirme system of, 134
Outline of Turkish History (Türk Tarihinin Ana Hatları), 26. See also Turkish Historical Society
Özakman, Turgut, 62
Özal, Turgut, 7–8, 35, 36, 128, 202n48
Özcan, Yusuf Ziya, 134
Özel, Soli, 104–106, 170, 193; 194
Özgür, 195, 196
Özsoy, Ömer, 49, 69
Özyürek, Esra, 80, 93, 94, 207–208n48

Pamuk, Orhan, 56
Panorama 1453 History Museum, 9
Parla, Ayşe, 154
parliament, Ottoman, 25
parliament, Turkish, 13, 14, 34, 35, 45, 46, 51, 63, 74, 78, 83, 87, 142, 156, 199n43, 204n17, 213n9; debate about women's clothing in, 156; women and, 176. See also Grand National Assembly
Parthians, 26
patron-client systems, 174
Pavey, Şafak, 213n17
Pax Ottomania, 50–51
Peres, Shimon, 86
"personalism," 100

personhood, 49, 77, 187; and community, 97, 99–101; Islamic personhood, 216n8
Phrygians, 26
piety, 5, 88, 118, 120, 122, 123, 128, 168, 174, 192; Islamic piety, 171, 216n8; and women, 169–170
pissoirs, as un-Islamic, 211n51
PKK. See Kurdistan Workers' Party (Partiya Karkerên Kurdistan [PKK])
pluralism, 13, 20, 44, 73, 100, 208n61
pollution (racial), and the lost city, 114–118, 120–121; and arabesk, 117; and the maganda, 117–118, 210–211n48; and the process of unmixing, 118; role of the yemeni in, 116–117; and the romanticizing of village life, 116; squatter areas and gecekondu, 117, 118; and varoş characteristics/areas, 118, 120
population exchange, 25, 29, 92, 107, 147
postcolonialism, 95, 188
Potuoğlu-Cook, Öykü, 129, 130–131
Powell, Colin, 52
Poyraz, Ergun, 92
primordial networks, 167
primordial patronage groups, 166, 167
Princes' Islands, 108
privatization: of Islam, 5; of state industries, 26, 42, 127
Protestants, 87, 93
purity: and belonging, 6; and the nation, 132–135; and the link to Republican nationalism, 134–135; sexual purity, 150, 151–152, 161–162

Quran, 138, 143, 169
Qutb, Sayyid, 36

Rabia, 165, 166, 169, 171
race/racism, 2, 60, 66, 67, 114, 197n10; and communities, 30; and the "racial moment," 30; racialism, 54; racialized nationalism, 91–92, 186
Radikal, 1
Ram, Uri, 191, 192, 216n15
Ramazan, 111, 124
rape, 83, 150, 151, 154, 161, 176
"raving Turks" (çılgı n Türkler), 62
religion, 4–5, 18, 44, 69, 125–126; cultural religiosity (Turkish Islam), 91; in the educational system, 71; and Jewish nationalism, 191; Kemalist view of as dangerous, 28; percentage of Turks defining themselves as religious,

religion (*cont.*)
201n39; secularization of in Turkey, 5–6; and Turkish nationalism, 94, 148; use of ethno-religious categories to characterize someone as un-Turkish, 91–92. *See also* missionaries, fear of
Republic Meetings (*Cumhuriyet Mitingleri*), 61, 64, 141
Republican People's Party (*Cumhuriyet Halk Partisi* [CHP]), 32, 33, 62, 65, 88, 99, 137
Rize, 81
Roma, 15, 129, 199n35
Rum, 25, 57, 84, 107, 110–111, 148, 149, 151. *See also* Greek Orthodox
Russia, 25, 188

Sabah, 125
Samanyolu, 123–124
Samast, Ogün, 2, 197n9
Santoro, Andrea, 78, 82, 90, 197n4
Saraçoğlu, Şükrü, 83
Sarıgül, Mustafa, 106
Sassanians, 26
Saudi Arabia, 63
Scott, Joan Wallach, 89
secular/sacred, blurring of the line between (*aggiornamento*) , 5–6, 192
secularism, 46, 51, 189, 190, 192; categories of, 181–182, 198n16; Kemalist secularism, 6; Muslim secularists, 43–46; and religion, 4–5; secular modernity, 5; secularists, in Turkey, 10–11, 19
Seligman, Adam, 5, 198n16
Seljuks, 26
Şencan, İrfan, 134
Separation (*Ayrılık*) television series, 110
Seufert, Günter, 126
sexuality, 151, 153–154, 158, 183, 184; male sexual agency, 152; sexual boundaries, 23. *See also* masculinity, women
shamanism, 66, 195
shari'a law, 36, 43
Şık, Ahmet, 216n10
Şimşirli, 81
Sipahi, Erdal, 152
Şirin, Selçuk, 175
social justice, 42, 148, 167, 171, 192
socialization, 69; and induction into the military, 77–78
society: as a disordered system, 193; as "us and them," 210n33

Solak, Ayşenur Bilgi, 136–137, 138
solidarity, 20, 60, 64, 103, 104, 144, 149, 166–167, 172, 173, 182, 183, 186–187, 188, 195; communal solidarity, 12, 101, 194, 196; lineage solidarity, 174; soil-based solidarity, 148, 174; and Turkishness, 148; as unity of blood and race, 3
Somer, Murat, 13
Sophie's World (Gaarder), 163, 164
sperm donation, 134
Spickard, Paul, 2, 30
Starr, Deborah A., 113, 210n36
State Ministry for Women's Issues and Women's Status, 177
Strategic Depth (Davutoğlu), 50
subjectivity. *See* national subjectivity
suburbanization, 129–132
Sufism, 91
Sulaimaniya, 152
Sultan Selim, 68–69
Sulukule, 129
Sumerians, 26, 57
Sun Language Theory, 26–27, 57
Syria, 51
Syriac Monastery of Mor Gabriel, 83
Syrian Catholics, 87

takiyye, 44
Tanyeri-Erdemir, Tuğba, 27
Tarlabaşı, 129
television/radio, 35–36, 147; deregulation of, 127
Temelkuran, Ece, 1, 2
Tercüman, 1, 2
tesettür. See headscarves
The Alchemist (Coelho), 163–164
Thrace, 25
Tophane street battle (2010), 131–132
Toprak, Binnaz, 109, 199–200n44, 200n48
treason, 5, 14, 93, 196, 198n19
trust, 20, 59, 78, 84, 87, 94, 166; lack of in Turkish society, 105, 109, 195, 196, 209n14; and religiosity, 109, 160
truth(s), 18, 22, 57, 65, 75, 113, 135, 180, 182; as relative, 194; "truth" of Turkishness, 194
Tuksal, Hidayet Şefkatlı, 142–143, 146–147, 173
Tunisia, 184, 190
Türkeş, Alparslan, 66
Turkey, 5, 15, 29, 31, 50, 109, 110, 214n9; anti-Americanism in, 152–153; Christian population in, 81–82; community pressure in, 7, 69,

100, 123, 187; conquest of Christian Byzantium (1453), 83; discourses of divisiveness in
(categories of citizens), 63–65; divestiture of
non-Muslim citizens' rights in, 86; expansion
of international role under the AKP government, 11–12; and EU accession procedures,
188–189; fear of "decivilization" in, 63; gender empowerment in, 211n55; intolerance in,
199–200n44; lack of interpersonal trust in,
105; lack of support for Islamist law in, 43;
minorities in, 56; mistrust of the United
States in, 59; negative feelings in for other
countries and religions, 7, 108–109, 198n23,
209n24, 215n1; non-Muslims as the "enemy
within" Turkey, 186; Ottoman imperial past
of, 28, 201n17; percentage of citizens who are
Muslim, 81, 189; personalization of Turkish
society, 100; political extremism in, 33–34;
privatization of state industries in, 127; relationship with Islam, 22, 126–127; and "social
fragmentation," 59; attitudes toward joining
the EU in, 99; support for social change in,
211n63; and the "threat paradigm," 59–60;
Turkish cultural complexity, 58–59; unemployment in, 126; unfavorable opinion of
Jews and Christians in, 108–109; weak sense
of citizenship in, 94; wine industry of, 133;
youth and the new economy of, 36, 202n49;
youth unemployment in, 104, 209n10. See
also conservatism, types of in Turkey; Turkey,
education in; Turkey, First Republic; Turkey,
Second Republic; Turkey, Third Republic;
Turkish identity
"Turkey for the Turks," 10, 53, 59–61, 100
Turkey, First Republic, 6, 24–32; importance of
history and literature to the founding of, 93–
94; importance of a shared language to the
founding of, 93; and "proving" the prior existence of a homogenous language, culture, and
religion in, 25–26; unity of Turks in, 27
Turkey, Second Republic, 4, 32–35; leftist politics
in, 34; multiparty elections in, 32; right-wing
politics in, 34
Turkey, Third Republic, 4–11, 19, 35–38, 69,
103, 187; Islamic presence in, 35–36; primary
changes that occurred in Turkey during, 7–8;
violence of the coup that precipitated the
Third Republic, 35
Turkification, 84; basis of, 29; Turkification policies targeting Kurds and Alevis, 108
Turkish Anthropology Association, 55

Turkish army/military, 59, 189, 204n7; criticism
of, 78; anti-U.S. sentiment in, 60, 152; as a
closed institution, 59; and the "hooding incident," 152–153, 213n9; induction into, 77–
78; view of the threat paradigm, 59–60
Turkish flag: as the "blood-flag," 1–2; teaching in
schools concerning the Turkish flag and its
red color, 74
Turkish Historical Society (Türk Tarih Kurumu),
26
Turkish History Thesis (Türk Tarih Tezi), 26, 31,
48, 57, 96, 195
"Turkish-Islamic Synthesis," 8, 35, 41, 71,
127–128
Turkish national identity 2, 29, 95, 135, 183, 185,
187, 188, 204n17; and academic disciplines,
57, 203–204n3; among high school students,
174–175; and the authentic Turkish self as
Muslim, 84; building blocks/markers of (history, blood, culture, language, Muslimness,
and Westernness), 79, 101, 185–186; Turks
as simultaneously liberal and conservative, 17;
collective identity, 103–104; early attempts to
establish a national identity, 26–27; as embodied in religion and race/bloodlines, 102–
103; emphasis of on blood, purity, boundaries, and honor, 2, 22, 65–66; fear of losing
national identity, 89–95, 103; incorporation
of Western practices and lifestyles into Turkish modernity as "civilization" (medeniyet),
27; international modernist style of architecture as the "Turkish" national style, 27; and
Islam, 197n10; and national power, 26; pollution of national identity, 28; survey results of
the "most important identity" for Turks, 21,
200n52; Turkish national essence, 27–28; use
of ethno-religious categories to characterize
someone as un-Turkish, 91; and üst kimilik
(upper identity), 205n18. See also "Turkey for
the Turks"; Turkishness (Türklük)
Turkish Language Association (Türk Dil Kurumu), 28
Turkish model, for the Middle East, 188–190
Turkish Parliament. See Grand National Assembly, parliament
Turkish social/political life, contradictory nature
of, 23
Turkish Supreme Court of Appeal (Yargıtay), 86
Turkishness (Türklük), 2, 3, 21, 22, 24, 28, 29, 32,
49, 53, 57, 60, 66, 69, 71, 100, 103, 115, 135,
141, 173, 180, 187, 193, 195; basic compo-

Turkishness (*Türklük*) (*cont.*)
    nents (blood, culture, language, Muslimness,
    secularity, and Westernness) of, 79, 101, 185–
    186; contestation of the nature of, 8–9; cul-
    tures of, 18; fear of losing Turkishness, 89–95,
    101; and forms of, 22, 79, 113–114; as an in-
    clusive concept, 27; law concerning (Article
    301 of the Penal Code), 2, 3, 163, 185; Otto-
    man Turkishness, 101, 183; as a product of
    the media, 183; schools as arenas for express-
    ing Turkishness, 75; as solidarity, 195, 196;
    "truth" of, 194
Türkiyeli (Turkish citizen), 64, 136–137, 204n17,
    205n18
Türkyılmaz, Yektan, 114

ultranationalism, 34, 54, 56, 102, 137, 207–
    208n48; fracturing among ultranationalists,
    67; right-wing ultranationalists (*ülkücü*), 60,
    64, 65, 66, 67; Kemalist ultranationalists, 53.
    See also Green Wolves
ulusalcı (left-wing neonationalist, secularist, sup-
    porter of a strong state and military, anti-
    West), 64
Union of Civilizations Project, 136
United States, 7, 51, 62, 63, 134, 186; and the
    "hooding incident," 152–153; mistrust of in
    Turkey, 59; "passive secularism" of, 198n16;
    and women in the labor force, 215n5
urbanity, 111, 113, 117, 120, 131
urbanization, 194
Üstel, Füsün, 109, 111
Uzbeks, and Turkish citizenship, 29

Valley of the Wolves (*Kurtlar Vadisi* [2006]), 82,
    109–110, 120
Valley of the Wolves: Iraq, 152
Van, 108
Varagavank (Seven Churches) monastery, 108
vatandaş (citizen), 64; as used by women, 64. *See*
    also citizenship
Venezuela, 11
"vernacular politics," 127
Veronika Decides to Die (Coelho), 163, 164
village guards, 91, 207n33
Village Institutes, 57–58
"village-ification" (*köylaştırması*), 115
virginity tests, forced, 154
Virtue Party (*Fazilet Partisi* [VP]), 43–44, 99,
    127
Vural, Oktay, 102, 103

Wealth Tax (1942), 83, 85, 92, 108
Welfare Party (*Refah Partisi* [WP]), 40–41, 44,
    127; antisystem stance of, 41; appeal of to
    nonreligious voters, 41; election success of,
    40–42; political style of, 41–42; radicalism of
    as cause of its demise, 42–43
Westernization, 40
whirling dervishes. *See* Mevlevi
White Turks, 47, 48
Woman Has No Name, The (*Kadının Adı Yok*
    [Asena]), 215n21
women, 15, 21, 61, 120, 131, 176–177, 183,
    185, 213n12; activism of, 16–17, 65, 122–
    123, 142, 167, 184–185; as alienated from
    Turkish nationalism and as lesser citizens,
    141–142; and artificial insemination, 133–
    134; and belly dancing, 130–131; and chas-
    tity (*ırz*), 150; conservative view of, 177;
    and the experience of Islamic modernity, 20;
    female virtues of the Islamic woman, 122;
    and choice (freely chosen actions), 169–
    173, 186–187; in the Gülen Movement,
    167–168, 169, 172; home-based roles of,
    122; and *iffet*, 150; labor force participation
    rate of, 122, 209n10, 211n55, 215n5; lob-
    bying of for Penal Code reform, 142; the
    "new Islamic woman," 122, 123; opportuni-
    ties for mixing with those of different races
    and lifestyles, 148–149; and personal
    choice, 186–186–187; and piety, 170; rape
    of, 83, 150, 151, 154, 161, 176; role of in
    Alevi religious ritual, 14; subjectivity and fe-
    male choice, 171–172, 173; and subordina-
    tion as a means to identity, 169–170;
    women as symbols of the nation, 161, 178,
    183, 185; as *vatandaş*/citizen, 64, 184; views
    of nationalism, 138–141; women's rights
    and their status in a community, 177–178,
    211n55. *See also* women, under Kemalist
    nationalism
women, under Kemalist nationalism: and the
    cultural marker of breastfeeding, 157,
    213n20; focus on Ataturk's mother in school
    textbooks, 157; and the *makbul* (acceptable)
    woman, 141–142, 156; marginalization of
    women as national subjects, 160; and the
    moral obligation between mother and child
    (the "milk debt"), 157–158; and mother-
    hood as a "national mission," 161; and the
    rearticulation of motherhood (from "mother
    of sons" to "mother of martyrs"), 156–157;

as representative of national vulnerability, 161, 189; roles available for women, 156–162

World Bank (WB), 77

World Economic Forum (2008), 177

World Expo Shanghai 2010, 96–97

World War I, 30, 62, 84; occupation of Istanbul and Izmir by Allied Forces during, 32

World War II, and women in the labor force, 215n5

Yazıcıoğlu, Mushin, 67

Yeditepe University, architecture of, 54

Yemen, 184–185

Young Turks (*Jeunes Turcs*), 25; influence of the French Revolution on, 28

Youth, Turkish, 3, 36, 65, 80, 100, 104, 111, 171, 174–175, 183, 196, 209n10, 215n1

YouTube, 1, 3

Zaghlul, Safiyya, 161

Zaman, 7, 123–124

Zionism, 92

PRINCETON STUDIES IN MUSLIM POLITICS

Diane Singerman, *Avenues of Participation: Family, Politics, and Networks in Urban Quarters of Cairo*

Tone Bringa, *Being Muslim the Bosnian Way: Identity and Community in a Central Bosnian Village*

Dale F. Eickelman and James Piscatori, *Muslim Politics*

Bruce B. Lawrence, *Shattering the Myth: Islam beyond Violence*

Ziba Mir-Hosseini, *Islam and Gender: The Religious Debate in Contemporary Iran*

Robert W. Hefner, *Civil Islam: Muslims and Democratization in Indonesia*

Muhammad Qasim Zaman, *The 'Ulama in Contemporary Islam: Custodians of Change*

Michael G. Peletz, *Islamic Modern: Religious Courts and Cultural Politics in Malaysia*

Oskar Verkaaik, *Migrants and Militants: Fun and Urban Violence in Pakistan*

Laetitia Bucaille, *Growing Up Palestinian: Israeli Occupation and the Intifada Generation*

Robert W. Hefner, ed., *Remaking Muslim Politics: Pluralism, Contestation, Democratization*

Lara Deeb, *An Enchanted Modern: Gender and Public Piety in Shi'i Lebanon*

Roxanne L. Euben, *Journeys to the Other Shore: Muslim and Western Travelers in Search of Knowledge*

Robert W. Hefner and Muhammad Qasim Zaman, eds., *Schooling Islam: The Culture and Politics of Modern Muslim Education*

Loren D. Lybarger, *Identity and Religion in Palestine: The Struggle between Islamism and Secularism in the Occupied Territories*

Augustus Norton, *Hezbollah: A Short History*

Bruce K. Rutherford, *Egypt after Mubarak: Liberalism, Islam, and Democracy in the Arab World*

Emile Nakhleh, *A Necessary Engagement: Reinventing America's Relations with the Muslim World*

Roxanne L. Euben and Muhammad Qasim Zaman, eds., *Princeton Readings in Islamist Thought: Texts and Contexts from al-Banna to Bin Laden*

Irfan Ahmad, *Islamism and Democracy in India: The Transformation of Jamaat-e-Islami*

Kristen Ghodsee, *Muslim Lives in Eastern Europe: Gender, Ethnicity, and the Transformation of Islam in Postsocialist Bulgaria*

John R. Bowen, *Can Islam Be French? Pluralism and Pragmatism in a Secularist State*

Thomas Barfield, *Afghanistan: A Cultural and Political History*

Sara Roy, *Hamas and Civil Society in Gaza: Engaging the Islamist Social Sector*

Michael Laffan, *The Makings of Indonesian Islam: Orientalism and the Narration of a Sufi Past*

Jonathan Laurence, *The Emancipation of Europe's Muslims: The State's Role in Minority Integration*

Jenny White, *Muslim Nationalism and the New Turks*

Lara Deeb and Mona Harb, *Leisurely Islam: Negotiating Geography and Morality in Shi'ite South Beirut*